"THE SUPREME HARMONY OF ALL"

"The Supreme Harmony of All"

THE TRINITARIAN THEOLOGY
OF JONATHAN EDWARDS

Amy Plantinga Pauw

WILLIAM B. EERDMANS PUBLISHING COMPANY

GRAND RAPIDS, MICHIGAN / CAMBRIDGE, U.K.

Wm. B. Eerdmans Publishing Co.
255 Jefferson Ave. S.E., Grand Rapids, Michigan 49503 /
P.O. Box 163, Cambridge CB3 9PU U.K.
www.eerdmans.com

Printed in the United States of America

07 06 05 04 03 02   7 6 5 4 3 2 1

Library of Congress Cataloging-in-Publication Data

Pauw, Amy Plantinga.
The Supreme harmony of all : the Trinitarian theology
of Jonathan Edwards / Amy Plantinga Pauw.
p.   cm.
Includes bibliographical references.
ISBN 0-8028-4984-9 (pbk. : alk. paper)
1. Trinity — History of doctrines. 2. Edwards, Jonathan, 1703-1758.
I. Title.
BT111.3 .P38 2002
231'.044'092 — dc21
2002067151

For Alan

CONTENTS

ACKNOWLEDGMENTS

The research for this book was guided and abetted by a wonderful group of scholars associated with the Works of Jonathan Edwards project at Yale. Within this larger community, Tom Schafer, Ken Minkema, and Ava Chamberlain deserve my special thanks. From the beginning of my interest in Jonathan Edwards, Harry Stout and David Kelsey have been supportive and enthusiastic mentors, even while they wondered if I would ever finish this book.

An ATS Lilly Faculty Fellowship provided me with time to write and confirmed my sense of the project's importance. Louisville Presbyterian Seminary granted me a sabbatical leave to work on it. My long-suffering colleague Kathryn Johnson read some awful early drafts and offered invaluable guidance throughout. Other colleagues, including Joe Coalter, Burton Cooper, Chris Elwood, Susan Garrett, and John Mulder, read parts of the manuscript and found numerous ways to help and encourage me. I am grateful for the wise counsel I received at crucial points from John Carman, Sarah Coakley, Sang Hyun Lee, George Marsden, Richard Muller, Bill Placher, and Miroslav Volf. Melisa Scarlott was of great assistance in preparing the manuscript. The good humor and expertise of my editors at Eerdmans, Jon Pott and Jennifer Hoffman, made them a pleasure to work with.

My extended family also deserves my deep thanks. Neal Plantinga first seeded my interest in the doctrine of the Trinity. Carol and Don Mead, Leon Plantinga and Ellen Ryerson, and Alan and Jan Pauw all provided various forms of encouragement and support while I was writing. I dedicate this book to my husband, Alan. Our "uncommon union," and the joy and distraction provided by our three children, Clara, Andrea, and Emily, have helped sustain me every step of the way.

INTRODUCTION

"God has appeared glorious to me, on account of the Trinity. It has made me have exalting thoughts of God that he subsists in three persons; Father, Son, and Holy Ghost."

EDWARDS, *Personal Narrative*

The flow of a living tradition is fascinatingly unpredictable.[1] Sometimes it broadens and merges with other streams; sometimes it constricts or takes sharp bends. At other times parts of it seem to dry up altogether. The focus of this book, the trinitarian theology of Jonathan Edwards (1703-1758), has been one of the parched places in the Edwardsean tradition. The mainstream of his theological legacy has followed other channels, into explorations of human will and virtue, morphologies of spiritual revival, and assertions of divine sovereignty. Edwards's trinitarianism was largely neglected by his immediate New Divinity successors, who found themselves more interested in Edwards's reflections on human nature than on divine nature.[2] His later

---

1. Edwards himself used the metaphor of a "large and long river, having innumerable branches" to describe the flow of human history. See John F. Wilson, ed., *A History of the Work of Redemption*, The Works of Jonathan Edwards, vol. 9 (New Haven: Yale University Press, 1989), p. 520. (After the first citation, subsequent references to the Yale edition of the Works of Jonathan Edwards will be indicated by Works, followed by volume and page number.)

2. See Bruce M. Stephens, *God's Last Metaphor: The Doctrine of the Trinity in New England Theology* (Chico, Calif.: Scholars Press, 1981).

nineteenth-century custodians were uncomfortable with his trinitarian musings and attempted something of a cover-up.[3] With renewed attention to the Trinity in western theology, and with the accessibility of previously unpublished writings of Edwards, his creative trinitarian reflection has begun to claim its rightful place in his theological legacy and in wider theological discussion.[4]

In a study of Edwards's cultural and theological legacy, Joseph A. Conforti shows how, in the nineteenth century, Edwards's writings on popular piety (above all, his *Life of David Brainerd*) and his major Stockbridge writings (above all, *Freedom of the Will*) met the needs of diverse constituencies, and formed the center of his legacy. As Conforti points out, tradition "is historically constructed, contingent, negotiated, and instrumental."[5] The center of Edwards's theological legacy is again shifting, as the corpus of published writings increases, and as new cultural and theological interests are brought to bear. This book is a participation in the continuing work of its reconstruction.

The diversion of the Edwardsean tradition away from the doctrine of the Trinity is explicable in part by its relative inaccessibility within Edwards's life and writings. Though by no means absent, Edwards's explicit trinitarianism was a prominent theme neither in his preaching nor in the writings published in his lifetime.[6] Its richness remained

3. An interesting account of the controversy surrounding the nineteenth-century publication of some of Edwards's trinitarian writings can be found in Richard D. Pierce, "A Suppressed Edwards Manuscript on the Trinity," *Crane Review* 1 (Winter 1959): 66-80.

4. The Trinity figures significantly in studies of Edwards by Robert W. Jenson, *America's Theologian: A Recommendation of Jonathan Edwards* (Oxford: Oxford University Press, 1988); Stephen Holmes, *God of Grace and God of Glory: An Account of the Theology of Jonathan Edwards* (Grand Rapids: Eerdmans, 2001); and Sang Hyun Lee, *The Philosophical Theology of Jonathan Edwards* (Princeton: Princeton University Press, 1988). See also Lee, "Jonathan Edwards's Dispositional Conception of the Trinity: A Resource for Contemporary Reformed Theology," in David Willis and Michael Welker, eds., *Toward the Future of Reformed Theology: Tasks, Topics, Traditions* (Grand Rapids: Eerdmans, 1999), pp. 444-55.

5. Joseph A. Conforti, *Jonathan Edwards, Religious Tradition, and American Culture* (Chapel Hill and London: University of North Carolina Press, 1995), p. 7.

6. It is likely that Edwards's extended pieces on the Trinity were not published along with his more polemical writings because he planned to include them in his all-encompassing work on the History of Redemption. In the interests of accessibility, rather than textual accuracy, references to two of Edwards's major writings on the Trinity, "Treatise on Grace" and "Discourse on the Trinity," will be taken from Paul

largely hidden behind the public exterior of his life, emerging more in the privacy of his study and on his solitary rides and walks, than in his Northampton pulpit or in the Edinburgh printing houses. These trinitarian reflections surfaced explicitly at times in his public voice, but, as in the case of his apocalypticism, his characteristic style was one of "conjecture in private and discretion in public."[7] His trinitarianism ran like a subterranean river throughout his career as a pastor and polemicist; it did not dominate his public discourse.

Yet Edwards's trinitarian reflections provide a strong link between two aspects of his thought that often have seemed disconnected: his profound metaphysical musings and his zeal for the church and the Christian life. Edwards's philosophical explorations and his ardent pastoral efforts both funded and were funded by his extended reflections on the Trinity. In a figure as complicated as Edwards, it is unreasonable to expect to discover one interpretive window into all the facets of his life and thought.[8] But some windows are bigger than others. I argue that Edwards's trinitarianism provides an unusually wide view of his deepest philosophical, theological, and pastoral inclinations. The Trinity was for Edwards "the supreme harmony of all,"[9] and in his trinitarian thought the various facets of his life and genius — his philosophical explorations, his vital interest in discerning true religious affections, his critical appropriation of the Reformed tradition, and the affective, mystical element in his faith — moved toward harmonious resolution.

Anyone who has read a biography of Jonathan Edwards knows that "harmony" is not one of the major themes in his career as pastor. His yearnings for earthly anticipations of trinitarian harmony proved hard to satisfy, except in his marriage with Sarah Pierpont. Glorious Chris-

---

Helm, ed., *Treatise on Grace and other posthumously published writings including Observations on the Trinity* (Greenwood, S.C.: Attic Press, 1971). Henceforth, Helm, *Trinity*.

7. "Editor's Introduction," in Stephen J. Stein, ed., *Apocalyptic Writings*, The Works of Jonathan Edwards, vol. 5 (New Haven: Yale University Press, 1977), p. 19.

8. Michael J. McClymond, *Encounters with God: An Approach to the Theology of Jonathan Edwards* (Oxford: Oxford University Press, 1998), p. 28, notes the difficulty of "isolating and identifying such a fundamental motif" in Edwards's theology, and briefly notes particular accents in recent books on Edwards.

9. Thomas A. Schafer, ed., *The "Miscellanies," a-z, aa-zz, 1-500*, The Works of Jonathan Edwards, vol. 13 (New Haven: Yale University Press, 1994), p. 329 (no. 182).

tian communion modeled after the harmonious society of the Trinity seemed to come to easier expression in Edwards's private notebooks than in his actual intercourse with Northampton parishioners. The harmonious interiority of Edwards's trinitarian reflection does not disclose the "real Edwards," hidden behind an artificial public persona. Not the least of the obstacles to realizing earthly forms of harmony were located within Edwards himself, in what Ola Winslow has described as his "sense of justice to the letter, a pastoral urge toward the reproof and correction of others, and a lamentable lack of any sense of humor."[10] The irritability and social ineptness of Edwards the pastor were also "the real Edwards." Indeed, the two sides seemed often to reinforce each other. Edwards's trinitarian vision of heavenly Christian union was at times a hindrance to patient and charitable dealings with his all too earthly parishioners.[11] Likewise his frustrations with congregational disharmonies drew him away from duties like pastoral visitation to the serenity of his private musings. Edwards's trinitarian reflection sheds new light on both his happiness in marriage and his frustrations and failings in the pastorate.

The basic outlines of Edwards's trinitarian thought were established when he was only twenty years old, in an entry in his notebooks the "Miscellanies."[12] There he made the daring assertion that "if God loves

10. Ola Elizabeth Winslow, *Jonathan Edwards: 1703-1758* (New York: Macmillan, 1941), p. 69. See also "Editor's Introduction," in David D. Hall, ed., *Ecclesiastical Writings*, The Works of Jonathan Edwards, vol. 12 (New Haven: Yale University Press, 1994), pp. 1-90; and Patricia J. Tracy, *Jonathan Edwards, Pastor: Religion and Society in Eighteenth-Century Northampton* (New York: Hill and Wang, 1979).

11. For example, it will be argued in Chapter 5 that this vision played a role in his bitter conflict with his Northampton congregation over the sacrament of communion.

12. The "Miscellanies" are a series of notebooks of miscellaneous theological reflections that Edwards kept throughout his life. Quotations from *Miscellany* entries a-500 will follow Works, 13. This volume also contains the "Table" Edwards produced to arrange the entries topically. See the entries listed under "Trinity" in Works, 13, p. 149. Quotations from *Miscellany* entries 501-832 will follow Ava Chamberlain, ed., *The "Miscellanies" 501-832*, The Works of Jonathan Edwards, vol. 18 (New Haven: Yale University Press, 2000). Quotations from Miscellanies 833-1152 will follow Amy Plantinga Pauw, ed., *"Miscellanies," 833-1152*, The Works of Jonathan Edwards, vol. 20 (New Haven: Yale University Press, 2002). References to later "Miscellanies" will rely on the Schafer transcripts, deposited at Beinecke Library, edited in accordance with Yale edition criteria. References to entries 833 and higher will be indicated by *Misc.*, followed by the number Edwards assigned.

himself and delights in himself, there is really a triplicity, three that cannot be confounded, each of which are the Deity substantially."[13] Throughout his twenties, Edwards returned to the doctrine of the Trinity frequently, exploring the connections between the eternal "triplicity" in God and his root metaphysical notions of proportion, relation, and excellency. These deep correlations between his metaphysics and his doctrine of the Trinity were thus in place before his major treatises were written. Even where the doctrine is not mentioned explicitly, Edwards's abundant use of terms like love, idea, consent, unity, and beauty in his later writings has a distinctively trinitarian cast to it.

In the early 1730s, Edwards began his *Discourse on the Trinity*, a work that he never published, but to which he returned repeatedly over the next decade with clarifications and additions.[14] In it he attempted a correlation between his philosophical idealism and the notion of the Son as God's Idea. He also developed the analogy of the Holy Spirit as God's Love, an understanding of the Spirit that proved critical in the 1740s as Edwards confronted the pastoral conundrums of the revivals and the nature of true religion. In the 1730s and again in the late 1740s he took up more generally the question of the trinitarian economy, the division of labor within the Godhead for the work of creation and redemption, this time with special attention to the role of the Son. Towards the end of his life, in response to growing deist challenges, Edwards devoted energy to defending the reasonableness of the Trinity, both on historical and philosophical grounds. His interest in the Trinity never flagged, though some of his polemical works bear scant evidence of it. Even in the last years of his life, Edwards was busily copying long excerpts from Chevalier Ramsay on the "eternal commerce of the coeternal three."[15]

Attention to Edwards's trinitarianism nuances our understanding of his Puritan inheritance. My reading of Edwards will give special emphasis to the group of divines, centered in the Cambridge colleges in England, whom William Haller has termed the Spiritual Brethren.[16] Richard Sibbes, John Cotton, John Owen, and even the English nonconformist Thomas Goodwin, usually a marginal figure in Edwards

13. Works, 13, p. 262 (no. 94).
14. See Helm, *Trinity*, pp. 99-131.
15. *Misc.*, no. 1253.
16. William Haller, *The Rise of Puritanism* (New York: Columbia University Press, 1938).

studies, will receive special attention in this study because of their elaborate use of the Trinity. The Spiritual Brethren emphasized the intimate union of the persons of the Godhead, and found in the unity of the triune God "a pattern for our unity."[17] In listening for the resonances between the Spiritual Brethren and Jonathan Edwards, I am indebted to Janice Knight's book *Orthodoxies in Massachusetts*.[18] She lifts up the themes of love, communalism, and grace in the piety of the Spiritual Brethren, and argues that "on almost every important issue, Edwards gave new voice to the principles of the Cambridge faith."[19]

In their vision of the Christian hope as one of communal love and glory, a reflection of the eternal love and glory of the Trinity, the Spiritual Brethren articulated a theology and piety that resonate strongly with Edwards's trinitarianism. God, for Edwards, was "a full and overflowing and an inexhaustible fountain of love." This divine love has its source in the eternal life of the Trinity: it "has its seat in the Deity as it is exercised with the Deity, or in God toward himself. But it does not remain in such exercises only, but it flows out in innumerable streams toward all the created inhabitants of heaven."[20] In Edwards's trinitarian reflections, love replaces power as the primary divine attribute, setting the relationship between God and humanity in a much larger frame: God is not only a "glorious being infinitely superior," but also One who desired to be "familiarly conversed with and enjoyed."[21] The source and raison d'être for the creation and redemption of humanity are the eternal love and harmony of the Godhead, and the ultimate goal of the work of redemption is the saints' joyful participation in the overflowing harmony of the divine life.

Knight makes a (too) sharp distinction between the Spiritual Brethren and the group she calls the "Intellectual Fathers" of Puritanism — men like William Perkins, William Ames, Thomas Hooker,

17. Alexander Grosart, ed., *The Complete Works of Richard Sibbes*, 7 vols. (Edinburgh: James Nichol, 1862), 3, p. 194. Henceforth, Sibbes, *Complete Works*.

18. Janice Knight, *Orthodoxies in Massachusetts: Rereading American Puritanism* (Cambridge, Mass.: Harvard University Press, 1994), especially the Epilogue.

19. Knight, *Orthodoxies*, p. 199. Because of their geographical center in Cambridge, England, Knight sometimes refers to the Spiritual Brethren as the Cambridge Brethren.

20. Paul Ramsey, ed., *Ethical Writings*, The Works of Jonathan Edwards, vol. 8 (New Haven: Yale University Press, 1989), pp. 369, 373.

21. Works, 18, p. 54 (no. 510).

Thomas Shepard, John Winthrop, and Peter Bulkeley. In contrast to the love and communion of the Spiritual Brethren, Knight locates the theology of the Intellectual Fathers in "its celebration of divine power, its elaborated system of contractual covenants, and its tribal nationalism."[22] The extent to which this division in early-seventeenth-century New England Puritanism can be historically sustained, especially in the case of ambiguous figures like Thomas Shepard, is a matter for scholars of Puritanism to sort out. For the purposes of this book, it is enough to note that Edwards was profoundly indebted to figures among both the Spiritual Brethren and the Intellectual Fathers. In *Religious Affections,* for example, he freely appealed to Intellectual Fathers Shepard, Ames, and Perkins as well as to Spiritual Brethren Owen, Preston, and Sibbes in making his theological case. The genius of Edwards, as Norman Pettit affirms, "lay in his ability to select from the many strains of nonconformity and to combine those strains in such a way as to gain new insight into the spirituality of his own time."[23]

My intent, in listening for echoes of the Spiritual Brethren in Edwards's trinitarianism, is to complement, rather than replace, more usual readings of Edwards that attribute to him a celebration of divine power. In Edwards's concentrated reflections on freedom of the will, original sin, and the "extremity of hell torments," there is admittedly little attention to themes of trinitarian love and union.[24] Here his emphasis on sheer divine sovereignty supports a common interpretation of Edwards's theology as centered in "the rhetorical climax of the God of power." Amanda Porterfield is not wrong to find places in Edwards where an emphasis on the "uncompelled power of God" is so absolute that it results in a profound divine "deafness to human complaint," a total lack of emotional vulnerability.[25] Fueled by the perennial use of the sermon "Sinners in the Hands of an Angry God" as the standard representation of Edwards's theology, this vision of the inscrutable

22. Knight, *Orthodoxies,* pp. 1-2.

23. Review of Knight, *Orthodoxies in Massachusetts,* in *The New England Quarterly* 68 (March 1995): 150.

24. Though I agree with Michael McClymond's assertion that Freedom of the Will and Original Sin are "not nearly as central to Edwards's lifelong intellectual concerns as is commonly thought" (*Encounters with God,* p. 6).

25. Amanda Porterfield, *Female Piety in Puritan New England: The Emergence of Religious Humanism* (Oxford: Oxford University Press, 1992), pp. 155-56.

God of power has alternately dominated theological interpretations of Edwards, or served as a basis for severing his mystical piety from the Puritan tradition altogether.

A trinitarian reading of Edwards demonstrates the existence of other deep veins in his theology besides the stress on monarchial, uncompelled divine power,[26] and indeed provides leverage from within his theological reflections for critiquing this emphasis. Edwards's sermon "Heaven Is a World of Love," while equal to the "Sinners" sermon in sheer rhetorical power, exemplifies the markedly different theological tone of his explicitly trinitarian reflections.[27] Attending to Edwards's trinitarianism requires the rejection of monological interpretations of his theology and provides a wider perspective on his Puritan inheritance. Though Edwards made intellectual acquaintance with his seventeenth-century Sibbesian forebears on both sides of the ocean, and found in Cotton Mather a model for appropriating their thought, my aim is not to demonstrate direct historical links between Edwards and the Spiritual Brethren, but to exhibit their profound rhetorical and theological resonances on the doctrine of the Trinity.

These resonances are strongest in the Spiritual Brethren's depictions of the Trinity's work of human redemption. Christian theology has distinguished the inner life of the Godhead, the immanent Trinity or God *ad intra*, from God's dealings with creation, referred to as the economic Trinity, or God *ad extra*. In their descriptions of God's economic outworkings, such as God's purpose in creation, or the Holy Spirit's work of sanctification, there is a remarkable confluence of theological emphasis and rhetoric between the Cambridge Brethren and Edwards. Like the Spiritual Brethren, Edwards articulated a confident "unapologetic theology"[28] of the Trinity. He simply proceeded on the assumption that the Trinity is in fact at the center of Christian faith and de-

---

26. Burton Z. Cooper, in *Why, God?* (Atlanta: John Knox Press, 1988), uses this image to make a similar point about the biblical tradition.

27. Both sermons are conveniently accessible in Wilson Kimnach, Kenneth Minkema, and Douglas Sweeney, eds., *The Sermons of Jonathan Edwards: A Reader* (New Haven: Yale University Press, 1999).

28. I borrow this phrase from William C. Placher, *Unapologetic Theology: A Christian Voice in a Pluralistic Conversation* (Louisville: Westminster/John Knox, 1989). I find that Edwards's unapologetic theology is of more enduring interest than his ardent apologetic theology.

voted himself to showing connections between a trinitarian vision of God's communal love and questions of religious experience, ecclesiology, and eschatology. Edwards, however, was considerably bolder than the Cambridge Brethren in articulating the harmony between the trinitarian economy and the Godhead *ad intra,* and in exploring the metaphysical implications of his trinitarian vision.

Edwards's trinitarianism also intersected with later rationalist currents in English Christianity. In his trinitarian reflections, as in many of his other theological endeavors, Edwards was working against the tide. He lived in an age driven by a strong impulse to rid Christianity of its recondite metaphysical riddles and reduce it to a simple and reasonable faith. The Trinity, as an exhibit *par excellence* of metaphysical abstruseness, was a prime target of this theological reconstruction.[29] In the aftermath of the Enlightenment, the Trinity would lose its position of doctrinal centrality in much of western theology. Indeed, into the early twentieth century it was often regarded as "either a postscript to Christian faith of merely historical or antiquarian interest, or as a mental construct that is not an essential ingredient of faith itself, even if it serves a certain utilitarian purpose in giving expression to what is of faith."[30]

Like other orthodox Christians during the English Enlightenment, Edwards thought it appropriate to counter attacks on reasonableness of the doctrine of the Trinity with reasonable arguments. Though the tide of antitrinitarianism did not rise in New England until after Edwards's death, he was acquainted with the earlier attacks on the doctrine by British deists. As early as 1724, Edwards planned to write a treatise entitled "A Rational Account of the Principles and Main Doctrines of the Christian Religion," with the aim of showing that "the present fashionable divinity is wrong."[31] In an outline to this projected work,

29. Roland N. Stromberg, *Religious Liberalism in Eighteenth-Century England* (Oxford: Oxford University Press, 1954), p. 36: "The trinity was to become the most perplexing problem of all that plagued the Church in this era of rationalism. It was never settled, and it led honest Christians to despair."

30. William J. Hill, *The Three-Personed God: The Trinity as a Mystery of Salvation* (Washington, D.C.: Catholic University of America Press, 1982), p. 83. See also Claude Welch, *In This Name: The Doctrine of the Trinity in Contemporary Theology* (New York: Scribner, 1952), esp. ch. 2.

31. Works, 18, p. 546 (no. 832). See Ava Chamberlain's description of this projected treatise in Works, 18, pp. 24-29.

Edwards reminded himself "[t]o explain the doctrine of the Trinity before I begin to treat of the work of redemption."[32] Though by 1740 Edwards abandoned his plans to write this treatise and "explain the doctrine of the Trinity," he never gave up his conviction that belief in the Trinity was reasonable and he experimented with various arguments on its behalf.

In the 1740s he shifted his trinitarian apologetics away from rational arguments to historical ones. Edwards found confirmation of the reasonableness of trinitarian doctrine in the striking similarities between Christian orthodoxy and the utterances of the ancient heathens.[33] This shift mirrors his decision to abandon "A Rational Account" and instead to write "a body of divinity in an entire new method, being thrown in the form of an history."[34] His hopes of writing this "great work," *A History of the Work of Redemption* "beginning from eternity" and ending with the "consummation of all things," were likewise unrealized. Though this projected work used a different apologetic strategy, his intentions to refute deist arguments against central doctrines of the faith, including the Trinity, remained constant.[35]

Edwards's trinitarian reflection also has a contribution to make to more recent theological discussion. For someone familiar with the twentieth-century renaissance in trinitarian theology, one of the most striking features of Edwards's trinitarianism is his refusal to take sides in the debate between theologians who emphatically affirm a social plurality in the Godhead and those who in various ways put greater stress on the unity of the Godhead.[36] Starting with his earliest reflec-

32. Wallace E. Anderson, ed., *Scientific and Philosophical Writings,* The Works of Jonathan Edwards, vol. 6 (New Haven: Yale University Press, 1980), p. 396.

33. See "Editor's Introduction," in Works, 20.

34. George S. Claghorn, ed., *Letters and Personal Writings,* The Works of Jonathan Edwards, vol. 16 (New Haven: Yale University Press, 1998), p. 727.

35. Gerald R. McDermott persuasively argues that much of Edwards's corpus represents a concerted effort to respond to deist attacks on Christian orthodoxy. See *Jonathan Edwards Confronts the Gods: Christian Theology, Enlightenment Religion, and Non-Christian Faiths* (Oxford: Oxford University Press, 2000).

36. For an introduction to the general twentieth-century trinitarian discussion, see Ted Peters, *God as Trinity: Relationality and Temporality in Divine Life* (Louisville: Westminster/John Knox, 1993); Catherine Mowry LaCugna, "Philosophers and Theologians on the Trinity," *Modern Theology* 2, no. 3 (April 1986): 169-81, and "Current Trends in Trinitarian Theology," *Religious Studies Review* 13, no. 2 (April 1987): 141-47; David S. Cunning-

tions, Edwards employed two distinct models of the immanent Trinity, both with deep roots in the Christian tradition. One model portrayed the Son and Spirit as the Wisdom and Love of the one God, thus emphasizing divine unity. The other model emphasized relationality within God by depicting the Godhead as a society or family of persons. Edwards alternated or modulated between them depending on the immediate theological and cultural context of his writing, but never repudiated either one.

That Edwards refused to choose between them is an indication of his high tolerance for theological tension. Perhaps he sensed, as the twentieth-century theologian Hans Urs von Balthasar has asserted regarding these two models, that the image of the Trinity "can only be developed in two opposite lines of being and thought that point to each other."[37] He appealed to the two models not as conflicting blueprints of the inner life of the Godhead, but as complementary linguistic idioms for narrating a basic soteriological story line, according to which "God having from eternity from his infinite goodness designed to communicate himself to creatures," chose

> to unite himself to a created nature, and to become one of the creatures, and to gather together in one all elect creatures in that creature he assumed into a personal union with himself, and to manifest to them and maintain intercourse with them through him.[38]

Edwards was willing to live with the theological tension between these two models for the Trinity because he found them each indispensable for telling the story of God's great work of redemption through Christ.

Since the interplay between Edwards's two basic models for the Trinity will be the focus of the following chapters, I will introduce them briefly here. Like much of the contemporary trinitarian debate, Edwards's two models mirror the two significant trinitarian traditions in western medieval theology: the Augustinian, and the alterna-

---

ham, "Trinitarian Theology since 1990," *Reviews in Religion and Theology* 4 (November 1995): 8-16.

37. Hans Urs von Balthasar, *Theo-Drama: Theological Dramatic Theory*, Vol. III, *The Dramatis Personae: The Person in Christ*, trans. Graham Harrison (San Francisco: Ignatius Press, 1992), p. 525.

38. Works, 18, p. 389 (no. 744).

tive initiated by Richard of St. Victor in the twelfth century. The Augustinian model, as it was adopted and refined by the later tradition, has come to be called the psychological analogy of the Trinity, although the term suggests a much higher degree of theological confidence and linguistic precision than Augustine (354-430) himself accorded it. According to this model, the human mind knowing itself and loving itself provides a most fitting image of the Godhead. Among the myriad images for God explored in his classic reflections on *The Trinity*, Augustine found in the "inferior image" of the human soul an especially appropriate model of the distinctions and mutual relations of the divine persons:

> when the mind knows itself and loves itself, a Trinity remains: the mind, love, and knowledge; and there is no confusion through any commingling, although each is a substance in itself, and all are found mutually in all.... These three, therefore, are in a marvelous manner inseparable from one another; and yet each of them is a substance, and all together are one substance or essence, while the terms themselves express a mutual relationship.[39]

In comparing the Trinity to a human mind and its internal operations of knowledge and love, Augustine depicted the Son as the Idea or Image of God, and the Spirit as the divine Love or Joy.

Edwards appealed to the understanding of the Son as the Word or Idea of God in various apologetic arguments. In *Discourse on the Trinity*, he brought together Augustine's understanding of the Son and the vocabulary of philosophical idealism to argue that "that idea which God hath of Himself is absolutely Himself."[40] In his *Miscellanies*, he found here a common ground between Christian trinitarianism and the insistence of "the heathen philosophers" such as Plato on "the Son of God as Wisdom or Idea or Logos," and the "Holy Spirit as Love."[41]

Though the psychological image was a model of the immanent Trinity, it had strong implications for God's redemptive presence in the

---

39. Saint Augustine, "The Trinity," trans. Stephen McKenna, in *Fathers of the Church*, vol. 45 (Washington, D.C.: Catholic University of America Press, 1963), pp. 277-78 (IX.v.8).

40. Helm, *Trinity*, p. 103.

41. *Misc.*, no. 955.

world, since, in Edwards's phrase, "God is a communicative being."[42] Following the Augustinian tradition, Edwards identifies the manifestation of God's truth with "Christ's being in the creature, in the name, idea or knowledge of God being in them." Likewise, the communication of God's grace is connected with "the Holy Spirit's being in them, in the love of God's being in them."[43] The double flowing forth of God outwards toward the creature is thus a repetition of the internal flowing forth of the Son and Holy Spirit within the Godhead.

The communication of divine wisdom is by the Son, who communicates "himself in an image of his own excellency." While this communication occurs "properly only to spirits," the Son as Wisdom also imparts "a sort of a shadow or glimpse of his excellencies to bodies."[44] This image of the Son as the communication of divine Wisdom funded Edwards's theology of preaching. It is also the basis for his pervasive use of typology. Since Christ is the full revelation of God to the world, the ultimate antitype, all other manifestations of God in Scripture and in the created order are types of this perfect and eternal wisdom, "images and shadows of divine things."[45]

Likewise, Edwards's identification of the Holy Spirit with immanent divine love was profoundly correlated with the Spirit's economic work as aimed at loving union among the saints and with God. "'Tis in our partaking of the Holy Ghost that we have communion with the Father and Son and with Christians: this is the common excellency and delight in which they all [are] united."[46] The centrality of love in Edwards's ethical, metaphysical, and millenarian thought has been commented on many times.[47] The inseparability of this pervasive emphasis on love from the role of the Spirit in the psychological model for the

42. Works, 13, p. 410 (no. 332).

43. *Misc.*, no. 1084. See also nos. 1082, 1151.

44. Works, 13, p. 279 (no. 108).

45. See Wallace E. Anderson, Mason I. Lowance, and David H. Watters, eds., *Typological Writings*, The Works of Jonathan Edwards, vol. 11 (New Haven: Yale University Press, 1993), for Edwards's notebook bearing this title.

46. Works, 13, p. 448 (no. 376).

47. E.g., Alan Heimert and Andrew Delbanco, eds., *The Puritans in America: A Narrative Anthology* (Cambridge, Mass.: Harvard University Press, 1985), p. 411: "if any single thread unites all his utterances it is the one encapsulated in a single entry in his private notebooks — 'gravity,' he declared after exploring the inherent qualities of Newton's universe, 'is a type of love.'"

Trinity has not been recognized as frequently.[48] As we shall see, the role of the Holy Spirit is in many respects the most original and the most problematic aspect of Edwards's trinitarianism.

Edwards also employed a social model of the immanent Trinity that emphasized the love and intimate fellowship among the members of the Trinity by likening them, not to a single human soul, but to a family, a society, or a communion of friends. According to this model the Father, Son, and Holy Spirit form a "family of three,"[49] a divine society marked by love, consent, and unity of will. As Edwards wrote in a 1751 letter to Lady Mary Pepperell, "The eternal and immutable happiness of the Deity himself is represented in Scripture as a kind of social happiness, in the society of the persons of the Trinity."[50] The social model echoes the trinitarian arguments that Richard of St. Victor (d. 1173) put forth as an alternative to the Augustinian model that prevailed in his day. Richard insisted that God, who is love (1 John 4:8), is necessarily a community of persons, since the perfection of any person is found in loving another person. Furthermore, "in a mere duality, neither of the two would have a person to whom he could communicate the supreme delights of his happiness."[51] Therefore the Trinity must consist of three persons, united by perfect confluence of love and purpose. Richard of

48. Rowan Williams cautions readers against reading Augustine's trinitarian writings in abstraction from his ecclesial situation, in which he was struggling against the Donatist schismatics: for Augustine, love has "a strongly 'public,' even institutional dimension" as the bond of peace in the church. "The Paradoxes of Self-Knowledge in the *De trinitate*," in *Augustine: Presbyter Factus Sum*, ed. Joseph T. Lienhard, S.J., Earl C. Muller, S.J., Roland J. Teske, S.J. (New York: Peter Lang, 1993), p. 132. Similarly, for Edwards, even more consistently than for Augustine, the love of the Trinity had a practical institutional dimension.

49. See, for example, Edwards's descriptions of the Trinity as "the society and family of the three," Helm, *Trinity*, p. 122, and as "that society of the three persons in the Godhead," Works, 13, p. 110 (no. 571).

50. Works, 16, p. 415.

51. Richard of St. Victor, "De Trinitate," trans. Gaston Salet, in *Sources Chrétiennes*, No. 63 (Paris: Éditions du Cerf, 1959), p. 208 (III.xviii). English translations are mine. Edwards's emphasis on love and communion within the Trinity also echoes themes from the eastern Cappadocian tradition. Patricia Wilson-Kastner, in "God's Infinity and His Relationship to Creation," *Foundations* 21 (October-December 1978): 317, points to the Cappadocian theologian Gregory of Nyssa (c. 330-395) as a "major but mediated influence" on Edwards, and speculates that Edwards "almost surely had some consciousness of his debt."

St. Victor's trinitarianism was clearly the minority view in the West, and it has been slighted in accounts of Edwards's trinitarianism as well.[52] Yet the social dimension of the Godhead had profound correlations with Edwards's metaphysics, his ethic of human community, and his vision of God's great work of redemption, and will receive new emphasis in this study.

The Trinity was for Edwards a "useful" doctrine, and attention to its theological contours cannot be separated from the way it functioned in his historical and cultural context. The link between Edwards's use of both the psychological and social models of the Trinity was the notion of divine love, whether personified in the Holy Spirit, or exemplified in the harmonious communion of the trinitarian persons. Their unity for him was rooted less in conceptual harmony than in practical outworkings: both models fueled his account of God's amazing work of redemption, the loving consent inherent in true sainthood, and the ultimate fulfillment of the elect in the "world of love" called heaven.

To adopt the phrase Brooks Holifield has applied to the earlier Puritans, Edwards was an "ambidextrous theologian," who tailored a variety of rhetorical modes to specific polemical, pastoral, and intellectual contexts: in Edwards's depictions of the God of Christian faith, "what the right hand took away, the left hand could retrieve."[53] While Edwards's treatment of the doctrine of the Trinity provides an important link among seemingly disparate areas of his thought, it also throws the unsystematic, situational character of his theology into sharper relief. The pervasiveness of trinitarian reflection in Edwards's writings is due in part to his flexible array of theological images for the Godhead, and his willingness to live with discursive tensions that resulted.

52. For example, Sang Hyun Lee, *Philosophical Theology,* slights the social aspect of Edwards's trinitarianism by his focus on dispositional ontology; Conrad Cherry, *The Theology of Jonathan Edwards: A Reappraisal* (Bloomington: Indiana University Press, 1990), aligns Edwards's trinitarianism with his consideration of faculty psychology; Stephen H. Daniel, *The Philosophy of Jonathan Edwards: A Study in Semiotics* (Bloomington: Indiana University Press, 1994), lifts up the image of the Son as Word to portray Edwards the semiotician.

53. E. Brooks Holifield, *The Covenant Sealed: The Development of Puritan Sacramental Theology in Old and New England, 1570-1720* (New Haven, Conn.: Yale University Press, 1974), pp. 27-28. This ambidexterity helps account for both the stunning disparities in interpretations of Edwards and his perennial appeal to a wide cast of readers.

I am one of the tribe that David Hall has termed seminary historians,[54] and this requires me to be an "ambidextrous theologian" in my own way: I find myself writing for two different audiences simultaneously. On the one hand, I claim that an examination of this neglected part of Edwards's theological legacy can shed new light on his life, writings, and Puritan inheritance, and thus be of interest to scholars of American religion. Though studies of his social context and the literary, political, and aesthetic dimensions of his thought have contributed greatly to our knowledge of Edwards, any endeavor to understand him historically must reckon with the fact that his own principal interest was theological. On the other hand, I write for Christian theologians and their faith communities. Contemporary western theology has seen tremendous renewed interest in the doctrine of the Trinity, but this great theological revival has occurred almost completely without reference to American theology before the twentieth century. A central claim of this book is that Edwards's trinitarianism has a place in this discussion, and offers largely untapped resources for understanding the complex issues of Christian practice and communal life.

The sequence of chapters in this book parallels the outline Edwards provided to the Princeton trustees regarding the "body of divinity" he hoped to write. It begins "from eternity," starting with an examination of the immanent Trinity. It moves through a consideration of the intratrinitarian covenant of redemption — a setting forth of God's "grand design" for human redemption — that is poised between the immanent and economic Trinity. The sequence continues with an exploration of the Trinity's economic work of redemption — "the summum and ultimum of all the divine operations and decrees," and ends in the "consummation of all things" in heaven.[55] This sequence means that focused attention on the relationship of the Trinity to Edwards's participation in the revivals and his Northampton pastorate does not occur till the fifth chapter. But even views of the immanent Trinity are embedded in particular historical contexts, and so throughout I will be assuming that the doctrine's social function, while often difficult to discern, is an integral part of its theological intricacies.

54. David D. Hall, "On Common Ground: The Coherence of American Puritan Studies," *William and Mary Quarterly* 3, no. 44 (1987): 193-229.
55. Works, 16, pp. 727-28.

The first chapter will focus on Edwards's use of Scripture in his development of models for the immanent Trinity. Chapter 2 will discuss the impediment that the tradition of divine simplicity presented for Edwards's metaphysical correlations between excellency and the Trinity. The third chapter will examine the role of the Trinity in covenant theology, paying particular attention to Edwards's development of the covenant of redemption. Chapters 4 and 5 will shift to the economic work of the Trinity to demonstrate how, for Edwards, the union of the persons of the Trinity had direct relevance for the unions ordinary Christians were concerned about: the union of Christ with sinful human nature, the redemptive union of the elect with God, and the union of saints in a rapidly changing society. The fourth chapter will describe the role of the Trinity in the divine work of creation, election, and incarnation. In the fifth chapter, the focus will shift from the Trinity's eternal nature and past actions to the phase of God's great work of redemption that was contemporaneous with Edwards's life, the conversion and sanctification of human sinners. In these two chapters, the theological resonances with the Spiritual Brethren are so frequent that they will ordinarily be relegated to footnotes, so as not to disturb the flow of the text. In the last chapter, I argue that Edwards's vigorous trinitarianism and his spirit of theological adventure are things contemporary theologians would do well to imitate, even if they find, as Edwards himself did in the case of John Calvin, that they "cannot justly be charged with believing in everything just as he taught."[56]

56. Paul Ramsey, ed., *Freedom of the Will*, The Works of Jonathan Edwards, vol. 1 (New Haven: Yale University Press, 1957), p. 131.

Chapter 1

THE TRINITY AND THE BIBLE

". . . I am not afraid to say twenty things about the Trinity which the Scripture never said."

EDWARDS, "Miscellanies," no. 94

Though explicit trinitarian doctrine developed gradually over centuries of theological reflection and dispute, the Christian church confessed God as both one and three from its earliest expressions of faith. Early Christians had to integrate their belief in the one Creator God revealed in the Hebrew Scriptures, with their faith in the salvific work of Jesus of Nazareth. "For us," the Apostle Paul writes, "there is one God, the Father, from whom are all things and for whom we exist, and one Lord, Jesus Christ, through whom are all things and through whom we exist" (1 Cor. 8:6).[1] The early Christians were also convinced of the Holy Spirit's continuing presence in their midst, as reflected in the triadic blessing of 2 Corinthians 13:13: "The grace of the Lord Jesus Christ, the love of God, and the communion of the Holy Spirit be with all of you." As 1 John 5:7, a late addition to the Latin text of the New Testament, puts it: "For there are three who bear witness in heaven, the Father, the Word, and the Holy Spirit, and these three are one."[2] The patterns of

1. All biblical citations will follow the New Revised Standard Version.

2. This text, known as the "Johannine Comma," was not recognized as an interpolation until the early modern period. It was included in the King James translation of the Bible, and widely appealed to by Puritans in support of trinitarian doctrine.

early Christian baptism, prayer, and outreach all reflected this complex experience of God's presence. Worship provided a powerful impulse to trinitarian reflection, and rich traditions developed in both the eastern and western church through the medieval period.

The earliest Protestant Reformers inherited the western tradition of this reflection, particularly as it had been developed by medieval scholasticism.[3] The magisterial Reformers did not perceive themselves as theological innovators regarding the doctrine of the Trinity; they positioned themselves within the western tradition, but did not significantly extend it. Most Protestant Christians agreed with their fellow Catholics that the doctrine of the Trinity was "biblical," in the sense that it reflected or summarized biblical teaching about God. Sixteenth-century Calvinist Reformers such as Heinrich Bullinger, John Calvin, and Ulrich Zwingli, along with their early-seventeenth-century heirs, stoutly defended trinitarian orthodoxy, but showed little inclination to theological reflection on the doctrine. As the twentieth-century theologian Karl Barth has noted, John Calvin's interest in the Trinity was "not exactly burning."[4] Calvin's rather brusque counsel to the readers of his *Institutes* to be content with traditional creedal language for the Trinity is typical: "Say that in the one essence of God there is a Trinity of persons; you will say in one word what Scripture states, and cut short empty talkativeness."[5] In a similar way, Zwingli and Bullinger affirmed the received trinitarian doctrine in a way that protected divine oneness, but showed little interest in developing its larger theological implications.

The links between Scripture and trinitarian doctrine were forged

3. Catholic scholasticism reached its height in the thirteenth century. Particularly influential in the development of Reformed orthodoxy were the Franciscans, such as Alexander of Hales and Bonaventure, who stressed the practical side of theology as a discipline oriented toward the ultimate goal of humanity's union with God.

4. Karl Barth, *Church Dogmatics* I/1, trans. G. T. Thomson (Edinburgh: T. & T. Clark, 1936), p. 477. But see Philip W. Butin, *Revelation, Redemption, and Response: Calvin's Trinitarian Understanding of the Divine-Human Relationship* (New York: Oxford University Press, 1994), who argues for the centrality of the Trinity in Calvin's theology. Perhaps it may be said that Calvin anticipates the pattern in Puritan theology of reliance on the Trinity for describing the economy of divine grace, without much interest in its place in the doctrine of God.

5. John Calvin, *Institutes of the Christian Religion,* Library of Christian Classics, ed. John T. McNeill (Philadelphia: Westminster Press, 1960), I.xiii.5. Henceforth, *Institutes.*

over centuries by a hermeneutic that affirmed "the unity of Scripture and identity of all Scripture as the Word fulfilled in Christ."[6] Yet the widespread concern of the early magisterial Reformers to uphold the authority of Scripture as the preeminent source for all theological reflection foreshadowed later Protestant critiques of trinitarian doctrine. During the Reformation period, this principle of *sola Scriptura* did not extend to the technical vocabulary of trinitarian doctrine, which remained in use in Lutheran and Reformed circles. But as theologians after John Calvin heeded his warning not to "take it into our heads either to seek out God anywhere else than in his Sacred Word, or to think anything about him that is not prompted by his Word, or to speak anything that is not taken from that Word,"[7] questions about the tradition's reliance on nonbiblical vocabulary for the Trinity arose.

The doctrine of the Trinity came under fierce attack in seventeenth-century Europe, as small but influential numbers of Christians began to question allegiance to a trinitarian orthodoxy based on "Unscriptural Terms and Phrases" justified as "Scriptural consequences."[8] According to H. John McLachlan, "the rejection of scholastic theology and attachment to a purely scriptural basis of belief is characteristic of all who in the seventeenth century made their protest against the accepted doctrines of the Trinity and the atonement."[9] The accessibility of the Bible in vernacular translation was itself an important element in the spread of Arianism and other forms of antitrinitarianism during and after the Reformation.[10] But the growing suspicions about the

6. Richard Muller, *Post-Reformation Reformed Dogmatics,* 2 vols. (Grand Rapids: Baker, 1987), 2, p. 210. I am indebted to Muller's exposition of the waning of the Reformation hermeneutic and its consequences for trinitarian doctrine.

7. Calvin, *Institutes* I.xiii.21.

8. Hubert Stogdon, *Seasonable Advice Relating to the Present Dispute about the Holy Trinity, Address'd to Both Contending Parties* (London, 1719), p. 23. Quoted in *Works,* 13, p. 256, n. 2. Stogdon was a Dissenting pastor who reacted favorably to the outcome of the Salters' Hall dispute, discussed below.

9. H. John McLachlan, *Socinianism in Seventeenth-Century England* (Oxford: Oxford University Press, 1951), p. 39.

10. Arius was a fourth-century Christian anathematized for asserting that the Son was not fully God. The Arian position, condemned by the church at the Council of Nicea in 325 C.E., received renewed support among some of the radical sixteenth-century Reformers, both Catholic and Protestant, on biblical grounds. George H. Williams has referred to them as "Evangelical Rationalists," noting that "eventually the program-

doctrine of the Trinity also stemmed from a profound shift in ways of reading the Bible. The long tradition of Christian typological exegesis, particularly the affirmation of trinitarian and christological motifs in the Old Testament, was the target of growing criticism. The more grammatical, historical approach to Scripture that took its place seemed to open a gulf between the biblical text and received trinitarian orthodoxy. By Edwards's time, many Protestants lacked Calvin's confidence that to affirm "a Trinity of persons . . . in the one essence of God" was to "say in one word what Scripture states."

Edwards's trinitarian reflections reflect an awareness of this sea change in Christian doctrine. As he commented in a notebook entry written in the early 1720s, "there has been much cry of late against saying one word, particularly about the Trinity, but what the Scripture has said."[11] By that time intermittent battles had raged in England over the doctrine of the Trinity for three decades.[12] English doubts about the Trinity were fed by various sources, including a stream of Socinian literature from Holland, the republication of John Biddle's antitrinitarian work in 1691, and an anti-Catholicism that set trinitarian dogma alongside the doctrine of transubstantiation as yet another unscriptural offense to human reason. It did not help matters that three of the greatest English minds of the day, Isaac Newton, John Milton, and John Locke, lined up against the doctrine of the Trinity, all expressing doubts about its reasonableness and its basis in Scripture.

---

matic abandonment of the doctrine of the Trinity became their distinguishing mark." George H. Williams and Angel M. Mergal, eds., *Spiritual and Anabaptist Writers,* Library of Christian Classics (Philadelphia: Westminster Press, 1957), p. 24. This Reformation movement represents the beginnings of Unitarianism.

11. *Works,* 13, p. 256 (no. 94). Edwards may well be referring to Samuel Clarke's *The Scripture-Doctrine of the Trinity* (1712), which is discussed below.

12. William S. Babcock, "A Changing of the Christian God: The Doctrine of the Trinity in the Seventeenth Century," *Interpretation* 45, no. 2 (April 1991): 135, rightly asserts that the English trinitarian controversy "has so far been charted in only the most rudimentary fashion; and its specifically theological dimensions have hardly been plotted at all." Partial accounts can be found in McLachlan, *Socinianism;* Roland N. Stromberg, *Religious Liberalism in Eighteenth-Century England* (Oxford: Oxford University Press, 1954); John Redwood, *Reason, Ridicule and Religion: The Age of Enlightenment in England, 1660-1750* (London: Thames and Hudson, 1976); and Roger Thomas, "The Non-Subscription Controversy amongst Dissenters in 1719: The Salters' Hall Debate," *Journal of Ecclesiastical History* 4 (1953): 162-86.

Anglican disputes over the Trinity flared up in Oxford in 1691, when Rector Arthur Bury was expelled from Exeter College for his book, *The Naked Gospel*, which was charged with denying the divinity of Christ and "defiling the venerated mystery of the faith."[13] As the pamphlet war that followed his dismissal indicates, Bury was not alone in his doubts about the doctrine of the Trinity. Other prominent Anglicans were rumored to share them, including Dr. Tillotson, the Archbishop of Canterbury. In 1714 Bishop Samuel Clarke faced milder disciplinary proceedings as a result of the publication of *The Scripture-Doctrine of the Trinity* in 1712. After a diligent search, Clarke professed to find no definite biblical statement to support the Athanasian orthodoxy that the Son was of one divine substance with the Father.[14] Clarke's advice to treat the trinitarian question as a nonessential of the faith, on which Christians could reach their own conclusions, proved a more crushing blow for orthodoxy than an outright denial of the Trinity. Conrad Wright has described Clarke's *Scripture-Doctrine of the Trinity* as "a pervasive influence, spreading anti-Trinitarianism in the Church of England and dissenting circles alike for two generations after its publication."[15]

In combating attacks on trinitarian orthodoxy, its defenders found appeals to church tradition ineffective and scriptural arguments for the Trinity inconclusive. So they "gambled on reason,"[16] confident that the central truths of Christian faith could be vindicated by rational argument. To their great humiliation, and to the delight of their opponents, trinitarian apologists found themselves in contradiction and heated disagreement with each other. A prime example is the work of the orthodox apologist Bishop William Sherlock,[17] which was accused

13. Quoted in Redwood, *Reason, Ridicule and Religion*, p. 255, n. 11.

14. "What the proper Metaphysical Nature, Essence, or Substance of any of these divine Persons is, the Scripture has no where at all declared, but describes and distinguishes them always by their personal Characters, Offices, Powers, and Attributes." *The Scripture-Doctrine of the Trinity*, 3rd ed. (London, 1737), p. 234. The orthodoxy of Athanasius's view of the Godhead was established at the Council of Nicea in 325 C.E., which declared the Son "of the substance of the Father, God of God, Light of Light, true God of true God."

15. Conrad Wright, *Beginnings of Unitarianism in America* (Boston: Beacon Press, 1966), p. 201.

16. Stromberg, *Religious Liberalism*, p. 12.

17. *A Vindication of the Doctrines of the Holy and Ever Blessed Trinity, and of the Incarnation of the Son of God* (London, 1690); *A Defence of Dr. Sherlock's Notion of a Trinity in Unity, In An-*

by his fellow trinitarians of promoting tritheism. Roland Stromberg wryly suggests that "the doctrine of the Trinity undoubtedly suffered more from Bishop Sherlock's defense than from Stephen Nye's attack."[18]

Among Dissenting circles, the precarious "happy union" between Presbyterians and Independents was shattered in the early eighteenth century by disputes over the Trinity. Independents tended to defend trinitarian orthodoxy, while Presbyterians, among whom there was a great yearning to reduce requirements for Christian belief to a "few and plain" truths, tended to claim religious liberty in this area.[19] The Dissenters' disputes over the Trinity culminated in the controversy at Salters' Hall, in which a slim majority decided to "stand on the Scriptures alone, rather than on the Scriptures as interpreted in the light of the historic creeds,"[20] and rejected calls for subscription to a trinitarian article. By no means all of the "Non-Subscribers" denied the doctrine of the Trinity. But it is perhaps fair to say, to paraphrase the judgment of a contemporary Dissenter, that "tho' they confessed the truth of the doctrine they quitted the importance of it."[21]

---

swer to the Animadversions upon His Vindication of the Doctrine of the Holy and Ever Blessed Trinity (London, 1694).

18. Stromberg, Religious Liberalism, p. 36. Though Edwards disagreed with figures like Newton, Tillotson, Clarke, and Nye on the Trinity, he drew on them appreciatively in defense of the reasonableness of other Christian doctrines in his "Miscellanies" notebooks, demonstrating his willingness to borrow good arguments where he could find them.

19. Stromberg, Religious Liberalism, p. 39.

20. Horton Davies, Worship and Theology in England: From Watts and Wesley to Martineau, 1690-1900, vol. 2 of Worship and Theology in England (Grand Rapids: Eerdmans, 1996), p. 83.

21. Roger Thomas, "The Non-Subscription Controversy," p. 185. Thomas is quoting the opinion of Thomas Reynolds on his assistant, James Read. McLachlan, Socinianism, pp. 333-34, argues that the force of liturgy should not be underestimated in accounting for the easy spread of antitrinitarianism among Dissenters in the eighteenth century. Among Anglican circles, there were several proposals, both public and private, to revise the Prayer Book so as to eliminate, or at least blunt, its trinitarian force. But these never carried the day, and so worshipers continued to be formed by address and petitions to the three persons of the Trinity, regardless of what their Anglican parson did or did not say from the pulpit. By contrast, among Presbyterians and other members of the old Dissent, the metrical version of the Psalms took the place of the Prayer Book and the hymn book. The lack of trinitarian reference in this part of the liturgy was reinforced by the absence of reading of the creed or catechism during worship services.

New England was not impervious to English antitrinitarian currents, although the main disagreement between theological liberals and conservatives in the first half of the eighteenth century concerned human, not divine, nature.[22] It was the Arminianism of Samuel Clarke, not his trinitarian views, which first appealed to New England liberals.[23] However, Arminian tendencies in New England, at least among the seekers of a more "reasonable" faith, proved to be harbingers of antitrinitarianism.[24] By the end of Edwards's life, this rising consciousness about the problems of moving from Scripture to trinitarian doctrine spilled over into New England. Jonathan Mayhew scandalized the Massachusetts clergy by boldly asserting that "my Bible saith not . . . that there is any other true God, besides '[Jesus'] Father and our Father, his God and our God.'"[25] It was the defenders of classical trinitarianism, Mayhew insinuated, who were unscriptural: those who "contend, and foam, and curse their brethren, for the sake of the Athanasian Trinity . . . do not love and fear the ONE living and true God as they ought to do."[26] The 1756 Boston republication of Thomas Emlyn's *Humble Inquiry* into Christ's "Deity and Glory," with a preface challenging theologians to refute the Arian position, also troubled New Eng-

22. Daniel Walker Howe, *The Unitarian Conscience: Harvard Moral Philosophy, 1805-1861* (Cambridge, Mass.: Harvard University Press, 1970), p. 5. Boston and its surrounding towns were the focal point for the development of religious liberalism in New England.

23. Wright, *Beginnings of Unitarianism,* p. 202. Arminianism was a Reformed movement of revolt against a stricter Calvinist doctrine of irresistible grace, which was thought to vitiate all human responsibility in salvation. In eighteenth-century New England it became a derogatory catch-all term for confidence in the human ability to win divine approval by moral striving.

24. According to Wright, *Beginnings of Unitarianism,* p. 200, though Arminianism and antitrinitarianism were logically distinct, "temperamentally and historically they went together." By the end of the eighteenth century the pietistic streams of Arminianism in Massachusetts had been channeled into the "new" revivals and Methodism; Baptist and Methodist churches had emerged as the popular alternatives to the Standing Order. What remained of this once comprehensive and monolithic structure was then split by Arianism.

25. Jonathan Mayhew, *Sermons upon the Following Subjects, Viz. On Hearing the Word* (Boston, 1755), p. 269.

26. Mayhew, *Sermons,* p. 268. The 1805 appointment of Henry Ware as Hollis Professor of Divinity at Harvard is usually seen as the precipitating factor in the Unitarian controversy. In Connecticut the encroachment of Arianism was much less pronounced; there were only three Unitarian churches in the state by the end of the century.

land defenders of orthodoxy.[27] In a 1757 letter to Prof. Wigglesworth at Harvard, Edwards expressed his uneasiness after reading a book by Mayhew, "wherein he ridicules the doctrine of the Trinity," and, in response to Emlyn's book, sounded "the call of God that some one should appear in open defense of this doctrine."[28]

However, many of the scandalized New Englanders who shared Edwards's concern for theological orthodoxy found the doctrine of the Trinity necessary to affirm but convenient to ignore.[29] As Conrad Wright has noted, "the Trinity was a part of Puritan theology, but it never took up much of the attention of the first settlers. Neglect of it was an established custom long before any Arians appeared on the scene."[30] Puritan writings provide ample documentation for Wright's thesis. However, this judgment needs to be qualified when considering the New England members of the Spiritual Brethren such as John Cotton.[31] As Cotton's English counterpart Thomas Goodwin insisted, "the great and mysterious truth of the trinity of persons in one God . . . is not a mere speculative notion, but a truth, in which the faith and practice of a Christian is concerned."[32] Like Goodwin and others of the Cambridge Brethren, Edwards paid a good deal of theological attention to the doctrine, not simply for the sake of preserving orthodoxy, but because of his conviction of the Trinity's profound practical value for Christian faith and life.

27. Thomas Emlyn, *An Humble Inquiry into the Scripture-account of Jesus Christ; or, A Short Argument concerning His Deity and Glory, according to the Gospel*, 5th ed. (Boston, 1756).

28. Works, 16, p. 699.

29. As Paul Tillich asserted, "Protestantism generally did not attack the dogma, but it did not use it either." *Systematic Theology*, 3 vols. (Chicago: University of Chicago Press, 1963), 3, p. 291. For a larger-scale discussion of the loss of the Trinity as a practically relevant doctrine, see Catherine Mowry LaCugna, *God for Us: The Trinity and the Christian Life* (San Francisco: Harper Collins, 1991).

30. Wright, *Beginnings of Unitarianism*, p. 203.

31. See the Introduction for a description of the Spiritual Brethren and their theology.

32. John C. Miller, ed., *The Works of Thomas Goodwin, D.D.*, 12 vols. (Edinburgh: James Nichol, 1861-67), 6, p. 5. Henceforth, Goodwin, *Works*.

The Practical Value of the Trinity

Jonathan Edwards's lavish praise of Peter van Mastricht's *Theoretico-practica Theologia* as "much better than Turretin or any other book in the world, excepting the Bible, in my opinion,"[33] may come as a surprise to those who have accepted the common portrayal of the Reformed scholastics as abstract speculators in the dusty realms of theological arcana. In fact, for many of these late-sixteenth- and seventeenth-century codifiers of Calvinism, the task of theological reflection had a decidedly practical orientation.[34] As van Mastricht wrote, echoing William Ames, "Christian theology is nothing other than the doctrine of living to God through Christ; or, the doctrine that follows the way of piety."[35] In the theological system so admired by Edwards, van Mastricht developed a four-part architectonic that included an exposition of the practical implications for each theological locus, including the doctrine of the Trinity. Edwards's debt to the Reformed scholastics has been largely overlooked in interpretations of his thought, not least because many of them remain in untranslated Latin.[36] The Reformed scholastics took on the intellectual task of shaping the received trinitarian tradition to the contours of Reformed Protestantism, particularly its teachings on Scripture and grace, and its emphasis on God's unity and sovereignty. In different ways, Edwards shared with continental theologians like Francis Turretin and Peter van Mastricht the task of building on the relatively unformed trinitarianism of the sixteenth-century Protestant Re-

---

33. 1746/47 letter to Joseph Bellamy, in Works, 16, p. 217.

34. I am following Richard Muller's periodization of Reformed theology after the Reformation era (ca. 1517-1565). The period of early orthodoxy (ca. 1565-1640) includes, among others, William Ames, Bartholomaeus Keckermann, William Perkins, and Johannes Wollebius. The high orthodox period (ca. 1640-1700) includes Johann Heidegger, Peter van Mastricht, and Francis Turretin. Figures in late orthodoxy (1700-1790) include John Owen and Francis Turretin's son, Jean François. See *Post-Reformation Reformed Dogmatics*, 1, pp. 40-52. Edwards drew on the writings of figures from all of these periods.

35. Peter van Mastricht, *Theoretico-practica Theologia* (Utrecht, 1724), I.i.xxxvi.

36. Norman Fiering estimates that "not half of the basic academic sources in Latin that the Puritans themselves relied on have been studied, and all sorts of claims are made without the authors most of the time having the vaguest idea of what was *distinctively* New England Puritan or simply a commonplace of Protestant scholasticism." "Early American Philosophy vs. Philosophy in Early America," *Transactions of the Charles S. Peirce Society* 13 (1977): 229.

formers, using new philosophical tools and responding to new cultural and theological contexts. Their trinitarian convergences deserve more notice than they have received.

With van Mastricht, Jonathan Edwards was convinced that "a true knowledge of God and divine things is a practical knowledge."[37] Even the doctrine of the Trinity needed to "follow the way of piety." To be sure, demonstrating the practical value of the doctrine of the Trinity was a particularly delicate task in late-seventeenth-century Europe. Van Mastricht's antitrinitarian opponents, the Socinians, were arguing the strictly practical nature of theology as a basis upon which to dispense with doctrines such as the Trinity. We have already seen Edwards's willingness to take on various opponents of trinitarianism in his own day. At the root of his vigorous defense of doctrinal orthodoxy was the practical conviction that a trinitarian vision of God lay at the heart of Christian worship and ethics.

In an early entry in his "Miscellanies" notebooks, written while he was a tutor at Yale, Edwards ruminated: "I used to think sometimes with myself, if such doctrines as those of the Trinity and the decrees are true, yet what need was there of revealing them in the gospel? what good do they do towards the advancing [of] holiness?" He proceeded to answer his own question in typically Puritan fashion. "I know by experience," Edwards insisted, "how useful these doctrines be":

> such doctrines as these are glorious inlets into the knowledge and view of the spiritual world, and the contemplation of supreme things; the knowledge of which I have experienced how much it contributes to the betterment of the heart.[38]

As he asserted in a slightly later entry, since "Duties are founded on doctrines, . . . the revelation we now have of the Trinity, of the love of God, of the love of Christ to sinners . . . make[s] a vast alteration with respect to the reason and obligations to many amiable and exalted duties, so that they are as it were new."[39] Here the question of the value of the doctrine of the Trinity was asked and answered from the "way of piety."

This chapter and the next will focus on two impediments to appro-

37. Works, 8, p. 296.
38. Works, 13, p. 328 (no. 181).
39. Works, 13, p. 416 (no. 343).

priating trinitarian doctrine according to the "way of piety" — the Reformed wariness of nonscriptural images for the Trinity, and the divine simplicity tradition. The majority of Puritans and Reformed scholastics chose one of two routes: either they pursued the practical implications of the Trinity at the cost of great theological tension with their views of Scripture and divine simplicity, or they downplayed the theological importance of the Trinity. Edwards took a different approach. His metaphysical vision funded both a free use of nonscriptural trinitarian images and a markedly casual attitude towards the divine simplicity tradition, permitting him to explore boldly what "betterment of the heart" and ethical guidance the Trinity might provide.

Reformed Distrust of Trinitarian Analogies

John Calvin's prescription against thinking or speaking about God in ways not directly prompted by Scripture[40] made later Reformed theologians distinctly uneasy with the congruence Catholics found between Scripture and human traditions. Polemics against the Catholic appeal to reason and church tradition in defending Christian doctrine were commonplace in Puritan writings.[41] As John Cotton, a prominent member of the Spiritual Brethren, insisted,

> for our Religion, if wee cannot fetch it from the Apostles first Doctrin, and from the Prophets and Apostles of old, wee will renounce it, but when we can bring for all our Doctrin, the seal of the Prophets and Apostles, we have a sure note of the truth, wee preach no truth, but what Christ and his Apostles taught.[42]

In the case of the Trinity, the Reformed insistence on teaching only what "Christ and his Apostles taught" became evident in their wariness

40. Calvin, *Institutes,* I.xiii.21.

41. Edwards shared in the general anti-Catholicism of his Puritan heritage. See his account of the gradual "rise of Antichrist" in the Roman church, as "superstition and ignorance more and more prevailed" and "the holy Scripture by degrees was taken out of the hands of the laity, the better to promote [the privileges of the clergy]." Works, 9, pp. 412-15.

42. John Cotton, *A Practical Commentary . . . upon the First Epistle Generall of John* (London, 1656), p. 189. Henceforth, *First John Generall.*

about the Catholic use of nonscriptural analogies for the Trinity. Puritans were quick to see in the Catholic tradition of natural images of the Trinity the arrogant attempt of human reason to discern divine mysteries apart from the guidance of Scripture.

The Reformed scholastics shared the general Reformed reluctance to pursue created images for the Trinity. An index of their wariness is that this subject was one of the few places in their theological systems in which the Reformed scholastics criticized Augustine. Van Mastricht is typical in his caution that "the Trinity can neither be investigated nor solidly proved by natural reason."[43] Despite the strong theological taboos against using natural images for the Trinity, both Puritan and Reformed scholastic theologians employed them to some extent. The centrality of the Trinity for their understanding of God and the way of "living to God through Christ" encouraged an expansion of theological vocabulary and images beyond scriptural boundaries. In this way, the two main streams of nonscriptural analogies for the Trinity — the social and the psychological — both made their way into Reformed trinitarian reflection, albeit furtively.

The Social Vein

The social vein of trinitarian analogy emphasized the love and intimate fellowship among the members of the Trinity, by likening them to a family, a society, or a communion of friends. The first thing to recognize is how rare it is in Reformed writings to find the Godhead explicitly referred to as a family or other social entity. That believers are the children of God is a commonplace in almost all expressions of Christian theology. That the Godhead itself is a family is not. Scriptural, theological, and cultural factors all play into the rarity of this locution.

The Puritans found indirect biblical support for social images of the Trinity in the Johannine writings of the New Testament, where the relationship between the Father and Son is depicted as a loving and intimate union. As Jesus prays to the Father on behalf of his followers, "The

---

43. *Theoretico-practica Theologia*, II.xxiv.21. (Trinitatem ratione naturali, nec investigari, nec solide demonstrari posse.) Unless otherwise noted, English translations of Reformed scholastic works are my own.

glory that you have given me I have given them, so that they may be one, as we are one, I in them and you in me, that they may become completely one, so that the world may know that you have sent me and have loved them even as you have loved me" (John 17:22-23). The step from the biblical language of Father and Son to calling the Godhead a family or society may seem like a small one. In fact, within the Reformed theological framework, it was a large one, and rarely ventured. God is never referred to in the Bible as a family or society; despite the concentration of *Father-Son* language for God in certain books, the New Testament canon reflected the strong monotheism of the Hebrew Scriptures. The Reformed emphases on *sola Scriptura* and the oneness of God, combined with theological convictions about human sinfulness and a corresponding distrust of human analogies for God, made direct references to the Godhead as a family or society unusual, and even daring.

However, there were both theological and cultural factors that tempted Reformed theologians to at least implicit use of the social analogy. Social images of the Trinity fit well within the framework of covenant theology that was broadly adhered to by both the Puritans and the Reformed scholastics. In particular, the notion of the *pactum salutis*, the eternal covenant of redemption made between the Father and the Son on behalf of human sinners, lent itself to a variety of explicitly social metaphors for the Godhead. As the Scottish Puritan David Dickson asserted, God's "way to save sinners" was "by virtue of and according to the tenor of the covenant of redemption, made and agreed upon between God the Father and God the Son, in the council of the Trinity before the world began."[44] Edwards described it as an "agreement which the persons of the Trinity came into from eternity as it were by mutual consultation and covenant."[45] Protestant scholastic treatments of the covenant of redemption often suggested a social view of the Trinity, though scholastic theology's strong emphasis on divine oneness, combined with a theological method that strove for linguistic precision and consistency, made overt use of social images rare. Refer-

44. David Dickson, *The Sum of Saving Knowledge,* with an introduction by John MacPherson (Edinburgh: T. & T. Clark, n.d.), p. 54. See Chapter 3 for an explication of the covenant of redemption.

45. *Misc.,* no. 993. Nos. 1064 and 1091 explore the relations between the intratrinitarian covenant of redemption and the covenant of grace that binds believers to Christ.

ences to the Trinity as a council in which plans for human redemption were purposed, and to the Father and Son as distinct covenant partners in this affair, had obvious practical value in assuring believers of their salvation. "It is a comfortable consideration," Richard Sibbes declared, "to see how our salvation . . . stands upon the unity of the three glorious persons in the Trinity, that all join in one for the making of man happy."[46] But the social images of the Godhead funded by the covenant of redemption strained Reformed rules about divine oneness and nonscriptural language for God to the breaking point. While there was ample scriptural precedent for the idea of a covenant between God and human persons, Reformed theologians could muster only the skimpiest biblical support for the idea of an intratrinitarian covenant of redemption. It seemed to be more the result of wishful theological speculation than honest searching of Scriptures.

The tremendous emphasis on familial and communal bonds within Puritan society also encouraged social images. David D. Hall has pointed to the close "interweaving of the family and religion" in the popular piety of Puritan New England. Family was for these Puritans "the most important bridge between religion and society," and the centrality of these familial bonds was often reflected in their language for God.[47] As John Cotton exclaimed,

> I will be thy God, that is, not only a good Father, a good Mother, a good King, a good friend, but whatsoever is good in the creature, that he promiseth to be to us, he will be a good Father, and Ruler, and Friend, and Husband to us, partly in his own person, that if all those fail, he will be all these to us, or else he will dispense himself so in those instruments, that we shall see Gods goodnesse in every creature.[48]

Cotton's effusiveness reflects the richness, but also the twists and tensions in Puritan patterns of familial imagery for God. These patterns mirrored both biblical precedents and Puritan social realities.

Following the biblical example, familial language for God in Puritan

---

46. Sibbes, *Complete Works*, 4, p. 294.

47. David D. Hall, *Worlds of Wonder, Days of Judgment: Popular Religious Belief in Early New England* (New York: Alfred Knopf, 1989), p. 241.

48. Cotton, *First John Generall*, p. 382.

writings was predominantly masculine, depicting God as father and husband, and Christ as son, husband, and brother. The male voices of the biblical and Puritan writers encouraged a propensity to describe believers in similarly masculine terms, as sons of God and younger brothers of Christ. Occasionally maternal images were used,[49] but God was not portrayed as sister, daughter, or wife. Rejecting the Catholic tradition of Marian devotion, the Puritans did not appropriate the notions of Mary, Jesus, and Joseph as a "holy family," or of Mary in particular as the "mother of God." But they did draw on the larger biblical and theological tradition of depicting believers as the bride or wife of God and Christ in order to fill the large vacuum in feminine imagery for God in both Scripture and Puritan writings.

In her study of female piety in Puritan New England, Amanda Porterfield notes that, "as the most fundamental unit of social organization in Puritan societies, and as a model for church and state as well, the marriage bond was the principal referent of Puritan experiences of God."[50] This remarkable claim finds considerable support in Puritan literature, though the imagery of Father and child runs a close second. The fact that spousal imagery for describing the believer's relation to God is abundant in Scripture no doubt encouraged its prominence.[51] The

49. For an account of Puritan maternal images for God, see David Leverenz, *The Language of Puritan Feeling: An Exploration in Literature, Psychology, and Social History* (New Brunswick, N.J.: Rutgers, 1980).

50. Amanda Porterfield, *Female Piety in Puritan New England: The Emergence of Religious Humanism* (Oxford: Oxford University Press, 1992), p. 11.

51. See Richard Godbeer, "'Love Raptures': Marital, Romantic, and Erotic Images of Jesus Christ in Puritan New England, 1670-1730," *New England Quarterly* 68 (1995): 355-84. On pp. 373-74 he discusses Puritan appeals to Scripture to justify the use of the marriage trope as appropriate to depict the union between redeemer and redeemed. There is a burgeoning body of literature on the intersections of gender and religion in Puritan society. The classic is Edmund Morgan, *The Puritan Family: Religion and Domestic Relations in 17th-century New England* (1944; reprinted, New York: Harper and Row, 1966). See also Carol Karlsen, *The Devil in the Shape of a Woman: Witchcraft in Colonial New England* (New York: Norton, 1987); Kathleen Verduin, "'Our Cursed Natures': Sexuality and the Puritan Conscience," *New England Quarterly* 56 (1983): 220-37; Janet Wilson James, ed., *Women in American Religion* (Philadelphia: University of Pennsylvania Press, 1980); Margaret W. Masson, "The Typology of the Female as a Model for the Regenerate: Puritan Preaching, 1690-1730," *Signs* 2, no. 2 (Winter 1976): 304-15; Laurel Thatcher Ulrich, *Good Wives: Image and Reality in the Lives of Women in Northern New England, 1650-1750* (New York: Oxford University Press, 1980).

church is often portrayed as Christ's bride in Johannine writings,[52] and the Puritans were particularly fond of reading this relationship back into the love poetry of the Song of Songs. Here, as Richard Sibbes declared,

> the union between Christ and his spouse is so familiarly and livelily set forth by that union which is between the husband and the wife, that, though ungodly men might take offense at it, yet the godly may be bettered by it.[53]

The heavy concentration of familial language in Puritan writings for depicting God's relations with believers makes the rarity of overt portrayals of the Godhead as a family all the more striking. The lack of scriptural precedent seems an obvious factor.

It is tempting to extend this argument a bit further. Porterfield astutely observes that the Puritan appeals to the marriage bond exalted a form of social relationship that was hierarchical as well as affectionate, reinforcing at the same time both true piety and appropriate patterns of social deference. As Sibbes declared, "He is our husband, and we give our consent to take Christ to be so, that he shall rule and govern us. . . . There is no relation, nor any degree of subjection and subordination, but it sets forth this sweet union and agreement between Christ and us."[54] In explicating how "the believing soul is the bride and spouse of the Son of God," Edwards was even more explicit about the woman's appropriate subjection:

> Thus it's against nature for a man to love a woman as wife that is rugged, daring and presumptuous, and trusts to herself, and think she is able to protect herself and needs none of her husband's defense or guidance. And it is impossible a woman should love a man as an husband, except she can confide in him, and sweetly rest in him as a safeguard. . . . Wherefore, the dispositions of soul which Christ looks at in his spouse are a sweet reliance and confidence in him, a humble trust in him as her only rock of defence, whither she may flee.[55]

---

52. See John 3:29; Revelation 21:2, 9; and 22:17; also Ephesians 5:25-32.
53. "The Spouse, Her Earnest Desire after Christ," in Sibbes, *Complete Works*, 2, p. 201.
54. Sibbes, *Complete Works*, 4, pp. 24-25.
55. *Works*, 13, pp. 220-21 (no. 37).

The relations between parent and child in the Puritan family were also characterized by both affection and hierarchy, and calls for Christians to be loving and obedient children of God the Father were likewise abundant. In this way, the imagery of the saint as bride of Christ or as child of the Father reinscribed the patterns of Puritan family life.

But for profound theological reasons, images of the Godhead as a family or society could not mirror Puritan social hierarchies. The pronounced lack of feminine imagery in mainstream trinitarianism yielded what was for the Puritans the social oddity of an all-male household. Even the familiar parental relationship of the Father to the Son resisted traditional patterns of social deference. The persons of the Trinity were all of the same divine essence and thus equal to each other in power, wisdom, and goodness; to insist on the subordination of the Son to the Father risked charges of Arianism, the denial that the Son is fully God with the Father. As Edwards insisted, the beautiful harmony of the divine society required the ontological equality of its members — if the persons are not of the same essence, they "don't infinitely consent."[56]

Arian views were gaining new currency among antitrinitarians, beginning in the Reformation period. The antitrinitarians found social instantiations of their theological claim that the Son is subordinate to the Father close at hand. Defenders of orthodoxy, by contrast, had to distinguish between human familial patterns and trinitarian relations. To the objection that sons and fathers are often not equals, John Cotton replied, "True, amongst men, but in the God-head no Person can be superiour to another, there are no distempers, nor misery."[57] The loving union of the persons of the Trinity was a union of equals. Thus Richard Sibbes's exclamation that "the Trinity should be the pattern of our unity"[58] represented a subtle threat to established social patterns, rather than a reinforcement of them. The subversive undertones of appeals to the Trinity as the perfect model of society and loving communion may also have stanched the flow of social images for the Trinity in much Puritan piety.

The scriptural, theological, and cultural factors that discouraged so-

---

56. Works, 13, p. 283 (no. 117).
57. *First John Generall,* p. 182.
58. Sibbes, *Complete Works,* 3, p. 194.

cial trinitarianism make its presence in Reformed scholastics like van Mastricht and the Cambridge Brethren all the more striking. A passage Edwards cited from van Mastricht in his private notebooks described the trinitarian economy after the analogy of a household: van Mastricht referred to the first person of the Trinity as the *Pater-familias,* and noted "the eternal fellowship and society of this family, into which the church was adopted in time."[59] Thomas Goodwin, to whom Edwards referred in several late "Miscellanies" entries, portrayed the persons of the Trinity as "three blessed Companions of a knot, and Society among themselves; enjoying Fellowship, and Delights accordingly in themselves."[60]

Richard Sibbes, Goodwin's older Cambridge contemporary, appealed to John 17:21 in urging the church to let the Trinity serve as the pattern of Christian unity. "The sum" of Christ's heavenly prayer, "That they may be one, as we are one," is "the unity of the church to the end of the world."[61] New England's Cotton Mather, grandson of John Cotton, would later appeal to the same verse in urging that "our Union with one another must carry a Resemblance to the Union between the Father and the Son in the Eternal God-head. This is the pattern for our Union given here, As thou, Father, are in me, and I in thee." Using the Father and Son as a model, Mather argued, the union of the saints must provide "a near Perception of one anothers Cases" and fill them "with Joy in and Love to one another."[62] In churches rent by "hateful . . .

---

59. *Theoretico-practica Theologia,* II.xxiv.11. (In hujus familiae KOINONIAN et quasi societatem, in tempore adscivit Ecclesiam.) Edwards refers to this passage in Works, 13, p. 524 (no. 482).

60. *A Discourse of the Knowledge of God the Father, and His Son Jesus Christ,* in *The Works of Thomas Goodwin,* 5 vols. (London, 1682), 2, p. 7. The first edition of Goodwin's works is a five-volume folio edition, published posthumously. Unfortunately, most of my citations from Goodwin will rely on the nineteenth-century Nichol's edition, which, like nineteenth-century editions of Edwards's works, considerably "improved" the fresh images and colloquial syntax of the first edition.

61. Sibbes, *Complete Works,* 3, p. 194.

62. Cotton Mather, *Blessed Unions* (Boston, 1692), pp. 45, 49. Edwards was probably introduced to Cotton Mather's works in Timothy Edwards's library. Thomas Schafer, *Works,* 13, p. 256, thinks this may have been a proximate source for Edwards's trinitarianism. Cotton Mather's emphasis on trinitarian union suggests that he shared something of his grandfather's "particular and perpetual" admiration of Richard Sibbes. See *Magnalia Christi Americana; or, the Ecclesiastical History of New England,* 2 vols., ed. Thomas Robbins (London, 1702), 1, p. 255.

schism and division," the Trinity was to serve as a pattern for joyful and loving union.

Edwards also seems to have found Johannine language especially apt for undergirding the use of social metaphors for the Trinity. In the *Treatise on Grace* and the *Discourse on the Trinity*, Edwards made three times as many references to John as he did to the synoptic gospels and Acts combined. There are distant echoes of Richard of St. Victor in Edwards's reference to 1 John 4:16:

> That in John God is love shews that there are more persons than one in the deity, for it shews love to be essential and necessary to the deity so that His nature consists in it, and this supposes that there is an eternal and necessary object, because all love respects another that is the beloved.[63]

Like Sibbes and Mather, Edwards also drew extensively on the "high priestly prayer" in the gospel of John in urging believers to be one, even as the Father and Son are one: the Trinity was the paradigm for earthly Christian unity. But in referring to the Trinity as "a family of three" and as "a society of three persons," Edwards also signaled his willingness, along with the Cambridge Brethren, to go beyond what has "been said in Scripture in express words."[64]

It is hard to reconcile this strikingly social view of the Godhead with traditional Reformed views of Scripture and affirmations of divine oneness. The appeal of familial images in developing a "practical" understanding of the Trinity is evident for both van Mastricht and the Spiritual Brethren. Yet overt use of social images is rare in van Mastricht, reflecting the Reformed scholastic striving for theological precision. The Cambridge Brethren, who tended to be less concerned with linguistic exactness and the interconnections among theological doctrines, used social images for the Trinity a bit more freely. But in neither case was there any theological justification given for bending traditional rules for theological discourse.

Edwards, by contrast, justified his willingness to use nonscriptural language for the Godhead by articulating a distinctive view of typology. In a typological worldview, "the things of the world are ordered [and]

63. Helm, *Trinity*, p. 100.
64. Works, 13, p. 257 (no. 94).

designed to shadow forth spiritual things."[65] John F. Wilson has noted the development of typology among the Reformed scholastics and Puritans beyond the earlier Reformers' austere adherence to literal or historical interpretation of Scripture. He argues that "a marked expansion of the tradition of typological interpretation . . . enabled later Protestants, especially English Puritans and their New England descendants, to find sufficient latitude to work imaginatively with biblical materials."[66] A typological interpretation of the Old Testament permitted them to find in Christ the fulfillment of God's promises to Israel. Scottish and English theologians took the further step of "reading their immediate struggles and goals in terms of apocalyptic symbols in the Bible."[67] Wilson finds that Edwards "accepted and wholeheartedly embraced — indeed developed significantly — the typological approach to Scripture which came to him from Puritan-Protestant figural sources."[68]

But he "also moved beyond and transformed" this approach in various ways. Most significantly for our purposes, "Edwards detached the typological framework from its exclusive linkage to scriptural sources," finding "images of divine things" in nature, human history, and current events.[69] Thus Edwards found it unreasonable "to say that we must not say that such things are types of these and those things unless the Scripture has expressly taught us that they are so."[70]

I expect by very ridicule and contempt to be called a man of a very fruitful brain and copious fancy, but they are welcome to it. I am

65. Works, II, p. 53. For Edwards's use of typology see the "Editor's Introduction" to *Images of Divine Things* and *Types of the Messiah* in Works, II. See also Stephen H. Daniel, *The Philosophy of Jonathan Edwards: A Study in Divine Semiotics* (Bloomington: University of Indiana Press, 1994); and Janice Knight, "Learning the Language of God: Jonathan Edwards and the Typology of Nature," *William and Mary Quarterly* Third Series, 48, no. 4 (October 1991): 531-51.

66. Works, 9, p. 47. For the development in Protestant typology see Wilson's "Editor's Introduction," Works, 9, pp. 40-50, and Mason I. Lowance, Jr., *The Language of Canaan: Metaphor and Symbol in New England from the Puritans to the Transcendentalists* (Cambridge, Mass.: Harvard University Press, 1980).

67. Works, 9, p. 46.

68. Works, 9, p. 49.

69. Works, 9, p. 49.

70. Works, II, p. 152.

not ashamed to own that I believe that the whole universe, heaven and earth, air and seas, and the divine constitution and history of the holy Scriptures, be full of images of divine things, as full as a language is of words; and that the multitudes of those things that I have mentioned are but a very small part of what is really intended to be signified and typified by these things.[71]

As Mason Lowance affirms, "the world of nature became a vast book now available to the elect saints through the 'new sense of things.'"[72]

Edwards's expansive transformation of typology was integrally related to his trinitarian view of God. The cornerstone of his typological trinitarianism is that "God is a communicative being." For intelligent creatures, God's "communication of himself to their understandings is his glory, and the communication of himself with respect to their wills, the enjoying faculty, is their happiness."[73] This twofold communication parallels Edwards's articulation of the psychological analogy. As he noted in the notebook entry immediately preceding this one, the Logos is "God's perfect understanding of himself" and the Holy Ghost is "the love, the joy, the excellence, the holiness of God."[74] The eternal communication of wisdom and love within God finds fitting external expression in God's communication of wisdom and love to the creation. Indeed, for Edwards, "the great and universal end of God's creating the world was to communicate himself."[75]

In communicating divine truth to human understanding, God employs types. As Edwards declared in his "Types" notebook, "Types are a certain sort of language, as it were, in which God is wont to speak to us."[76] While this divine speaking is paradigmatically put forth in Scripture, it is not exclusively confined there. Like a grammar teacher who writes out the conjugations of only a few paradigm verbs, God "han't expressly explained all the types of Scriptures, but has done so much as is sufficient to teach us the language."[77] As God's pupils, believers are

71. Works, 11, p. 152.
72. Works, 11, p. 180.
73. Works, 13, p. 410 (no. 332).
74. Works, 13, pp. 409-10 (no. 331).
75. Works, 13, p. 410 (no. 332).
76. Works, 11, p. 150.
77. Works, 11, p. 151.

to acquire an ear for this divine language in the rest of Scripture, but also in other arenas in which God's voice is still sounding. For Edwards, "very much of the wisdom of God in the creation appears in his so ordering things natural, that they livelily represent things divine and spiritual. . . ."[78] "'Tis very fit and becoming of God, who is infinitely wise, so to order things that there should be a voice of his in his works instructing those that behold them, and pointing forth and showing divine mysteries and things more immediately appertaining to himself and his spiritual kingdom."[79]

Edwards's expanded view of typology provided authorization for his use of nonscriptural images for the Trinity. Noting that "we are expressly taught" in Scripture that marriage is a "type of the union between Christ and the church (Eph. 5:30-32)," he boldly amplified this assertion by adding, "And if God designed this for a type of what is spiritual, why not many other things in the constitution and ordinary state of human society, and the world of mankind?"[80] The lack of direct scriptural precedent is not a hindrance to identifying divine types embedded in "the ordinary state of human society." Freed from strict adherence to the limits of the scriptural canon, Edwards marveled at the "innumerable things in human affairs that are lively pictures of the things of the gospel, such as shield, tower, and marriage, family."[81] *Family,* as we have seen, served for him as a type not only of the union of saints with each other and with God, but also of the union among the persons of the Godhead. What is required for theological fluency is an intimate acquaintance with the particular "idiom" of God's language of types. Otherwise,

> We shall be just like one that pretends to speak any language that han't thoroughly learnt it. We shall use many barbarous expressions that fail entirely of the proper beauty of the language, that are very harsh in the ears of those that are well versed in the language.[82]

78. Works, 13, p. 284 (no. 119).
79. Works, 11, p. 67.
80. Works, 11, pp. 53-54.
81. Works, 13, p. 284 (no. 119).
82. Works, 11, p. 151.

Clearly, Edwards thought that *family* and *society* were images of the Godhead that reflected "the proper beauty" of the divine language. No doubt his "uncommon union" with Sarah and the happiness of his own family life inclined him to exalt these images.[83] But these images also mirrored the correlation between divine excellency and divine plurality that was woven into his metaphysics.[84]

The issue of the propriety of nonscriptural language for the Godhead has not gone away. In the twentieth-century western church, the theological and liturgical appropriateness of the traditional trinitarian formula "Father, Son, and Holy Spirit" has been a topic of heated debate. Opponents of its exclusive use point out that there are many other scriptural references to God from which to draw for theological constructions. Despite the formula's long theological pedigree, they argue that "Father, Son, and Holy Spirit" has in the contemporary context "lost most of [its] power to evoke the central claims upon which trinitarian doctrine is based."[85] By contrast, some proponents of the formula insist that "Father, Son, and Holy Spirit" is God's only "proper name," a permanent element of Christian grammar.[86] All alternative trinitarian locutions are, in Edwards's phrase, "barbarous expressions that fail entirely of the proper beauty of the language."

83. Edwards's marriage with Sarah will receive further attention in Chapter 5.

84. See Chapter 2.

85. David S. Cunningham, *These Three Are One: The Practice of Trinitarian Theology* (Oxford: Blackwell, 1998), p. 70. As Cunningham notes elsewhere, it is not sufficient to appeal to the non-patriarchal intent of classical *Father* language, when "The overwhelming effective-history of this usage, as demonstrated in verbal and representational images over the centuries, has clearly been toward the masculinizing of God." Review of Gerald O'Collins, *The Tripersonal God: Understanding and Interpreting the Trinity*, in *Modern Theology* 17, no. 2 (April 2001): 254.

86. See, for example, Robert Jenson's argument for the traditional formula, in which he combines rationales from Scripture with a socio-biological appeal to male "ontological inferiority"! *Christian Dogmatics*, Carl E. Braaten and Robert W. Jenson, eds. (Philadelphia: Fortress Press, 1984), vol. 1, p. 94. Happily, his most recent arguments in *Systematic Theology* (New York: Oxford University Press, 1997), vol. 1, are considerably more circumspect regarding the theological significance of human reproductive roles. Arguments that Jesus' use of *Father* was radically different from that of his Jewish and Greek contemporaries are historically suspect. See Mary Rose D'Angelo, "Abba and 'Father': Imperial Theology and the Jesus Tradition," *Journal of Biblical Literature* (1992): 611-30. In my view, arguments that Jesus' use of *Father* gives us direct access to a transhistorical intratrinitarian "naming" are untenable on both exegetical and theological grounds.

Edwards's expansive approach to typology provides an intriguing angle on current debates about nontraditional and nonscriptural images for the Trinity. He liberally employs the terminology of *Father, Son,* and *Holy Ghost,* echoing the chorus of church tradition and ecumenical consensus around the classical formula. The Christian conception of God is not simply a mirror of human aspirations, to be freely constructed and reconstructed according to our present needs and current wisdom.[87] The Spirit's witness to the community of faith over long generations and across great geographical and ecclesial distances demands a patient and grateful hearing. On the other hand, Edwards's "grammatical" understanding of Christian speech about God is truer to the character of language and language acquisition than traditionalist views.[88] The goal of learning a language is not to be able to repeat correct paradigms, but to speak "beautifully" in a multitude of particular, often unforeseen situations. Edwards's insistence that the complex grammar of Scripture is paradigmatic guidance regarding the "innumerable things in human affairs that are lively pictures of the things of the gospel" authorizes great theological freedom. As he exclaimed in a sermon on Psalm 95:7-8, "the whole creation of God preaches" and all of the "providence of God preaches aloud."[89]

This generously expansive, assimilative, and confident approach to theological language finds echoes in Rowan Williams's assertion that theology should equip us to construct "effective images of a new world like the parables of Christ." In our language, Christians should be "nourished by the theological grasp of what the life and death of Jesus are, by scripture and the wrestle with dogmatic and devotional tradition; but not confined by it." "Our own untheologized memories and context, the particularity of where we are, . . . the efforts at meaning of

87. For the idea that the "available God" is a symbolic construct, to be reshaped as our perceptions of our circumstances warrant, see Gordon D. Kaufman, "Constructing the Concept of God," in Axel D. Steuer and James McClendon, Jr., *Is God God?* (Nashville: Abingdon, 1981), pp. 111-43; and Kaufman, "Reconstructing the Concept of God: De-Reifying the Anthropomorphisms," in Sarah Coakley and David A. Pailin, eds., *The Making and Remaking of Christian Doctrine: Essays in Honour of Maurice Wiles* (Oxford: Clarendon Press; New York: Oxford University Press, 1993), pp. 95-115.

88. I am indebted to Kathryn Johnson for this point.

89. Wilson H. Kimnach, ed., *Sermons and Discourses 1720-1723,* The Works of Jonathan Edwards, vol. 10 (New Haven: Yale University Press, 1992), p. 443.

the rest of the human race," are all places to listen for these new parables.[90] Similarly for Edwards, all images for divine things that attend the pattern and presence of Christ, even if they lack direct scriptural precedent, can attain to the "proper beauty" of God's language. Thus learning the idiom of God's language requires searching the whole biblical warehouse and even venturing far outside it, confident that the whole universe is full of "images of divine things."

The Psychological Vein

The place of the Holy Spirit in Edwards's "family of three" was less than secure. Like John Owen and Thomas Goodwin, Edwards stressed at times that the Holy Spirit was a distinct divine person, a full member of the Trinity, and thus deserving of human worship and adoration. In his *Treatise on Grace,* Edwards noted that

> He is often spoken of as a person, revealed under personal characters and in personal acts, and it speaks of His being acted on as a person, and the Scripture plainly ascribes every thing to Him that properly denotes a distinct person.[91]

But in practice, Edwards often ignored the Holy Spirit in his development of social images for the Trinity, focusing on the intimate union between the Father and Son alone.

In doing so, Edwards evidenced the deep Reformed ambivalence about the status of the Holy Spirit, an ambivalence inherited from the larger Christian tradition. Despite their preoccupation with the temporal presence of the Spirit in the lives of believers, Reformed theologians frequently left the Spirit's eternal role in the Trinity undefined, lifting up the relationship between the Father and the Son, and portraying the covenant of redemption as a two-way covenant between them. At more than one point in his trinitarian reflections, Edwards went so far as to deny that the Spirit was a proper object of divine or human consent. In his *Discourse on the Trinity,* he declared,

90. Rowan Williams, *On Christian Theology* (Oxford: Blackwell, 2000), pp. 42-43. This chapter is in part a critique of George Lindbeck's understanding of "Christian grammar."
91. Helm, *Trinity,* p. 57.

> There is nothing in Scripture that speaks of . . . any mutual friend-
> ship between the Holy Ghost and either of the other persons, or
> any command to love the Holy Ghost or to delight in or have any
> complacence in; tho' such commands are so frequent with respect
> to the other persons.[92]

Paradoxically, by denying the Spirit a role as a divine consenter, Edwards hoped to remedy what he saw as the neglect of the Spirit in Reformed theology. But increasing the theological prominence of the
Holy Spirit required tapping into another fund of trinitarian metaphors.

In Scripture, Edwards observed, "God is never said to love the Holy
Ghost." Despite this, the persons of the Trinity "are every way equal in
the society or family of the three" because the Holy Spirit is God's "infinite happiness and joy itself."[93] Edwards's representation of the Holy
Spirit as divine love, rather than as a divine lover, was a carry-over
from the Reformed appropriation of a second rich vein of trinitarian
metaphors. Albeit in modest and tentative ways, Reformed trinitarianism embraced an alternative image of the Godhead, pioneered by Augustine, and favored by most of western Christendom before the Reformation.

The Holy Spirit on the psychological model was not a loving and beloved member of the trinitarian society, but the divine love itself.[94] In
his extended meditations on this cluster of metaphors, Augustine introduced an important variant in the role of the Holy Spirit that
moved the psychological model closer to social models of the Trinity.
Instead of portraying the Spirit simply as God's self-love, Augustine
frequently depicted it as "the ineffable communion of the Father and
Son,"[95] thus positing a mutual reciprocity between the Son and Father
that the original model did not contain. At times Augustine went so far
as to describe the third person of the Trinity as the "community" or

---

92. Helm, *Trinity,* p. 129.

93. Helm, *Trinity,* pp. 122-23.

94. This was in keeping with the tendency in Scripture to speak of God's Spirit as
"poured out" on human persons. As Robert Merrihew Adams notes, this "suggests a
model that is more hydraulic than personal." *Finite and Infinite Goods: A Framework for
Ethics* (New York: Oxford University Press, 1999), p. 42.

95. Augustine, *The Trinity,* p. 190 (V.xi.12).

"society" of the other two.[96] This "communal" understanding of the Holy Spirit as divine love was the characteristic mode in which Edwards employed the psychological image.

But as with social images for the Trinity, the psychological model also raised questions of biblical precedent. Augustine had claimed, in a burst of confidence, that "the truth itself has persuaded us that as . . . the Son is the Word of God, so the Holy Spirit is love."[97] In fact, the scriptural foundation for the psychological model was very uneven. While the prologue of John's gospel and the Wisdom traditions of the Hebrew Scriptures provided considerable support for the first identification, Augustine himself conceded that Scripture "has not said that the Holy Spirit is love; had it done so, it would have removed no small part of this problem."[98] This unevenness of scriptural support was reflected in Puritan and scholastic usage. Whereas elaborate theological attention was given to the Son as the understanding or Word of God, appeals to the Holy Spirit as the personified Love of God were infrequent.

Citing Proverbs 8:23-24, John Cotton affirmed that Christ "is the wisdome or reason to his Father." In elaborating on this metaphor, Cotton revealed his ties to the larger western trinitarian tradition: "they that write of the Trinity expresse it thus, the Father from eternity considering and understanding himself, from this conceiving of the Father resulted the Image of himself, that was his Son."[99] But in typically Reformed fashion, Cotton did not extend the analogy beyond the reach of Scripture to the Holy Spirit as love, merely noting that "from them both resulteth the holy Ghost." Van Mastricht noted approvingly the tradition of appropriating various attributes to different persons in the Trinity, including wisdom to the Son; but in his exegetical treat-

---

96. E.g., *The Trinity*, p. 207 (VI.v.7); *In Jo.*, tr. XCIX.7; *Corp. Christ.* 1.4-6; and *Sermo* 71:20, 33. Jean Châtillon has traced the theme of the Holy Spirit as "concordia" and "connexio" from Augustine through Lombard, Abelard, and Aquinas. See "Unitas, Aequalitas, Concordia vel Connexio: Recherches sur les Origines de la Théorie Thomiste des Appropriations," in *St. Thomas Aquinas: Commemorative Studies*, 2 vols. (Toronto: Pontifical Institute of Mediaeval Studies, 1974), I, pp. 337-80.

97. Augustine, *The Trinity*, p. 287 (IX.xii.17).

98. Augustine, *The Trinity*, pp. 491-92 (XV.xvii.27). Augustine did appeal to Ephesians 4:3, which found "the unity of the Spirit in the bond of peace."

99. Cotton, *First John Generall*, p. 365.

ment of the Trinity, he appropriated the attribute of love to the Father, following the pattern of the Pauline doxology in 2 Corinthians 13:13.[100]

Calvin had criticized "that speculation of Augustine, that the soul is the reflection of the Trinity" as "by no means sound."[101] Nevertheless, occasional appeals to a full version of the psychological model of the Trinity can be found in both Puritan and Reformed scholastic sources. Bartholomaeus Keckermann was a late-sixteenth-century scholastic who gave some consideration to created analogies for the Trinity. Edwards used Keckermann's logic text at Yale, and may have been familiar with his theology as well. Keckermann noted parallels between the threefold unity of the Godhead and the mind, understanding, and will, as well as between the Trinity and the sun, its light, and its heat. Edwards noted these same "eminent and remarkable images of the Trinity" in a later addition to his *Discourse on the Trinity*. In describing the generation of the Son, Keckermann wrote

> Thus God's knowledge returns and bends back from eternity upon itself, i.e., upon God. Just as the soul thinks of itself . . . and this thought or intellection is called reflex. . . . (All intellection is the conceiving of some image. Either, therefore, we must attribute such an image to God or make Him irrational and ἀνόητος.)[102]

Like Keckermann, Edwards wrote of God's "reflex act of knowledge" and compared it to human processes of reflection. Keckermann, however, thought that human reason could only illustrate the doctrine of the Trinity, not prove it, whereas Edwards, as we shall see, occasionally made rash claims about "the reach of naked reason" in perceiving the Trinity.

The much more familiar names of William Ames and Richard Baxter and Cotton Mather also deserve mention in this context. With some reticence, Ames, in his great textbook, noted that the trinitarian relations "may be sketched in part by a figure":

---

100. Mastricht, *Theoretico-practica Theologia,* II.xxiv.2.

101. Calvin, *Institutes,* I.xv.4.

102. Keckermann, *Systema Sacrosanctae Theologiae,* in *Opera Omnia,* 2 vols. (Geneva, 1611), 2, p. 72. Quoted in Heinrich Heppe, *Reformed Dogmatics,* trans. G. T. Thomson (Grand Rapids: Baker, 1978), p. 106.

The Father is, as it were, *Deus intelligens,* God understanding; the Son who is the express image of the Father is *Deus intellectus,* God understood; and the Holy Spirit, flowing and breathed from the Father through the Son, is *Deus dilectus,* God loved.[103]

In *The Reasons of the Christian Religion,* one of the first books in Edwards's early catalog of reading, Baxter considered at length "natural evidence" for the Trinity. Echoes of the psychological model are clear in his conclusion that "The Happiness of the first Being consisteth, I. in his Being Himself. 2. In his Knowing Himself. 3. In his Loving and Enjoying Himself."[104] Likewise, Cotton Mather's appeal to the broad Augustinian tradition is evident in a sermon on John 17:21:

> God cannot be Infinitely and Absolutely Perfect, without the Perception of Himself, and an Immense Joy and Love resulting therefrom, in finding Himself, The Alsufficient Good. . . . The Father is the Fountain of the Deity; The Son is the Express Image of the Father's Person, or God Essentially Representing of God . . . ; the Holy Ghost is that wonderful Joy and Love, which God has in Himself by the Grateful Perception which the Father and Son Eternally have of one another.[105]

Edwards's frequent portrayals of the Son as the image of God and the Holy Spirit as God's "love and delight in Himself" closely echo those of Ames, Baxter, and Mather.

In his earliest expositions of the Trinity, Edwards was content to preface his identification of the Spirit with God's "love of his own essence" with the claim, "'tis often said." This theological consensus was a development of what "the Scripture has implicitly told us."[106] As Edwards's theological dependence on this identification grew, the weakness of its scriptural support evidently troubled him, and he returned to it in later "Miscellanies" entries. Around the time of the Great Awakening, Edwards presented a long, convoluted scriptural argument for

---

103. William Ames, *The Marrow of Theology,* trans. and ed. John Dykstra Eusden (Durham, N.C.: The Labyrinth Press, 1968), p. 89.

104. Richard Baxter, *The Reasons of the Christian Religion* (London, 1667), p. 24.

105. Cotton Mather, *Blessed Unions,* pp. 47-48.

106. Works, 13, p. 261 (no. 94).

this part of the analogy in his *Treatise on Grace*. Claiming to "go no further than I think the Scripture plainly goes before me," this time he concluded that, just as the Son is called "the personal wisdom of God," so the Spirit of God "may with equal foundation and propriety be called the personal love of God."[107] Not many of his Reformed predecessors would have agreed.

Though his use of the psychological model was fluid and often understated, the constellation of images referring to God's understanding, word, and idea, on the one hand, and to God's love, will, holiness, and beauty, on the other, was integral to Edwards's entire theology. From his fascination with typologies to his ponderings on true virtue and the course of the revivals, a dependence on this conceptuality can be observed, even where Edwards did not appeal to the Trinity explicitly. Various strands of the psychological model had developed within the theological tradition, and these were picked up at different points in Edwards's writings.

At some points he emphasized the primacy of the Father as the fountain of the Godhead. In his *Discourse on the Trinity*, Edwards declared: "The Father is the deity subsisting in the prime, unoriginated and most absolute manner, or the deity in its direct existence."[108] The deity does not remain in mere "direct existence": through "reflex acts" of knowledge and love, God exercises the divine disposition to self-communication and begets the Son and Spirit.

> The Son is the deity generated by God's understanding, or having an idea of Himself and subsisting in that idea. The Holy Ghost is the deity subsisting in act, or the divine essence flowing out and breathed forth in God's infinite love to and delight in Himself.[109]

As Sang Lee has summarized this strand of Edwards's trinitarian reflection, the second and third persons of the Trinity are "the eternal and absolutely complete repetitions of the Father's self-existent actuality."[110]

107. Helm, *Trinity*, p. 59.
108. Helm, *Trinity*, p. 118.
109. Helm, *Trinity*, p. 118.
110. Sang Hyun Lee, *The Philosophical Theology of Jonathan Edwards* (Princeton: Princeton University Press, 1988), p. 189. To my mind, Lee exaggerates the primacy of the Fa-

However, appeals to "the Father's self-existent actuality" are rather rare in Edwards's trinitarianism, and, at other points in the same essay, he showed discomfort with the theological implications of this view of God for understanding love within the Trinity. As he stated in another insert, "all love respects another that is the beloved"; self-love is "very improperly called love."[111] At times he resolved the theological problem of "God's infinite love to Himself" by modulating into consent discourse, which permitted a notion of reciprocal love among the Father, Son, and Holy Spirit. For example, in *True Virtue* he wrote:

> it is evident that the divine virtue, or the virtue of the divine mind, must consist primarily in love to himself, or in the mutual love and friendship which subsists eternally and necessarily between the several persons in the Godhead, or that infinitely strong propensity there is in these divine persons one to another.[112]

More often, however, Edwards followed Augustine in portraying the Holy Spirit as the bond of love between the Father and Son. In *Charity and Its Fruits,* for example, Edwards portrayed the Holy Spirit as the reciprocal love of the Father and Son for each other, so that "the Son of God is not only the infinite object of love, but he is also an infinite subject of it. He is not only the infinite object of the Father's love, but he also infinitely loves the Father."[113] Here Edwards echoed the consent theme so prominent in his development of social images for the Trinity.

An Eclectic Synthesis

Edwards's freedom in transgressing the boundaries of strict scriptural precedent gave him ample room to explore how the psychological and

---

ther because of his focus on the dispositional and psychological aspects of Edwards's trinitarianism. He achieves better trinitarian balance in his later article, "Edwards's Dispositional Conception of the Trinity," where he attributes the coincidence of disposition and actuality to the Son and Spirit as well as to the Father. Even in its amended version, however, his interpretation does not easily accommodate the abundance of covenantal and social themes in Edwards's trinitarianism.

111. Helm, *Trinity,* p. 100.

112. Works, 8, p. 557.

113. Works, 8, p. 373.

social models of the Trinity might "contribute to the betterment of the heart."[114] From these two streams of trinitarian reflection, he created an eclectic synthesis, one that informed his theology generally and served as the cornerstone of his intellectual constructions. The organizing centers of Edwards's theology — God, redemption, and the Christian life — were all deeply informed by his twofold trinitarian vision.

Despite their power and versatility, Edwards's trinitarian reflections have a distinctly unsettled character. There is an experimental, *ad hoc* quality to his employment of theological traditions that stubbornly resists systematizing. The two sets of trinitarian images he employed required different theological vocabularies and different presuppositions about the Godhead, and his constant modulation between them was not always harmonious. The mutuality and interdependence of the triune persons on the social model was in tension with the Father's primordial effusiveness in the psychological analogy, where, instead of being full members of the trinitarian society or family, the Son and Holy Spirit become eternal divine dispositions to communicate knowledge and love. The role of the Holy Spirit, usually slighted in the social view of the Trinity, is greatly amplified in the psychological view. Edwards's writings give no hint that he was ever troubled by the dissonances between these models.[115] Since both of them, in different ways, served his practical aim of "living to God through Christ," he seemed willing to live with the tensions between them.

In this way, Edwards anticipated a trend in some contemporary theology to cultivate deliberately a plurality of models for God. In theology, William Placher points out,

> we can use different models without falling into contradiction. Anyone who asks, after reading the Gospels, "Well, is the kingdom of heaven like a mustard seed, or a father with two sons, or a treasure hidden in a field? Which is it?" has misunderstood the way models work. Each of these metaphors points to some features of the Gospels' understanding of the kingdom. We learn about the

114. Works, 13, p. 328 (no. 181).

115. William C. Placher has suggested ways in which the two images may be seen as complementary. See *Narratives of a Vulnerable God: Christ, Theology, and Scripture* (Louisville: Westminster/John Knox, 1994), pp. 53-86.

kingdom by thinking through the implications of all of them and by reflecting on their interrelationships.[116]

Similarly, the psychological and social models of the Trinity, in their differences and interrelationships, each point to aspects of "the glorious mystery" of the Trinity. Theological allegiance to one trinitarian model to the exclusion of others risks putting "human ideas about God in the place that only God should fill in Christian life."[117] Moreover, if the goal of Christian theology is not a blueprint for the Godhead but wisdom about "living to God through Christ," it may be impossible to specify in advance which model of the Trinity most closely "follows the way of piety" in a given instance. Edwards's trinitarian reflections have an unsettled character in part because his choice of which model to employ depended so heavily on his immediate theological context.

Edwards's trinitarian writings are also unsettled in their curious vacillation between overweening confidence in the reasonableness of the Trinity and pious humility concerning the doctrine's mystery. Though he was confident that the psychological analogy was "agreeable to the tenour of the whole New Testament,"[118] as we have seen, Edwards did not confine his trinitarian reflection to what has "been said in Scripture in express words." He boldly presented his exposition of the Trinity in no. 94 of the "Miscellanies" as "that which necessarily results from the putting [together] of reason and Scripture." On these terms, he was "not afraid to say twenty things about the Trinity which the Scripture never said."[119] At times, Edwards even left Scripture behind, claiming that "it is within the reach of naked reason to perceive certainly that there are three distinct in God."[120] In Edwards's theological exuberance, he sometimes started with God, not with the creature, in developing trinitarian analogies. For example, in no. 259 he stated that

---

116. William C. Placher, "The Cross of Jesus Christ as Solidarity, Reconciliation, and Redemption," in W. Brueggemann and G. Stroup, eds., *Many Voices, One God: Being Faithful in a Pluralistic World* (Louisville: Westminster/John Knox, 1998), p. 155.

117. Kathryn Tanner, *Theories of Culture: A New Agenda for Theology* (Minneapolis: Fortress Press, 1997), p. 126.

118. Helm, *Trinity*, p. 122.

119. Helm, *Trinity*, p. 103.

120. Works, 13, p. 257 (no. 94).

There is in resemblance to this threefold distinction in God a three-fold distinction in a created spirit, namely, the spirit itself, and its understanding, and its will or inclination or love; and this indeed is all the real distinction there is in created spirits.[121]

In Edwards's overreaching hands, the status of the social and psychological images as *human* analogies was sometimes obscured.[122]

The Trinity was the subject of some of Edwards's more idiosyncratic doctrinal experiments, which departed even further from cautious use of trinitarian analogies within the mainstream Reformed tradition, and created various unresolved tensions within his theology. An example of Edwards's boldness in testing new philosophical frameworks for theological fruitfulness was his attempt to explain the generation of the Son in the philosophical currency of idealism. Edwards started by insisting that God's knowledge, like ours, comes through ideas: "if it were not by idea, it is in no respect like ours; 'tis not what we call knowledge, nor anything whereof knowledge is the resemblance."[123] The notion of God's "having an idea of Himself," he suggested, "will more clearly appear if we consider the nature of spiritual ideas, . . . these that we call ideas of reflection."[124] Human ideas are only faint and obscure repetitions, encumbered by "many new references, suppositions, and translations."[125] But

if it were possible for a man by reflection perfectly to contemplate all that is in his own mind in an hour . . . a man would really be two during that time, he would be indeed double, he would be twice at once. The idea he has of himself would be himself again.[126]

121. Works, 13, p. 367.
122. Given the appeals to human experience in the long theological history of the psychological model, I find most puzzling R. C. De Prospo's claim that this analogy "is for Edwards pure speculation; it derives according to his theology from no experience he has, from no experience that ever any creature can have." *Theism in the Discourse of Jonathan Edwards* (Cranbury, N.J.: Associated University Presses, 1985), p. 97.
123. Works, 13, p. 257 (no. 94). There are evident similarities between Edwards's formulation and the Lockean view of the self. However, I agree with Thomas Schafer "that Edwards evolved his so-called 'idealism' without the benefit of Locke's ideas, against the background of his own previous conclusions about matter and more directly from his own single-minded contemplation of God and his works" (Works, 13, p. 47).
124. Helm, *Trinity*, pp. 100-101.
125. Works, 13, p. 354 (no. 238).
126. Helm, *Trinity*, p. 102.

"An absolutely perfect idea of a thing is the very thing, for it wants nothing that is in the thing, substance nor nothing else." And because God's self-contemplation *is* perfect, "that idea which God hath of Himself is absolutely Himself."[127]

Edwards's use of idealism in portraying the Son's generation posed unique problems. Paul Helm has found Edwards's distinctive explanation of the Son's generation "implicitly tritheistic":

> If a perfect idea of *x* entails that *x* exists then Edwards has proved too much — not the second person of a Trinity of persons but a second *theos*.[128]

According to his idealism, even a human person who had a perfect reflex idea for an hour "would really be two during that time." Similarly, God's eternally perfect self-reflection would seem to result in two Gods. And so Edwards had to correct himself in mid-sentence to avoid asserting more than one God — the result of God's perfect self-contemplation is "another infinite, eternal almighty and most holy *and the same* God."[129]

The rationalist pressures afoot in Edwards's day tended to work against a robust trinitarianism: portraying God as a solitary cosmic ruler and moral governor seemed more "reasonable" to many than entering into the mysterious complexities of a trinitarian Godhead. In the heat of Edwards's polemics against the antitrinitarians, rash confidence sometimes gave to way to an equally strategic insistence on the frailty of human reason. "The exceeding imperfect notions that we have of the nature or essence of God" compel us to "think of it far otherwise than it is."[130] In this mode, Edwards repeatedly pointed to the limitations of human reason in apprehending truths about God, arguing that "'tis unreasonable to object against the truth of the Doctrines of the Trinity, incarnation, etc."[131] on the grounds that they are not transparent to human reason. He cited the case of a thirteen-year-old

---

127. Helm, *Trinity*, p. 103.

128. Helm, *Trinity*, p. 21. Edwards responded to this criticism in Works, 13, p. 392 (no. 308).

129. Helm, *Trinity*, p. 103, emphasis added.

130. Works, 18, p. 190 (no. 650).

131. *Misc.*, no. 839.

boy who refused to believe that a two-inch cube was eight times as big as a one-inch cube, noting that "it was a much more difficult mystery to him than the Trinity ordinarily is to men." "Why should we not suppose," Edwards demanded, "that there may be some things that are true, that may be as much above our understandings and as difficult to them, as this truth was to this boy?"[132]

In a wide-ranging polemic against deist notions of the sufficiency of human reason, Edwards frequently appealed to the human need for divine revelation. In the case of the Trinity and other doctrinal mysteries, Edwards declared divine revelation to be "exceeding needful." He found deist Matthew Tindal's insistence that "reason is the judge where there be any revelation" to be "an unreasonable way of arguing."[133] Given the limitations of human reason, it was necessary

> That God should declare to mankind what manner of Being He is. For though reason may be sufficient to confirm such a declaration after it is given, and see its consistence, harmony and rationality in many respects, yet reason may be utterly insufficient first to discover these things.[134]

Therefore, "the word of God certainly should be our rule in matters so much above reason and our own notions."[135] Whereas his deist contemporaries argued the independence of the best pagan wisdom from revelation, Edwards was so impressed by the foreshadowings of trinitarian doctrine among the "heathen," that he concluded they must have had "some degree of inspiration of the Spirit of God which led 'em to say such wonderful things concerning the Trinity."[136] The abil-

---

132. Works, 18, pp. 192-93 (no. 652).

133. *Misc.*, no. 1340.

134. *Misc.*, no. 1338.

135. Helm, *Trinity*, p. 57.

136. *Misc.*, no. 1162. Edwards is here appealing to a long Christian tradition of *prisca theologia*, or ancient theology. On this apologetic theory, whose historical plausibility was already being undermined in Edwards's day, the human race originally received special revelation via God's people Israel, beginning with the sons of Noah after the Flood. This revelation passed down to the Greeks and other non-Christians was gradually diluted and corrupted by foreign elements. See Gerald R. McDermott, *Jonathan Edwards Confronts the Gods: Christian Theology, Enlightenment Religion, and Non-Christian Faiths* (Oxford: Oxford University Press, 2000).

ity to grasp the truth of the doctrine of the Trinity was a gift of the Spirit, not an inherent capacity of human reason.

The "mysteries in religion" that Christ taught "are not only so above human comprehension, that men can't easily apprehend all that 'tis to be understood concerning them" — they are also "difficult to be received by judgment or belief."[137] In Edwards's opinion, much of the human difficulty in receiving the doctrine of the Trinity was rooted in a sinful reluctance to accept divine revelation.

> If things which fact and experience make certain, such as the miseries infants sometimes are the subject of in this world, etc. had been exhibited only in a revelation . . . they would be as much disputed, as the Trinity and other mysteries revealed in the Bible.[138]

Given the pride of fallen human reason, "difficulty in believing" is by no means a conclusive indicator of incoherence or falsity.

Genuine humility seems present alongside strategic posturing in Edwards's confession that the Trinity remained for him "an incomprehensible mystery, the greatest and the most glorious of all mysteries."[139] As he admitted in his *Discourse on the Trinity*, "I am sensible a hundred other objections may be made and puzzling doubts and questions raised that I can't solve. I am far from pretending to explaining the Trinity so as to render it no longer a mystery."[140] Such humility seems only appropriate. Edwards's reflections on the social and psychological veins of trinitarian analogy in his private notebooks had many rough edges — unexamined presuppositions, deep internal tensions, rash statements left unsupported. In his trinitarian thought Edwards joined in the larger theological tumult of his day, an era torn between a desire for a "reasonable Christianity" and the comforts of a rich, finally ineffable tradition. The unsettled quality of Edwards's trinitarianism is also evident in his approach to the divine simplicity tradition, which is the focus of the next chapter.

---

137. *Misc.*, no. 839.
138. *Misc.*, no. 1171.
139. Works, 13, p. 393 (no. 308).
140. Helm, *Trinity*, pp. 121-22.

Chapter 2

A REDEFINITION OF DIVINE EXCELLENCY

"One alone cannot be excellent, inasmuch as, in such case, there can be no consent. Therefore, if God is excellent, there must be a plurality in God; otherwise, there can be no consent in him."

EDWARDS, "Miscellanies," no. 117

In his interpretation of Edwards's philosophical thought, Wallace E. Anderson quotes the above passage about divine excellency, remarking almost apologetically that "this is not the place to discuss Edwards's account of the Trinity as such."[1] Anderson's tone is understandable, as the doctrine of the Trinity rarely figures significantly in philosophical discussions. But in the case of Edwards, attention to the Trinity is requisite to understanding his metaphysics. As Anderson goes on to point out,

> it seems evident that his new concept of being, when applied to the divine perfections, stands in sharp contrast to the long tradition of philosophical theology into which he was born. God's goodness is not grounded in the absolute unity and simplicity of his being, but belongs to him only as he constitutes a plurality involving relations.[2]

1. Works, 6, p. 84.
2. Works, 6, p. 84.

The Trinity was the paradigm of Edwards's "new concept of being," in which "to be means to be intentionally related."[3] His conviction that consent was at the core of divine reality put him at odds with long theological traditions about what constitutes God's excellence.

Boldly affirming "plurality in God" also had dramatic and far-reaching implications for his view of all created reality. Anderson argues that Edwards articulated "a very different view of the formal and intelligible structure of reality from any that had been developed by the major philosophers of the seventeenth century, and even by those of his own time."[4] In Edwards's view, "The whole material universe is preserved by gravity or attraction, or the mutual tendency of all bodies to each other." Physical reality is not a collection of independent or self-contained substances. Rather, God made "one part of the universe" to be "beneficial to another," so that "the beauty, harmony, and order, regular progress, life and motion, and in short all the well-being of the whole frame depends on it."[5] Edwards's "new concept of being" is best described as a relational ontology.

Edwards's relational ontology is inseparable from his trinitarianism. The importance of Edwards's metaphysical alternative is evident from the struggles of van Mastricht and the Cambridge Brethren to give free rein to the deep trinitarian impulses they shared with Edwards within a more traditional metaphysic. The connections between Edwards's basic metaphysical claim "that every real being must, as a condition of its reality, stand in some relation to other things, and even to all other things"[6] and his trinitarian understanding of God's excellency are displayed in two ways in this chapter: in Edwards's criticisms of the tradition of divine simplicity, and in his relational alternatives to substance metaphysics.

---

3. Stephen H. Daniel, *The Philosophy of Jonathan Edwards: A Study in Divine Semiotics* (Bloomington: University of Indiana Press, 1994), p. 180.

4. Works, 6, p. 85.

5. Works, 11, p. 81.

6. Works, 6, p. 85.

The Reformed Tradition of Divine Simplicity

According to John Cotton, from eternity the persons of the Godhead "nourished, delighted, and solaced each other."[7] One of the most obvious ways of developing a doctrine of the Trinity that followed "the way of piety" was to see in this vision of divine relatedness a perfect model for human society. "As the Persons in the Trinity are three," Cotton declared, "and yet their nature such, as they cannot be but one, one holinesse, one goodnesse, one truth, so all that worship [God], though their persons be never so different, yet let their spirits be all one."[8] Richard Sibbes's exclamation that "the Trinity should be the pattern of our unity"[9] finds echoes throughout the writings of the Spiritual Brethren. Likewise, van Mastricht affirmed that the triune Godhead exemplified the sort of love that saints should have for God and each other. In making a point about the saints' union with God, van Mastricht held up the Trinity as a model of social relations: "the perfection of the holy Trinity consists chiefly in the most perfect society and communion of the divine persons."[10] Edwards cited a passage from this same chapter in van Mastricht in his private notebooks, noting the connection he made "concerning the economy of the persons of the Trinity and the church's communion with God."[11] Like Edwards, the Cambridge Brethren and van Mastricht saw trinitarian consent and communion as marks of God's excellency.

The previous chapter noted the obstacle that lack of scriptural precedent posed for Puritan and scholastic attempts to explore models for the Godhead that would nurture the way of piety. This chapter explores another obstacle. Appealing to the Trinity as a model for human social relations was in considerable tension with Reformed understandings of God's perfect oneness. Since the third century, Christian emphasis on the unity of God had been indebted to the notion of di-

---

7. Cotton, *First John Generall*, p. 12.

8. Cotton, *First John Generall*, p. 367.

9. Sibbes, *Complete Works*, 3, p. 194. As the next chapter will indicate, there are theological dangers in too direct a mapping of trinitarian society onto human societies.

10. Peter van Mastricht, *Theoretico-practica Theologia* (Utrecht, 1724), II.xxiv.28 (in perfectissima personarum divinarum societate et communione, praecipua consistit S. Trinitatis perfectio).

11. Works, 13, p. 524 (no. 482).

vine simplicity, particularly as mediated by the Neoplatonist philosopher Plotinus. Through Neoplatonism, an Aristotelian understanding of God that emphasized this construal of divine oneness came into the Christian tradition, and was adopted as part of the Reformed philosophical heritage.[12] The broad acceptance of the notion of divine simplicity in both Puritan and Reformed scholastic thought can be seen as an extension of the Reformers' adherence to earlier Christian tradition on the nature of God, especially as developed by medieval scholasticism.

The doctrine of divine simplicity functioned in Reformed theology as a reminder of the limits of human understanding of the divine nature: God transcends all the linguistic distinctions and modes of analysis that are used in comprehending finite objects. But it was also a vision of what constitutes divine excellency: metaphysical perfection requires that God be "one alone," without physical or metaphysical *parts* of any kind.[13] Just as God has no bodily parts, neither is God "composed" of various immaterial properties or substances. One of the basic theological intuitions behind the simplicity theory was that multiple instances of, or real distinctions within, the divine essence threatened its aseity and integrity. As David Cunningham has asserted, in "the dominant philosophical tradition of the West, . . . 'otherness' is associated primarily with fragmentation or revolt."[14] If God is excellent, according to this dominant tradition, there must *not* be any true plurality in God; nor should human speech about God imply this. In Reformed theology of the seventeenth century, the doctrine of divine simplicity was allied with substance metaphysics, which saw ultimate reality as self-existent, possessing its identity apart from the relations in which it stands to others. "Substances and forms are principles of inherence and self-containment, and thus relations are not internal —

12. For philosophical antecedents to this understanding of God, see Aristotle's *Physics* VIII 6, 260a 17-19; VIII 10, 266a 10-11; and Plotinus's *Enneads* VI.9.

13. Brian Leftow uses this locution in *Time and Eternity* (Ithaca, N.Y.: Cornell University Press, 1991). *Part* usually refers to a piece of matter, and thus only material substances are ordinarily considered composite. But Leftow points out that for medieval theologians, immaterial substances too had *parts,* if they had a distinct essence and properties.

14. David S. Cunningham, *These Three Are One: The Practice of Trinitarian Theology* (Oxford: Blackwell, 1998), p. 8.

that is, they do not affect an entity's being."[15] The Reformed doctrine of divine simplicity held that God, as the supreme being or ultimate substance, must be also the most unified and thus the most invulnerable to dependence and disintegration.

Within the larger tradition of asserting divine oneness, the doctrine of divine simplicity had a special prominence in Reformed theology. The Reformed scholastics did not treat simplicity merely as one among the various divine attributes. In fact, following the Catholic scholastic tradition, simplicity was often placed in a controlling position in their systems of theology. Van Mastricht and Francis Turretin, for example, both put simplicity at or near the head of the divine attributes treated in the doctrine of God. Thus it affected the understanding and articulation of all the other attributes of God, and of how these different attributes related to each other and to the divine essence.

This distinctive view of God's oneness had profound implications for the way in which the other divine attributes were viewed. Johannes Wollebius, whose theological system began to replace Ames's *Medulla* at late-seventeenth-century Harvard,[16] concluded that, "The properties of God are not qualities or accidents, or real entities, different from the essence, or from each other. . . . For there is nothing in God, which is not God himself."[17] Francis Turretin asserted that divine attributes that to us seem distinct and even in opposition to each other, such as mercy and justice, are in God "all one and the same."[18] It is our epistemological limitations, he insisted, that prevent us from conceiving of the simple Deity truly.

Simplicity was seen to uphold other characteristics of God affirmed

---

15. Sang Hyun Lee, *The Philosophical Theology of Jonathan Edwards* (Princeton: Princeton University Press, 1988), p. 184. The alliance between simplicity theory and substance metaphysics is powerful, but not necessary. For example, Lee's concept of God's dispositional ontology retains a role for simplicity while rejecting substance metaphysics.

16. Perry Miller, *The New England Mind: The Seventeenth Century* (Cambridge, Mass.: Harvard University Press, 1954), p. 96.

17. Wollebius, *Compendium Theologiae Christianae* (Amsterdam, 1638), I.i. (Proprietates in Deo, non sunt qualitates, aut accidentia, aut res ab essentia, aut a se invicem diversae. . . . Nihil ergo in Deo est, quod non sit ipse Deus.)

18. Turretin, *Compendium Theologiae Didactico-Elencticae* (Franquerae, 1703), III.vii.11. (Ut sunt in Deo, omnia unum et idem sunt, quae nos cogimur diversis conceptibus imaginari.)

in tradition and Scripture. Van Mastricht chronicled how simplicity undergirds the traditional affirmations of God's aseity, immutability, infinity, eternality, perfection, and wisdom.[19] For example, he argued that if God is *a se,* that is, truly independent and self-sufficient, God's existence and nature cannot be "dependent" on any constituent parts. Likewise God's immutability requires that God not be composed of parts subject to dissolution. Turretin found a correspondence between simplicity and the abstract terms attributed to God in Scripture, such as Life, Light, and Truth.[20] God is not only said to *have* Life, as one would affirm of a composite being; God is said in Scripture to *be* Life, which can only be said of a simple being, for whom there is no distinction between essence and properties.

The Johannine affirmations about God as Love and Life were also favorite entrée points for Puritan affirmations of divine simplicity. John Cotton, for example, found in the affirmation of 1 John 1:2, "Christ is life eternal," a proof of Christ's simplicity; "for," as Cotton declared, "these speeches are no Hyperbolies."[21] Though in a less systematic way than the Reformed scholastics, the Puritans also defined the "oneness" of God so as to accord with the doctrine of divine simplicity and were sensitive to the far-reaching theological implications of the doctrine. This concern to uphold divine simplicity does not appear connected to particular theological controversies or divisions within Puritan circles. Though it accommodated well emphases on divine sovereignty and power, it was also prominent in theologies that highlighted divine love. Cotton's broad assertion of divine simplicity is typical:

> God is not compounded, but free without mixture, he is without all causes besides himself, he is of himself, from himself, and by himself, and for himself: and as he is not compounded of causes, so he is not compounded of subject, and adjunct; man is one thing, and his learning and wisdome another thing: but God and his wisdome are not two distinct things; God and his love are the same.[22]

---

19. Mastricht, *Theoretico-practica Theologia* (Amsterdam, 1682), II.vi.21.
20. Turretin, *Institutio Theologiae Elencticae* (Geneva, 1688), III.xii.4.
21. Cotton, *First John Generall,* p. 11.
22. Cotton, *First John Generall,* p. 317.

Cotton admitted that the notion of God's simplicity breaks the "rule of Logick" concerning the proper predication of attributes, but he ascribed this to the divine mystery: "There is no reason of this truth, because he is above reason."

Following the four-part architectonic of his theological system, van Mastricht concluded his exposition on divine simplicity with a practical application: Christians need to cultivate a "simplicity of heart."[23] This rapprochement between metaphysical doctrine and practical spiritual concerns echoed Puritan treatments of divine simplicity. John Preston, another member of the Spiritual Brethren, urged his listeners that, "tho such a simplicity as is in almighty God you cannot reach to, yet to have a heart inmixed, to be cleansed from drosse as the gold is, such a simplicity of minde you should labour to get."[24] But, like Cotton, Preston was not content with drawing practical implications from the notion of divine simplicity. He also affirmed simplicity more broadly as

> that Attribute, by which [God] is one most pure and entire essence, one most simple, being without all composition; so that there is not substance, accident, matter, forme, body or soule in any; but hee is every way most simple, nothing in him, but what is God, what is himselfe.[25]

Though Puritan theologians did not always reflect adherence to the tenets of divine simplicity in their discussions of particular divine attributes, they displayed a remarkable consistency with the tradition in their direct assertions about the relationship between God's nature and attributes.

The exposition of divine simplicity occurred in scholastic systems in the section on *De Deo Uno,* the doctrine of the one God, where the basic Christian grammar for articulating divine oneness was set out; but it obviously had profound implications for the section that immediately followed, *De Deo Trino,* the doctrine of the triune God. Adherence to divine simplicity necessitated some puzzling statements concerning the metaphysical status of the various divine attributes; but even greater

---

23. Mastricht, *Theoretico-practica Theologia,* II.vi.27.

24. Preston, *Life Eternall or, A Treatise of the Knowledge of the Divine Essence and Attributes* (London, 1633), pp. 59-60.

25. Preston, *Life Eternall,* pp. 47-48.

exertions were required to reconcile simplicity with God's trinitarian "threeness." The tension between adherence to divine simplicity and the desire of van Mastricht and the Sibbesians that the Trinity serve as the pattern of human unity was clear. Whereas the first predicated divine unity on the absence of composition, the second understood it as the consenting union of diverse persons.

There was a lot at stake doctrinally for the Reformed scholastics and Puritans in their attempts to reconcile divine simplicity with trinitarian doctrine. Perplexing as it might be to assert that God's immutability was really "the same" as God's omnipotence, and that both were finally identical with God's own being, there was no history of controversy in the early Christian tradition on the subject and thus few creedal guidelines for correct linguistic usage.[26] The scholastics and Puritans were free to speak in a variety of ways about the relation of the divine attributes to each other and to the divine essence, some reflecting their adherence to divine simplicity and some not. However, christological and trinitarian issues had been at the heart of doctrinal controversy in the early church, and were again a subject of intense debate in their own time; as a result the boundaries for orthodox trinitarianism were much more clearly defined.

The Westminster Shorter Catechism, though written later than some of the scholastic and Puritan works considered here, can serve as a baseline for trinitarian orthodoxy. In its two brief and uncontroversial questions on the Trinity, it asks:

Q 5 Are there more Gods than one?
  A There is but one only, the living and true God.

Q 6 How many persons are there in the Godhead?
  A There are three persons in the Godhead: the Father, the Son, and the Holy Ghost; and these three are one God, the same in substance, equal in power, and glory.

Edwards recited this catechism weekly at Yale College chapel services, and, according to Samuel Hopkins, made use of it in teaching his own

26. The relatively late statements of the Councils of Toledo (685), Rheims (1148), and Trent (1555) were not at issue in the Reformed tradition.

children. Yet this notably irenic derivative of the Westminster Confession carefully skirted the pointed questions implicit in its trinitarian affirmations. In exactly what sense are the Father, Son, and Holy Ghost "persons"? What does it mean to say that they are "the same in substance"? How are "these three" yet "one God"?

The challenge for the Protestant scholastic theologians as they codified the trinitarianism of the early Reformers was to reconcile the genuine distinctness of the divine persons with the simplicity of the divine essence. This task was made distinctly easier by the fact that the sixteenth-century Reformers had retained much of the technical trinitarian vocabulary of medieval scholasticism, which had also faced the theological problem of reconciling the doctrine of the Trinity with divine simplicity.

The western church had introduced two terms to the trinitarian vocabulary that became foundational to both Catholic and Protestant scholasticism. *Subsistentia,* or subsistence, was introduced as a parallel to the Greek term, *hypostasis,* to denote the threeness within the Godhead; the Father, Son, and Holy Spirit are each a distinct subsistence within the one divine substance or essence. The term *modus subsistendi,* or mode of subsisting, was introduced to explain the relation between the three divine persons and the one divine essence. The Father, Son, and Holy Spirit are not different parts of the divine essence, nor is there a real distinction between the persons and the divine essence, for this would violate the rules of divine simplicity. Instead, they each represent a different mode of subsistence within the simple divine essence.

Though they used it frequently, the scholastics reflected some of Calvin's ambivalence about the term *persona* in the trinitarian vocabulary.[27] They preferred to describe the trinitarian distinctions in terms of different subsistences or modes of being of the one divine essence. It was the implications of distinct personal agency that made Reformed scholastics shy away from using *persons* language for God. According to

---

27. Calvin argued that "ce mot de personnes en ceste matière est pour exprimer les propriétez lesquelles sont en l'essence de Dieu" (this word *persons* in this case is for expressing the properties which are in God's essence). He cautioned that *person* was to be understood "non point comme nous parlons en notre langage commun appelant trois hommes, trois personnes" (not as we speak in our common language, calling three men, three persons). *Corpus Reformatorum* (Brunsvigae: C. A. Schwetschke, 1863-1900), 43, p. 473.

the rules of simplicity theory, the works of the Trinity are indivisible — all of them are the works of the entire Godhead. At most there was an "economic" appropriation of certain acts to particular members of the Trinity; the incarnation, for example, was appropriated to the Son. But these appropriations did not imply the existence of distinct personal agency within the Trinity, for that would disturb the uncompounded-ness of the Deity.

Van Mastricht reflected the scholastic consensus when he denied that Father, Son, and Spirit form "parts of one deity," as if the divine nature were divided up among them.[28] Wollebius elaborated the same point: "The divine person is neither a species of God, or of the Deity, nor a part thereof, nor another thing besides the Deity, nor a bare relation . . . , but the very essence of God, in a certain mode of subsistence."[29] Turretin likewise insisted that the divine persons differ from the simple divine essence only modally, not as one thing differs from another.[30] While affirming only a modal distinction between the divine persons and the divine essence, the Reformed scholastics attempted to preserve real distinctions *among* divine persons by delineating properties unique to each person. These are variously called personal, incommunicable, and relative properties. Wollebius stated that, "The persons of the Deity are subsistences, each of which hath the whole essence of God, though differing in their incommunicable properties."[31] Turretin also argued that the three persons are distinguished from each other by incommunicable properties or modes of subsistence.[32]

It is true that many Puritans did not pay a lot of attention to this rather abstruse trinitarian terminology. Yet when they were confronted with the problem of correct trinitarian vocabulary, they reflected to a

28. Mastricht, *Theoretico-practica Theologia*, II.xxiv.18, 19 *(partes unius deitatis)*.

29. Wollebius, *Compendium Theologiae*, I.ii. (Persona divina nec Dei seu Deitatis species est, nec pars ejus, nec res a Deitate alia, nec nuda relatio . . . , sed essentia Dei, cum certo τῆς ὑπάρξεως τρόπῳ.)

30. Turretin, *Institutio*, IV.i.6 (non realiter . . . ut res et res, sed modaliter, ut modus a re).

31. Wollebius, *Compendium Theologiae*, I.ii. (Personae Deitatis sunt subsistentiae, quarum quaelibet essentiam Dei totam habet, proprietatibus interim incommunicabilibus differentes.)

32. Turretin, *Institutio*, III.xxv.1. (Tres esse distinctas Personas, quae proprietatibus incommunicabilibus, sive modis subsistendi, ita inter se distinguantur.) See *Institutio*, III.xxv.1-2 for an exposition of the orthodox position.

remarkable degree the Reformed consensus concerning the divine persons' relationship to the divine essence and to each other. Whatever theological divisions existed between the Spiritual Brethren and the Intellectual Fathers on their approach to the economic Trinity, they showed impressive agreement when it came to accommodating the immanent Trinity to the notion of divine simplicity. John Cotton acknowledged the parameters of the discussion when he noted that the distinction between the Father and the Son "cannot be essential, for their Essence is one, neither can it be accidental, for no Accidents are in God"; it must, he concluded, lie in personal properties.[33] As his theological opponent Thomas Hooker explained more fully:

> For the substance of God, with this property to be of none, doth make the Person of the Father; the very self-same Substance in number with this property to be of the Father, maketh the Person of the Son; the same substance having added unto it the property of proceeding from the other two, maketh the Person of the Holy Ghost. So that in every Person there is implied both the Substance of God, which is one; and also that property which causeth the same Person really and truly to differ from the other two.[34]

At the end of the seventeenth century, John Flavel likewise insisted that the trinitarian persons subsist "in the most glorious and undivided Godhead," and that a divine person is not really distinct from the Godhead, but simply "the Godhead distinguished by personal Properties."[35]

This representative sampling of Reformed scholastic and Puritan views on the Trinity reflects a virtual unanimity in the Reformed attempt to reconcile Trinity and simplicity by holding that the divine persons are really distinct from each other by their personal properties but that each person of the Trinity is only modally distinct from the divine essence. The notions of personal properties and modes of subsis-

---

33. Cotton, *First John Generall*, p. 12.

34. Hooker, *Ecclesiastical Polity* (reprint; Oxford: Clarendon Press, 1993), 2, p. 200.

35. Flavel, "A Treatise on the Soul of Man," *The Whole Works of Mr. John Flavel* (London, 1716), I, p. 471; "Exposition of the Shorter Catechism," John E. Smith, ed., *Religious Affections*, The Works of Jonathan Edwards, vol. 2 (New Haven: Yale University Press, 1959), p. 563.

tence permitted the establishment of a correct trinitarian grammar within the framework of divine simplicity. But these inherited conceptualities did not accommodate easily the vivid images of love, society, and communion within the Godhead that the Cambridge Brethren employed in pursuit of a "practical" doctrine of the Trinity. It is hard to see how they left room for John Cotton to speak of the divine persons eternally nourishing, delighting, and solacing one another. In the theology of the Spiritual Brethren, straightforward affirmations of divine simplicity and appeals to the Trinity as a model of social relations remained in uneasy juxtaposition.

A more typical Puritan pattern was to uphold divine simplicity at the expense of communal trinitarian images for God. William Ames insisted that "all love, grace, and those things which pertain to living well come from the Father, Son, and Holy Spirit." But his theology provided few links between the overflowing love of persons of the economic Trinity and the perfect simplicity of the immanent Godhead. His careful language about the immanent Trinity as three "subsistences distinguished from each other as things connected by certain relative properties"[36] was designed to accommodate trinitarian doctrine to the demands of divine simplicity, not to point the way for Christians to "live unto God."

At the beginning of the eighteenth century, the Englishman Thomas Ridgley, a well-established independent pastor and tutor of divinity, published *A Body of Divinity,* one of the spate of commentaries being produced on the Westminster catechisms. It was noteworthy for the way it reflected the pressure that the doctrine of divine simplicity could exert on the exposition of the Trinity. Ridgley cautioned Christians "not to think or speak of God in such a way as tends to overthrow the simplicity of the divine nature."[37] In his treatment of the Trinity he seems to have followed his own advice to such an extent that his view was branded Sabellian by his opponents, and a furious tract war ensued.[38] But in milder forms, his advice broadly prevailed, so that the es-

36. William Ames, *The Marrow of Theology,* trans. and ed. John Dykstra Eusden (Durham, N.C.: The Labyrinth Press, 1968), p. 24.

37. Ridgley, *A Body of Divinity: Lectures on the Assembly's Larger Catechism* (London: 1731-33; reprint, Philadelphia: William Woodward, 1814), I, p. 203.

38. Richard Muller, private correspondence. Sabellius was a third-century Christian

tablished Puritan custom of neglecting the doctrine of the Trinity, noted by Conrad Wright, continued.

Edwards's Ambivalence Towards the Simplicity Tradition

On the issue of appropriate trinitarian language, among others, Edwards seemed quite indifferent to Ridgley's concern "not to think or speak about God" so as to threaten divine simplicity.[39] Though Edwards was clearly influenced by the prominence of simplicity doctrine in the Reformed scholastics and Puritans, the notion of divine simplicity was never truly incorporated into his theology. There are abundant indications of Edwards's departure from its strictures that are both more deliberate and more integral to his theology as a whole than his casual use of it. He freely rejected those parts of the simplicity theory he could make no sense of, and developed an alternative conception of divine oneness that revolved around the notions of excellency, harmony, and consent. This metaphysical alternative to the divine simplicity tradition permitted Edwards greater boldness in articulating the vision of trinitarian union that he shared with van Mastricht and the Cambridge Brethren.

In an early "Miscellanies" entry, later incorporated into his *Discourse on the Trinity,* Edwards signaled his startling departure from traditional Reformed notions of divine oneness: "If God has an idea of himself, there is really a duplicity. . . . And if God loves himself and delights in

---

accused of confounding the trinitarian persons by denying true distinctions within the Godhead.

39. Historical explanations for this strange indifference will not be attempted, but there are some intriguing resonances with other voices that deserve brief mention. The dissenting voice of the Cambridge Platonist Ralph Cudworth is one of these, though there is scholarly disagreement about when Edwards actually read Cudworth's *Intellectual System.* T. H. Johnson, "Jonathan Edwards's Background of Reading," *Publications of the Colonial Society of Massachusetts* 28 (December 1931): 194-222, and Emily Stipes Watts, "Jonathan Edwards and the Cambridge Platonists" (University of Illinois dissertation, 1963), have argued that Edwards was exposed to him in his teens or early twenties. Wallace Anderson, in Works, 6, p. 329, has surmised that Edwards did not actually read Cudworth until 1756 or 1757, when he copied long quotations from Cudworth into various writings. Though it is likely that Cudworth was not a formative influence on Edwards's trinitarianism, there are interesting convergences between them.

himself, there is really a triplicity, three that cannot be confounded."[40] By asserting triplicity in God, Edwards was flatly contradicting the tradition of divine simplicity; Turretin, for example, asserted that "simplicity and triplicity are opposed to each other, and cannot subsist at the same time."[41] Edwards rejected the broad Reformed tendency to tailor the doctrine of the Trinity to fit with divine simplicity. John Cotton's vision of the divine persons as eternally nourishing, delighting, and solacing one another required "three that cannot be confounded."[42]

Apart from his rehearsals of the standard arguments for God's existence, Edwards paid little attention to the doctrine of God in abstraction from the doctrine of the Trinity. But he exhibited an internal consistency in his use of key terms concerning the essence and attributes of God, reflecting the broad Christian consensus regarding the correct grammar of divine oneness. *Deity, being, nature,* and *essence* were Edwards's primary terms for describing the oneness of God. The unity of God's essence meant that the divine persons must never be thought of as "three distinct Gods, one to another."[43] Likewise, Edwards asserted that the affirmation of one Jehovah in Deuteronomy 6:4 was to guard Israel "against imagining . . . that there was a plurality of essences or beings, among whom they were to divide their affections and respect."[44] As these excerpts show, Edwards's conception of "plurality" in God did not imply a plurality of essences or beings. Rather, asserting plurality in God made room for particularity in intimate union: Edwards's trinitarian vision glimpses "the possibility of true mutual participation which somehow does not allow the Three to be eclipsed by the One, but calls us to rejoice in the communion of their perfect and glorious particularity."[45]

While not entirely absent, his use of the simplicity tradition was infrequent and idiosyncratic. He occasionally affirmed divine simplicity outright, though, I suspect, almost reflexively. For example, in *Freedom of the Will* he referred to God's "perfect and absolute simplicity," in contrast to the "derived dependent" existence of beings "who are com-

40. Works, 13, p. 262 (no. 94).
41. Turretin, *Institutio,* III.vii.9 ("Simplicitas et Triplicitas ita sibi opponuntur, ut non possunt simul subsistere").
42. Works, 13, p. 262 (no. 94).
43. Works, 18, p. 84 (no. 539).
44. *Misc.,* no. 1105.
45. Cunningham, *These Three Are One,* p. 195.

pounded."[46] And in an odd passage, perhaps reflecting the influence of Christian Platonism, he suggested that if our created faculties were enlarged infinitely, "the same simplicity, immutability, etc." that is in God would result.[47] But again there is no explanation of what he understood divine simplicity to entail.[48] Facets of Edwards's trinitarianism also reflect the legacy of divine simplicity. In no. 308 of the "Miscellanies" he rooted the relationship of the persons of the Trinity in the simple divine essence:

> We don't suppose that the Father, the Son, and the Holy Ghost are three distinct beings that have three distinct understandings. It is the divine essence understands and it is the divine essence is understood; 'tis the divine being that loves, and it is the divine being that is loved. The Father understands, the Son understands, and the Holy Ghost understands, because every one is the same understanding divine essence.[49]

He asserted in a sermon on John 16:8 that the Father, Son, and Holy Spirit "are all the same substance, the same divine essence; . . . each one has the divine nature; each one is the divine nature."[50] In these in-

46. Works, 1, p. 377.

47. Works, 13, p. 295 (no. 135). Leroy E. Loemker, *Struggle for Synthesis* (Cambridge, Mass.: Harvard University Press, 1972), p. 20, has asserted that seventeenth-century Christian Platonists promulgated "the doctrine that God's perfections are not only 'univocal' with the attributes of his finite creations, but are, with finite limitations, identical with them."

48. Edwards's use of the Lockean terminology of *simple idea* in reference to knowing God is not a statement about God's own being, but a way of insisting that human cognition of God is a gracious gift, not "compounded" out of various natural human experiences and deductions. Cf. Works, 2, p. 205, "through the saving influences of the Spirit of God, there is a new inward perception or sensation of their minds, . . . which is entirely of a new sort, and which could be produced by no exalting, varying or compounding of that kind of perceptions or sensations which the mind had before; or there is what some metaphysicians call a new simple idea."

49. Works, 13, p. 392. Edwards concludes this unusually muddled entry with the disclaimer, "But I would not be understood to pretend to give a full explication of the Trinity, for I think it still remains an incomprehensible mystery, the greatest and the most glorious of all mysteries."

50. Kenneth P. Minkema, ed., *Sermons and Discourses 1723-1729*, The Works of Jonathan Edwards, vol. 14 (New Haven: Yale University Press, 1997), p. 379.

stances Edwards affirmed in a standard way the identity of the trinitarian persons with the divine essence.

But while Edwards clearly reflected the influence of the simplicity tradition in developing some facets of his trinitarianism, he did not hesitate to reject it outright when it conflicted with his notion of divine excellency and his desire for a doctrine of the Trinity that followed the way of piety. In his *Discourse on the Trinity*, Edwards explicitly rejected the "maxim amongst divines" that required the identification of all of God's attributes with God:

> If a man should tell me that the immutability of God is God or that the omnipresence of God and authority of God, is God, I should not be able to think of any rational meaning of what he said. It hardly sounds to me proper to say that God's being without change is God, or that God's being everywhere is God, or that God's having a right of government over creatures is God.[51]

Here Edwards self-consciously departed from the scholastic and Puritan consensus regarding the identity of all of God's attributes with God. The only sense that Edwards could make of the "maxim amongst divines" that identified all of God's attributes with God's essence was a trinitarian one. In the case of the "real attributes of God," Edwards declared, the simplicity maxim holds: "God's understanding and love are God, for deity subsists in them distinctly; so they are distinct Divine persons."[52] Throughout his *Discourse on the Trinity*, Edwards was careful to protect the genuine distinctness of these two attributes. He invoked divine simplicity to infer, for example, that in God's Love there are no distinctions of "faculty, habit, and act, between will, inclination, and love, but that it is all one simple act."[53] But he never collapsed the "real distinction" in God between his attributes of understanding and love, for, he asserted, "they are distinct Divine persons."

The terminology of *relations* gradually developed within classical trinitarianism to express difference within the immanent Godhead in a way that accommodated the exigencies of divine simplicity. It showed how there could be true distinctions within the immanent Trinity,

51. Helm, *Trinity*, p. 119.
52. Helm, *Trinity*, p. 119.
53. Helm, *Trinity*, p. 99.

without suggesting any metaphysical "parts" in God. The three in God are not distinct "persons," but only distinct relations of the one divine essence. That Edwards knew this terminology is clear from a manuscript fragment on the equality of the members of the Trinity, in which he asserted that "their personal glory is only a relative glory, or a glory of relation, and therefore may be entirely distinct. . . . to apply distinct attributes in this sense in no wise implies an applying of a distinct essence, for personal relations are not of the divine essence."[54] Yet Edwards showed striking lack of interest in the traditional terminology of processions within God, or of the "real relations" within God (fatherhood, sonship, spiration) that these implied. In fact, he characteristically rejected the use of the terms *relation* and *mode* to signify the real distinctions within the Godhead. "'Tis evident," he declared, "that there are no more than these three really distinct in God: God, and his idea, and his love or delight." It is the remaining divine attributes that are "meer modes or relations" of God's essence. For example, God's goodness and mercy are simply "his love with a relation." Even in creatures, "duration, extension, changeableness or unchangeableness" are not real distinctions but "only mere modes and relations of existence."[55]

While Edwards rarely employed the traditional trinitarian terminology of *relations* for designating trinitarian distinctions in God, relationality was at the core of his "new concept of being." He clearly did not think of the trinitarian persons as distinct individuals that "*have* relations, or who make a decision to *come into* relation."[56] God's being as Trinity is "a 'being for'" in perfect loving communion, an "eternal identity in otherness."[57] Edwards's idiosyncratic way of expressing this relationality drew on the imagery of the psychological model. If the Son is the Father's wisdom, he declared, then the Father cannot be wise without the Son. "There is such a wonderfull union between them that they are, after an ineffable and inconceivable manner, one in another, so that one hath another and they have communion in

54. *Fragment on the Trinity*, Boston Public Library, c. early 1740s. Used by permission of The Works of Jonathan Edwards, Yale University.

55. *Works*, 13, p. 367 (no. 259). This passage is later inserted into the *Discourse on the Trinity*.

56. Cunningham, *These Three Are One*, p. 65.

57. Rowan Williams, *On Christian Theology* (Oxford: Blackwell, 2000), p. 72.

one another and are as it were predicable one of another."[58] The Father understands because the Son is in him, and the Son loves because the Spirit is in him, and so on. The Father, Son, and Holy Spirit are not wise and loving independently — their relations to each other constitute who they are.[59]

This understanding of trinitarian relationality brought Edwards again into conflict with the maxim of divine simplicity. His violation of the simplicity tradition can be seen by comparing it with Augustine's version. Augustine deemed it "absurd" that the Father is wise only through the Son and strongly warned against thinking about God "as though the Father does not understand nor love for Himself, but that the Son understands for Him, and the Holy Spirit loves for Him."[60] Because of the identity he posited between the divine nature and attributes, the Father, Son, and Spirit must each possess the essential attributes "in respect to themselves." If one of the divine persons were dependent on something or someone else for wisdom and love, there would be a distinction between personal essence and divine attributes. To avoid this conclusion, Augustine asserted that wisdom "is so retained in the nature of each one, as that He who has it, is that which He has, as being an unchangeable and simple substance."[61] We saw that Edwards took this route to avoid positing "three distinct beings" in God in no. 308 of the "Miscellanies." Van Mastricht and the other Reformed scholastics more consistently followed Augustine in protecting divine simplicity by insisting that all the divine attributes were common to the Father, Son, and Spirit, because they coincided with the divine essence.[62]

58. Helm, *Trinity*, p. 120.

59. In his study of Edwards's theology, the Dutch theologian Jan Ridderbos found in this appropriation of the psychological analogy an unseemly literalism; he charged that Edwards had abandoned metaphorical language and portrayed the Son and Holy Spirit as being literally attributes of the one God. Ridderbos was right to see that in refusing to identify wisdom and love with the divine essence, Edwards violated the tradition of divine simplicity. But rather than an unseemly literalism, the point of Edwards's use of the model was to stress the relationality and mutual dependence of the persons of the Godhead. See *De Theologie van Jonathan Edwards* ('s-Gravenhage: Johan A. Nederbragt, 1907), pp. 274, 277.

60. Augustine, *The Trinity*, p. 492 (XV.xvii.28).

61. Augustine, *The Trinity*, p. 493 (XV.xvii.28).

62. Mastricht, *Theoretico-practica Theologia*, II.xxiv.9. (Quia omnia attributa divina, quae cum essentia divina coincidunt, Patri, Filio et Spiritui S. facit communia.)

Van Mastricht and the Cambridge Brethren in effect had two visions of the perfections of the immanent Godhead: one rooted in the metaphysical conceptuality of the simplicity tradition, and the other in a loose group of social images lacking metaphysical definition, but fueled by their desires for a theology that "followed the way of piety." Edwards shared their theological conviction that "the perfection of the holy Trinity consists chiefly in the most perfect society and communion of the divine persons,"[63] and that positing dynamic relationality at the core of God's being had important implications for Christian attempts to "live unto God." But just as he was "not afraid" to transgress the boundaries of strict scriptural precedent in his trinitarian imagery, so he was not afraid to abandon the divine simplicity tradition either. His emphasis on both personal agency and deep relationality within the Godhead allowed him to bring together the social and psychological models for the Trinity in an imaginative way and plumb them as a resource for "living unto God."

Leaving behind the abstract terminology of *fatherhood, sonship,* and *spiration,* Edwards took his theological cues from the complexities of God's work of redemption. If in the work of redemption it is possible, in the words of Hans von Balthasar, "for the Persons within the Godhead to say 'Thou,'"[64] this must reflect something about the Godhead in itself. Edwards thought the I-Thou relations of the economic Trinity legitimated the use of *persons* language within the immanent Godhead. In a passage in *Treatise on Grace,* Edwards expressed his confidence regarding the appropriateness of this term to signify trinitarian distinctions:

> I believe that we have no word in the English language that does so naturally represent what the Scripture reveals of the distinction of the Eternal Three, — Father, Son, and Holy Ghost, — as to say they are one God but three persons.[65]

"The Scripture does sufficiently reveal the Holy Spirit as a proper Divine person," he asserted, "and thus we ought to look upon Him as a

---

63. Mastricht, *Theoretico-practica Theologia,* II.xxiv.28.

64. Hans Urs von Balthasar, *Theo-Drama: Theological Dramatic Theory,* Vol. III, *The Dramatis Personae: The Person in Christ,* trans. Graham Harrison (San Francisco: Ignatius Press, 1992), p. 526.

65. Helm, *Trinity,* p. 57.

distinct personal agent."[66] Edwards betrayed no unease with the term *person*, despite the strains it placed on the simplicity tradition.

Edwards's most fundamental theological rationale for speaking of *persons* in God was the aptness of that vocabulary for expressing trinitarian love:

> That in John God is love shews that there are more persons than one in the deity, for it shews love to be essential and necessary to the deity so that His nature consists in it, and this supposes that there is an eternal and necessary object, because all love respects another that is the beloved.[67]

There must be sufficient personal "difference" within the Godhead so that God's love does not become self-love, which in Edwards's view was "very improperly called love." Within the triplicity of the Godhead there is eros: reciprocal love and delight. As Edwards noted in a sermon on Acts 20:28, "the eternal infinite happiness of the divine being seems to be social, consisting in the infinitely blessed union and felicity of the person[s] of the Trinity so that they are happy in one another; God the Father, God the Son are represented as rejoicing from eternity one in another."[68] The "mutual propensity and affection of heart"[69] among the persons of the Godhead found its image in human longing and desire for the other. The eros of human desire for union with the other was not merely a creaturely limitation or a carnal distraction from the business of religion: desire for union "cannot be because of our imperfection, but because we are made in the image of God; for the more perfect any creature is, the more strong this inclination." Abandoning the metaphysical vision of God's solitary perfection, Edwards concluded that "Jehovah's happiness consists in communion, as well as the creature's."[70]

---

66. Helm, *Trinity*, p. 57. Edwards's students Joseph Bellamy and Samuel Hopkins also defended "persons language" for the Trinity on the basis of the scriptural representations of the divine economy; however, they were considerably more guarded than Edwards on this point. See Bellamy, *Works* (Boston: Doctrine Tract and Book Society, 1854; reprint, New York: Garland Publishers, 1987), 1, p. 417; and Hopkins, *Works* (Boston: Doctrinal Tract and Book Society, 1853), 1, pp. 65-66.

67. Helm, *Trinity*, p. 100.

68. Ms sermon, Beinecke Library, Yale University.

69. Works, 8, p. 564.

70. Works, 13, p. 264 (no. 96).

Edwards's use of *person* to express trinitarian distinctions had theological perils. Charles Taylor has described the rise of "atomistic individualism" among the intellectual elite of Europe during Edwards's time, a vision of society as constituted by individuals for the fulfillment of ends that were primarily individual.[71] On this view persons "start off as political atoms." A person is first of all an individual, and only subsequently in relations with others. Establishing the prior consent of individuals to form a community was thus the first step of seventeenth-century contract theory.[72] As we will see in the next chapter, Edwards's development of the covenant of redemption in isolation from the relational themes of the psychological model for the Trinity fell prey to this atomistic view of personhood.

Starting already in Edwards's day, the prevalence of an atomistic view of the self, which Taylor argues is now deeply embedded in the western psyche, has fueled arguments against the use of *person* for designating trinitarian distinctions. The great twentieth-century Reformed theologian Karl Barth, for example, asserted that

> By Father, Son and Spirit we do not mean what is commonly suggested to us by the word "persons." This designation was accepted — not without opposition — on linguistic presuppositions which no longer obtain to-day. It was never intended to imply — at any rate in the main stream of theological tradition — that there are in God three different personalities, three self-existent individuals, with their own special self-consciousness, cognition, volition, activity, effects, revelation and name.[73]

Barth thought that the term *person* was irredeemably tainted by atomistic individualism, so that to speak of three persons in God would be "to speak of three gods." To portray the "mutual inter-

---

71. Charles Taylor, *Sources of the Self: The Making of the Modern Identity* (Cambridge, Mass.: Harvard University Press, 1989). See also the discussion of Taylor in Fergus Kerr, *Immortal Longings: Versions of Transcending Humanity* (Notre Dame: University of Notre Dame Press, 1997), pp. 136-58.

72. Taylor, *Sources of the Self,* p. 193.

73. Karl Barth, *Church Dogmatics* IV/1 (Edinburgh: T. & T. Clark, 1956), pp. 204-5. I am indebted to Neal Plantinga for these references. One might wish that Barth had taken the problem of "floating signifiers" more into account in his defenses of immutable appropriateness of *father* language for God.

connexion and relationship" among the Father, Son, and Holy Spirit, he abandoned three-persons language in favor of "one personal God . . . in three different modes."[74]

Barth was right that, in an age of atomistic individualism, the traditional language of "God in three persons" has lost its relational resonance. It seems to imply "three self-existent individuals" in the Godhead, instead of a dynamic, loving relationality. But the problems of *persons* language for the Trinity are not simply a product of modern individualism. As Nicholas Lash argues, "Even if we brought off the massive cultural, economic and political transformation necessary in order to set at centre stage relationship and mutuality, rather than ownership and independence, it would still be true that human beings would exist as individual agents. Amongst us, three persons would still be three people."[75] Rejecting this language also has its theological perils, however. As Lash points out, God is not "three people," but neither is God "an individual with a nature."[76] When theologians retain the assumption that God is personal, while rejecting the notion of three persons in God, the tendency is to imply only one "person" in God. Barth, for example, fell into the trap of retaining the modernist "definition of a person" as "a knowing, willing, acting I,"[77] and then insisting that there is in the Godhead only "the one 'personality' of God, the one active and speaking divine Ego."[78] But surely the image of one atomistic individual in the Godhead is no improvement over three! Sarah Coakley has shown the perils of importing "the sovereignly-free 'individualism' of the Enlightenment 'man of reason'" into theological discussion.[79] Though Barth is not the direct object of her critique, his theology does not entirely avoid what she calls the "masculinist projections" of God as "'individual,' a *very large* disembodied spirit with ultimate directive power and freedom."[80]

74. Karl Barth, *Church Dogmatics* IV/1, p. 205.

75. Nicholas Lash, *Believing Three Ways in One God: A Reading of the Apostles' Creed* (London: SCM Press, 1992), p. 32. For all his polemic against *persons* language for the Trinity, Lash himself cannot entirely avoid it.

76. Lash, *Believing Three Ways in One God,* p. 33.

77. Karl Barth, *Church Dogmatics* II/1 (Edinburgh: T. & T. Clark, 1957), p. 284.

78. Karl Barth, *Church Dogmatics* IV/1, p. 205.

79. Sarah Coakley, "Kenosis and Subversion: On the Repression of 'Vulnerability' in Christian Feminist Writing," in Daphne Hampson, ed., *Swallowing a Fishbone? Feminist Theologians Debate Christianity* (London: SPCK, 1996), p. 101.

80. Coakley, "Kenosis and Subversion," p. 102.

Barth's language of "the one divine Ego" clashed with his deeply trinitarian perception of "the plurality in the divine being . . . , the differentiation and relationship, the loving co-existence and co-operation, the I and Thou, which first take place in God Himself."[81] In his tortured locution, "the relationship between the I and the Thou" in God must be "included in the one individual."[82] Strangely, Barth's view of the human person is much more relational than his view of the one divine person. "Man is not a person" in himself, Barth asserted, "but he becomes one on the basis that he is loved by God and can love God in return." Among human beings, personhood is derivative of our relations. But it is not so with God, who is a person, "without being limited or bound by this [human] other."[83] Rejecting the notion of "three persons" within the Godhead led Barth to assert that God's singular personhood is "capable of fellowship," but not inherently relational. Like the consenting individual in seventeenth-century contracts, God is first of all "Himself and as such can confront another, a Thou."[84] A relational concept of God is deeply embedded in Barth's theology, but his idiosyncratic use of *persons* language for God works against it.

Edwards presents the curious picture of a theologian who argued vigorously for the propriety of the traditional language of "God in three persons," but also was willing to abandon it and express God's internal relatedness in other terms. His extensive use of the psychological analogy for the Trinity shows that his deployment of *persons* language was neither exclusive nor literal. Even in a culture of "atomistic individualism," there is something to be said for continuing to struggle with the language of "God in three persons" because it "calls into question our assumption that the categories of oneness and difference are incommensurable, incompatible, or even necessarily in tension with one another."[85] God is personal in a way that defies our categories of both "one person" and "three persons." Yet it seems that our broken speech about God and to God cannot avoid the syntax of one or the other of these categories. As the fourth-century theologian Hilary of Poitiers

81. Karl Barth, *Church Dogmatics* III/1 (Edinburgh: T. & T. Clark, 1958), p. 196.

82. Karl Barth, *Church Dogmatics* III/1, p. 196.

83. Karl Barth, *Church Dogmatics* II/1, p. 284.

84. Karl Barth, *Church Dogmatics* II/1, p. 284.

85. David Cunningham, *These Three Are One*, p. 8. I should note that Cunningham joins Barth in rejecting *persons* language for the Trinity.

wrote, concerning the first and second persons of the Trinity, "If in these Two you shall recognize the Unity, instead of the solitude of God, you will share the Church's faith."[86]

A Relational Ontology

The primacy of the Trinity in Edwards's metaphysics reveals that his basic ontology is a relational one. In Edwards's thought, as Michael McClymond has noted, "every entity stands in direct and constant relation to God, and every instance of truth, beauty, or goodness in creatures participates in the supreme truth, beauty, and goodness of God."[87] I will be arguing below that his aesthetics, his philosophical idealism, and what Sang Hyun Lee has called Edwards's dispositional ontology are best understood as shifting expressions of this relational ontology. Edwards's metaphysics, like his theology, is more a connected set of miscellaneous reflections than an internally consistent whole. What holds it together is the conviction that relationality is at the heart of metaphysical excellence. As Daniel B. Shea, Jr., has affirmed, "It is appropriate to consider Edwards's thought, not as a system, but as the expression of a profound experience of the interrelatedness of things."[88]

With Edwards, metaphysics cannot proceed without reference to God. "God is the prime and original being, the first and the last, and the pattern of all, and has the sum of all perfection."[89] We have already seen that Edwards envisioned the perfection of God to reside in relations of harmonious consent within an irreducible plurality. "In a being that is absolutely without any plurality there cannot be excellency, for there can be no such thing as consent or agreement."[90] Excellency

86. St. Hilary of Poitiers, *On the Trinity,* trans. E. W. Watson, in *The Nicene and Post-Nicene Fathers,* second series, vol. 9 (Grand Rapids: Eerdmans, 1979), p. 97 (Bk. 5, 39).

87. Michael J. McClymond, *Encounters with God: An Approach to the Theology of Jonathan Edwards* (Oxford: Oxford University Press, 1998), p. 103.

88. "Jonathan Edwards: Historian of Consciousness," in *Major Writers of Early American Literature,* ed. Everett Emerson (Madison: University of Wisconsin Press, 1972), p. 180. Quoted in McClymond, *Encounters with God,* p. 5.

89. Works, 6, p. 363. See more generally Edwards's first entry on "Excellency" in *Notes on the Mind,* Works, 6, pp. 332-38.

90. Works, 6, p. 337.

was so important to his thought, Norman Fiering has suggested, that "Edwards perhaps intended to rank [it] with the classical transcendental attributes of being."[91] Nowhere is this notion more evident than in the harmonious relations of the persons of the Trinity.

Beauty was irreducibly relational for Edwards. His aesthetics "does not, therefore, begin with the assumption of the ontological independence of the [beautiful] thing; it is not a thing first and only afterwards designated as beautiful."[92] Rather, beauty is a matter of proportion and harmony within the thing itself, and in its relations with other objects. The beauty of the created world derives from the fact "that God does purposely make and order one thing to be in an agreeableness and harmony with another."[93]

> That sort of beauty which is called "natural," as of vines, plants, trees, etc., consists of a very complicated harmony; and all the natural motions and tendencies and figures of bodies in the universe are done according to proportion, and therein is their beauty.[94]

Anything that is beautiful exhibits consent and agreement, and so must be "distinguished in a plurality some way or other."

Beauty thus requires complexity. Within the divine simplicity tradition, complexity was a mark of creaturely limitation. Edwards practically reversed this, finding creaturely limitation reflected in the incapacity for complexity.

> We see that the narrower the capacity, the more simple must be the beauty to please. Thus in the proportion of sounds, the birds and brute creatures are most delighted with simple music, and in the proportion confined to a few notes.[95]

Human creatures already enjoy more complex beauties on earth than animals can; and the saints can hope for at least a partial overcoming of their creaturely limitations in heaven.

91. Norman S. Fiering, *Jonathan Edwards's Moral Thought and Its British Context* (Chapel Hill: University of North Carolina Press, 1981), p. 74. See also Thomas Schafer's discussion of excellency and its connection to the Trinity in Works, 13, pp. 53-58.
92. Daniel, *Philosophy of Jonathan Edwards*, p. 182.
93. Works, 11, p. 53.
94. Works, 6, p. 335.
95. Works, 13, p. 329 (no. 182).

Then perhaps we shall be able fully and easily to apprehend the beauty, where respect is to be had to thousands of different ratios at once to make up the harmony. Such kind of beauties, when fully perceived, are far the sweetest.[96]

Heaven, Edwards opined, will no doubt offer "external beauties and harmonies altogether of another kind from what we perceive here." "But how much more ravishing," he speculated, "will the exquisite spiritual proportions be that shall be seen in minds, in their acts; between one spiritual act and another, between one disposition and another. . . ."[97]

Physical beauty, however complex, was for Edwards only "secondary"; "when we spake of excellence in bodies we were obliged to borrow the word 'consent' from spiritual things."[98] Beauty more properly applies to "perceiving and willing being" than to material things: even the "notes of a tune or the strokes of an acute penman" are beautiful by appearing "like a society of so many perceiving beings, sweetly agreeing together."[99] God has made the "mutual consent and agreement of [physical] things beautiful and grateful" to us, because "there is in it some image of the true, spiritual original beauty, . . . consisting in being's consent to being, or the union of minds or spiritual beings in a mutual propensity and affection of heart."[100]

The aesthetic dimensions of Edwards's theology derived from the more basic category of loving consent, because "all the primary and original beauty or excellence that is among minds is love."[101] More specifically, they derived from his understanding of the Trinity: because

96. Cf. Sibbes, "The sweetness of music ariseth from many instruments, and from the concord of all the strings in every instrument. When every instrument hath many strings, and all are in tune, it makes sweet harmony, it makes sweet concord." *Complete Works* 3, p. 194. Sibbes goes on to draw social consequences about the beauty of social concord.

97. Works, 13, p. 328 (no. 182).

98. Works, 6, p. 362. I am indebted here to Norman Fiering's analysis in *Jonathan Edwards's Moral Thought*, pp. 80-82.

99. Works, 6, p. 382.

100. Works, 8, p. 564.

101. Works, 6, p. 362. I am here siding with Norman Fiering, *Jonathan Edwards's Moral Thought*, over Roland Delattre, *Beauty and Sensibility in the Thought of Jonathan Edwards: An Essay in Aesthetics and Theological Ethics* (New Haven: Yale University Press, 1968), pp. 105-8, who tends to elevate beauty to a primary category.

there is true "plurality" in God, there can be consent and thus true beauty within the Trinity itself.[102] God's "infinite beauty is his infinite *mutual* love of himself."[103]

> 'Tis peculiar to God that he has beauty within himself, consisting in being's consenting with his own being, or the love of himself in his own Holy Spirit; whereas the excellence of others is in loving others, in loving God, and in the communications of his Spirit.[104]

The beauty of God in human creatures is thus primarily social rather than physical, because it is an emanation of the beauty of the divine society of persons. All created things are beautiful insofar as they are "made in his image, and are emanations from him." "The beauty of the world is a communication of God's beauty."[105] Edwards's identification of "original beauty" with love meant that the communications of the Holy Spirit, both within the Godhead and towards creatures, were beautiful. As Edwards declared in a typically effusive way, "the Holy Spirit is the harmony and excellency and beauty of the Deity."[106]

The "plurality" required by divine excellency was evident in his portrayal of the various attributes of God. Edwards devoted considerable effort to showing the harmony and "consent" of the various divine attributes, rather than arguing for their metaphysical identity. One of the grandest, most elaborate examples of this can be found in his well-known sermon "The Excellency of Christ," in which he presented the "admirable conjunction of diverse excellencies in Christ," distinguishing between those excellencies that are diverse primarily "in our manner of conceiving" and those that are "really diverse."[107] Those in the

---

102. Roland Delattre missed the role of the Trinity in Edwards's argument here. And so he mistakenly asserted, *Beauty and Sensibility*, p. 24, that "even the beauty of God . . . is not self-contained, for it consists more properly in his effulgence and propensity to creative self-communication than in his self-sufficiency." Rather, the Holy Spirit is "primarily" the exercise of mutual love within the Trinity, and only "secondarily" the repetition of this love towards creatures.

103. Works, 6, p. 363 (emphasis added).

104. Works, 6, p. 365.

105. Works, 13, p. 384 (no. 293).

106. Works, 13, p. 384 (no. 293).

107. M. X. Lesser, ed., *Sermons and Discourses, 1734-1738*, The Works of Jonathan Edwards, vol. 19 (New Haven: Yale University Press, 2001), p. 565. See John B. Carman's inci-

second group are unique to Christ, being "conjoined in no other person whatever, either divine, human, or angelical."[108] These truly diverse attributes are presented in pairs, such as "infinite glory and lowest humility," "infinite majesty and transcendent meekness," and "absolute sovereignty and perfect resignation." There is no argument, such as the one noted in Turretin, that these seemingly opposed attributes are really identical with each other and with the divine essence. Edwards nowhere claimed, for example, that majesty and meekness are diverse only according to our limited human conception. To the contrary, the excellency of Christ resides in the fact that, in him, these *truly* diverse attributes are perfectly conjoined.

Admittedly, the case of the incarnate Son is unique within the Trinity; neither of the other divine persons exhibits such perfect humility and resignation. Still, Edwards made similar arguments concerning the first person of the Trinity, in discussing the "Harmony of God's Attributes in the Work of Redemption."[109]

> These attributes being thus united in the divine nature and not interfering one with another is what is a great part of their glory: God's awful and terrible attributes, and his mild and gentle attributes. They reflect glory one on the other; and 'tis the glory of God that those attributes should always be exercised and expressed in a consistence and harmony one with the other.[110]

For the Father as well, in "this wonderful meeting of diverse excellencies," the beauty of the whole is one of complex harmony, not simplicity.

But in using the notions of consent and excellency to describe a union of attributes within God, Edwards was extending their meaning. For him, these words primarily denoted *interpersonal* union. Divine excellency required a genuine trinitarian sociality. There must be "an object from all eternity which God infinitely loves." A creature would not be a fitting object of this love, for it is not of the same divine essence,

---

sive analysis of this conjunction in *Majesty and Meekness: A Comparative Study of Contrast and Harmony in the Concept of God* (Grand Rapids: Eerdmans, 1994), pp. 231-51.

108. Works, 19, p. 567.

109. Title of "Miscellanies," no. 38 (Works, 13, p. 221). See also Edwards's sermon "God's Excellencies" in Works, 10, pp. 415-35.

110. Mark R. Valeri, ed., *Sermons and Discourses, 1703-1733*, The Works of Jonathan Edwards, vol. 17 (New Haven: Yale University Press, 1999), p. 159.

and "if it be different, it don't infinitely consent."[111] Even the harmony among the attributes of Christ is finally a type of "the supreme harmony of all," which is found "among the persons of the Trinity."[112] It is on account of Edwards's view of the harmony of the Trinity that he could assert that "God is God, and distinguished from all other beings and exalted above 'em, chiefly by his divine beauty."[113]

Edwards's idealism is a second facet of his philosophical reflection that is helpfully understood within the framework of a relational ontology.[114] We have already seen how Edwards experimented with an idealist framework in explicating the psychological analogy for the Trinity: "An absolutely perfect idea of a thing is the very thing, for it wants nothing that is in the thing, substance nor nothing else." And because God's self-contemplation *is* perfect, "that idea which God hath of Himself is absolutely Himself."[115]

But Edwards was not content to delineate the origin of the Son as the Father's idea within the immanent Trinity. "God is a communicative being," and therefore God's perfect idea does not remain within the Godhead, but flows out towards creatures. The perfect fullness in God distinguishes God from everything creaturely, but it is this very fullness that enables God to overflow in gifts to us. "The great and universal end of God's creating the world was to communicate himself."[116]

> As there is an infinite fullness of all possible good in God, a fullness of every perfection, of all excellency and beauty, and of infinite happiness. And as this fullness is capable of communication or emanation *ad extra;* so it seems a thing amiable and valuable in itself that it should be communicated or flow forth, that this infinite fountain of good should send forth abundant streams, that this infinite fountain of light should, diffusing its excellent fullness, pour forth light all around.[117]

---

111. Works, 13, p. 283 (no. 117).
112. Works, 13, p. 329 (no. 182).
113. Works, 2, p. 298.
114. It is more customary to align Edwards's idealism with his convictions about divine sovereignty, as a radical claim for creation's absolute dependence on its Creator.
115. Helm, *Trinity*, p. 103.
116. Works, 13, p. 410 (no. 332).
117. Works, 8, pp. 432-33.

Like the great thirteenth-century Franciscan St. Bonaventure, Edwards posited in God an eternal desire to radiate outwards in emanations of understanding and love towards creatures who are able to receive these gifts, so that the circle of relation expands beyond the boundaries of the Trinity.

In explaining how God is communicated to creatures, Edwards rejected a substance metaphysic for understanding both God's communication and the creature's reception of it:

> We ought to conceive of God as being omnipotence, perfect knowledge, and perfect love, and not extended any otherwise than as power, knowledge, and love are extended, and not as if it were a sort of unknown thing that we call substance, that is extended.[118]

In the same way, in reflecting on the claim that "the substance of the soul" is what brings a thought forth, Edwards averred, "if it be God, I acknowledge; but if there be meant something else that has no properties, it seems to me absurd."[119] Instead, following the framework of the psychological analogy, Edwards asserted that the Godhead is extended and received through its trinitarian relations. He found "these two ways of God's flowing forth and being communicated": "Christ's being in the creature in the name, idea or knowledge of God being in them, and the Holy Spirit's being in them in the love of God's being in them."[120] God's perfect knowledge and love are extended beyond the society of the Trinity into the world through the indwelling of Christ and the Holy Spirit in the hearts and minds of believers. In this way the psychological model of the Trinity provided Edwards with a basic soteriological story line, a way of telling how the work of redemption is "the main great work of power, wisdom and grace that is the hinge of all" God's works.[121]

The knowledge and love of God are available only to intelligent creatures; "they only are capable of being proper images of [the Son's] excellency."[122] Only creatures with mental consciousness can render God

---

118. Works, 13, p. 335 (no. 194).
119. Works, 13, p. 373 (no. 267).
120. *Misc.,* no. 1084.
121. Works, 18, p. 402 (no. 752).
122. Works, 13, p. 279 (no. 108).

glory by receiving the manifestation of divine truth and the communication of divine love, and reflecting them back to God.[123] As Edwards reflected in one of the earliest "Miscellanies" entries, "senseless matter would be altogether useless if there was no intelligent being but God, for God could neither receive good himself nor communicate good."[124] He developed this notion a few entries later, concluding that "there can be no being, either God or the world, without a consciousness of it."[125] The roots of Edwards's idealism lie in his conviction that only intelligent creatures can be in true relation with Christ, God's perfect Idea, and the Holy Spirit, God's perfect Love. Stephen Holmes has suggested expanding Edwards's idealist metaphysics in an explicitly trinitarian direction, so that "Edwards' assertion that to be is to be known would have to become 'to be is to be known and loved' (esse est percipi et amari)."[126] As Michael McClymond argues,

> Idealism was simply the extension of Edwards's theological conviction that God's glory, to be truly glorious, must reverberate in the hearts and minds of his creatures. . . . Beginning with the notion that God's glory must be known and appreciated for it to have any significance, he generalized this notion into the sweeping principle that "nothing has any existence anywhere else than in consciousness." The concept of God as known, as manifest, as visibly glorious, proved so decisive a factor in Edwards's thinking that it gave birth to idealist metaphysics.[127]

The eternal self-repetition of God in the Son, God's perfect Idea, finds its further reiteration in the consciousness of intelligent creatures, whose "end must be to behold and admire the doings of God, and magnify him for them, and to contemplate his glories in them."[128]

---

123. "The glory of God implies these two things: manifestation and communication, the latter called grace, the former, truth" (*Misc.,* no. 1094).

124. Works, 13, p. 185 (no. gg). Edwards's earliest Miscellany entries were numbered alphabetically, starting with *a* through *z* and continuing with *aa* through *zz.*

125. Works, 13, p. 47.

126. Stephen Holmes, *God of Grace and God of Glory: An Account of the Theology of Jonathan Edwards* (Grand Rapids: Eerdmans, 2001), p. 87.

127. McClymond, *Encounters with God,* p. 34.

128. Works, 13, pp. 185 (no. gg). Edwards's declaration is reminiscent of Gregory of Nyssa's reasoning for why God created humanity: "For it was not right that light should

Another expression of Edwards's relational ontology is found in his deployment of disposition as a metaphysical alternative to substance. According to Sang Hyun Lee, who has pioneered this valuable interpretation of Edwards's ontology, Edwards posited disposition and habit rather than substance and form as the building blocks of reality, "thereby introducing a dynamic element into the very fabric of being."[129] Disposition, under which Lee subsumes Edwards's diverse references to "habit, tendency, inclination, temper, and law," "is an ontologically real, active principle that has a mode of reality apart from its manifestations in actions and events."[130] As "laws that God has fixed,"[131] dispositions abide even when they are not being exercised, and so "function as the principles of permanence" in place of the traditional notion of substance.[132] Whereas substance is a static and self-contained mode of being, dispositional being is interrelated and dynamic. "One of the important consequences of such a dispositional reconnection of reality is that being is inherently disposed for further and further activities and relationships."[133]

As with Edwards's aesthetics and philosophical idealism, his dispositional ontology is inseparable from his understanding of the Trinity. God's being is dispositional, and as such inclined to increases and repetitions of the divine actuality. A dispositional ontology thus provides a way of portraying God's internal interrelations. In *Discourse on the Trinity*, Edwards depicted the Son as "the intellectual self-repetition of the Father":[134] "And I do suppose the deity to be truly and properly repeated by God's thus having an idea of Himself."[135] The

---

remain unseen, or glory unwitnessed, or goodness unenjoyed, or that any other aspect we observe of the divine nature should lie idle with no one to share or enjoy it." Gregory of Nyssa, "An Address on Religious Instruction," trans. C. Richardson, in *Christology of the Later Fathers,* ed. Edward Hardy (Philadelphia: Westminster Press, 1954), p. 276.

129. Lee, *Philosophical Theology,* p. 170.

130. Sang Hyun Lee, "Jonathan Edwards's Dispositional Conception of the Trinity: A Resource for Contemporary Reformed Theology," in David Willis and Michael Welker, eds., *Toward the Future of Reformed Theology: Tasks, Topics, Traditions* (Grand Rapids: Eerdmans, 1999), p. 447.

131. Works, 13, p. 358 (no. 241).

132. Lee, "Jonathan Edwards's Dispositional Conception of the Trinity," p. 447.

133. Lee, "Edwards's Dispositional Conception of the Trinity," p. 447.

134. Lee, "Edwards's Dispositional Conception of the Trinity," p. 451.

135. Helm, *Trinity,* p. 100.

Holy Spirit is the self-repetition of the Godhead in its affectional or volitional exercise:

> The Godhead being thus begotten by God's loving an idea of Himself and shewing forth in a distinct subsistence or person in that idea, there proceeds a most pure act, and an infinitely holy and sacred energy arises between the Father and Son in mutually loving and delighting in each other, for their love and joy is mutual. . . . So that the Godhead therein stands forth in yet another manner of subsistence, and there proceeds the third person in the Trinity, the Holy Spirit, viz. The deity in act, for there is no other act but the act of the will.[136]

The divine inclination to repetition and increase within the Godhead implies that relational activity is intrinsic to God's being and will naturally seek external exercise. "The eternal act or energy of the divine nature within him, whereby he infinitely loves and delights in himself, I suppose imply fundamentally goodness and grace towards creatures, if there be that occasion which infinite wisdom sees fit."[137] In Lee's words, "God's creation of the world is to be conceived of as a repetition of a prior actuality — an 'increase, repetition or multiplication' in time of God's internal 'fullness.'"[138]

Neither Edwards's emphasis on beauty nor his idealist or dispositional ontology provides a sufficiently wide lens for understanding his metaphysic as a whole. Each of them is partially disclosive of his relational view of divine being and creaturely reality. Yet all of them reflect Edwards's desire that the "admirable contexture and harmony of the whole" of reality would shine forth,[139] to the glory of the triune God, "the supreme harmony of all."

What John Owen called the "fruits of the Trinity's love and goodness for the human soul" will be the theme of the next chapters, as the focus shifts from the inner harmony of the Trinity to the plans, dispositions, and acts of the Godhead regarding human redemption.

---

136. Helm, *Trinity*, p. 108.

137. Works, 18, p. 97 (no. 553).

138. Lee, "Edwards's Dispositional Conception of the Trinity," p. 453, quoting Works, 8, p. 433.

139. "Letter to the Princeton Trustees" (Works, 16, p. 728). This was Edwards's description of his aim in writing "a body of divinity in an entire new method."

Chapter 3

COVENANTAL HARMONIES

"When man was first created, there was a consultation among the persons of the Trinity. . . . So it is in the work of redemption."

EDWARDS, Sermon on John 16:8

In the previous chapter, we saw how Edwards's relational ontology formed a bridge between the internal reality of the Godhead's eternal knowledge and love and its external expressions in the created world. For the most part, however, Edwards's idealist and dispositional ontologies were unable to accommodate the social images that were crucial to his trinitarian reflection as a whole. To give these adequate expression, he needed another bridge between the immanent and economic Godhead, one that would play out his basic themes of relation and dynamism in an explicitly social way. Edwards found this bridge in the Reformed notion of an eternal covenant of redemption made between the Father and the Son on behalf of human sinners. Edwards's willingness to flout Reformed rules about divine simplicity and nonscriptural language for God encouraged his employment of this explicitly social image of divine "plurality." The covenant of redemption was an "agreement which the persons of the Trinity came into from eternity as it were by mutual consultation and covenant."[1] Poised be-

---

1. *Misc.,* no. 993. Nos. 617, 825, 919, 1064, and 1091 explore the relations between the intratrinitarian covenant of redemption and the covenant of grace that binds believers

tween the immanent and economic Trinity, this intratrinitarian covenant was for Edwards a perfect showcase for demonstrating the harmony and fittingness of God's being and works within the framework of the social model for the Trinity.

To reprise Edwards's basic soteriological story line in a more explicitly social way, the eternal being-with of God as Trinity finds its external expression in the desire to incorporate human creatures into the divine life. It was "God's design" in the work of redemption "to admit the church into the divine family as his son's wife."[2] But in a world marked by sin and death, this intention to bring humanity into "the divine family of three" requires a struggle against all that stands in the way of intimate union with God. The intrinsic self-giving character of the Trinity is thus communicated to human sinners in the extraordinary self-giving of the incarnate Son. The incarnate Son "empties himself" to share a life of vulnerability and suffering with sinners, so as to bring them into intimate union with the Godhead. The means by which God achieves this union is at the same time God's redemptive goal for us: what we receive in union with Christ is the perfect consent to God and neighbor that characterize Christ's own life. Edwards deployed the notion of a covenant of redemption to show how Christ's economic work to "bring God and man to each other, and actually unite them together"[3] is both consistent with and distinct from the eternal life of the immanent Trinity.

The Covenant of Redemption

Underlying all of God's redemptive dealings with human creatures was the eternal consent of the persons of the Trinity. To negotiate the passage between the inner life of the Godhead and its economic dealings with creation, Edwards drew on the Reformed tradition of covenant theology, particularly its notion of the covenant of redemption. Unlike the covenants of works and grace, which were established between God

---

to Christ. This theme also appears widely in Edwards's sermons. See, e.g., the sermons referenced by Carl W. Bogue, *Jonathan Edwards and the Covenant of Grace* (Cherry Hill, N.J.: Mack, 1975), pp. 95-124.

2. Works, 18, p. 367 (no. 741).

3. Works, 18, p. 422 (no. 773).

and human persons in time, the distinct parties in the covenant of redemption were the eternal persons of the Trinity, who agreed upon it "in the council of the Trinity before the world began."[4] Edwards effectively employed this covenant framework to extend the theme of God's social consent beyond the bounds of the immanent Trinity. While the covenant of redemption was agreed upon within the immanent trinitarian society, it concerned the pattern of God's redemptive actions in the created world.

The theological intent behind the development of the covenant of redemption was admirable.[5] It addressed the difficult gap between the assertions of ontological parity and unity among the members of the immanent Trinity, and the subordinationist themes and obvious differentiation within the Trinity's economic work. Human assurance of salvation demanded that there be a deep coherence between God's eternal being and the temporal work of redemption. Orthodoxy required that this coherence not be obtained at the expense of a subordination of the Son and Spirit that prevented them from being properly "worshiped and glorified together" with the Father. As a rather fanciful ornamentation of the Reformed covenant tradition, the covenant of redemption tried to bridge this gap between the immanent and economic Trinity. Edwards found this image of the perfect consent of the Trinity useful for protecting the Christian faith against the twin threats of Arminianism and Arianism. Against Arminianism, the covenant of redemption emphasized the prevenient grace of God in human salvation. Against Arianism, it protected the ontological equality of the Son and the Father within the Godhead.

In its various forms, the covenant was the foundation of Reformed practical theology, undergirding the understanding of all God's salvific dealings with human creatures. *Covenant* was originally developed as a systematic theological notion in continental Reformed thought by sixteenth-century theologians such as Heinrich Bullinger, John Calvin, Zacharius Ursinus, and Caspar Olevianus.[6] In their writings, a single

---

4. David Dickson, *The Sum of Saving Knowledge,* with an Introduction by John MacPherson (Edinburgh: T. & T. Clark, n.d.), p. 54.

5. This is also true of the ingenious but ultimately unsuccessful compromises of Isaac Watts and Thomas Ridgley discussed later in this chapter.

6. My account is indebted to John von Rohr, *The Covenant of Grace in Puritan Thought* (Atlanta: Scholars Press, 1986), and Richard Muller, *Christ and the Decree: Christology and*

covenant linked the Old Testament and New Testament narratives of salvation history as the instrument of God's dealings with both Israel and the church. Yet from the beginning, there were different understandings of this covenant. Calvin portrayed the covenant as God's gracious, unilateral action in saving the elect, tying the temporal outworkings of the covenant to God's eternal decree of election. By contrast, his Swiss colleague Bullinger tended to depict the covenant of grace more as a bilateral covenant, contingent upon the response of human faith.[7] During the late sixteenth and early seventeenth centuries more extreme versions of both Calvin's and Bullinger's views appeared on the continent, with yet stronger emphases on sovereign divine grace and free human response, respectively.

As covenant theology became established in Reformed circles, the notion of distinct yet related covenants appeared. In Germany, Zacharius Ursinus and Caspar Olevianus, the authors of the *Heidelberg Catechism,* developed the idea of a covenant with humanity that preceded the covenant of grace. By the end of the sixteenth century, the covenant of grace was commonly supplemented by a covenant of works.[8] The covenant of works was understood to take place between God and Adam before the fall into sin. After this covenant was broken by human sinful acts, the covenant of grace was established by divine mercy. Later still, the notion of a trinitarian covenant of redemption developed, as an eternal agreement within the Godhead to save humanity, with the covenant of grace being its temporal expression.

Though there were earlier foreshadowings, the covenant scheme also became established in English theology during the mid-sixteenth century.[9] Like the continental theologians, English covenanters initially

Predestination in Reformed Theology from Calvin to Perkins (Durham, N.C.: Labyrinth Press, 1986). See also J. Wayne Baker, *Heinrich Bullinger and the Covenant: The Other Reformation* (Athens, Ohio: Ohio University Press, 1980).

7. J. Wayne Baker, *Heinrich Bullinger and the Covenant,* disputes this reading of Bullinger, emphasizing his insistence on salvation by grace alone. In my view, Bullinger's covenant theology exhibits perennial theological tensions between the role of God's grace and human response.

8. Michael McGiffert, "Grace and Works: The Rise and Division of Covenant Divinity," *Harvard Theological Review* 75 (1982): 464; and Leonard Trinterud, "The Origins of Puritanism" *Church History* 20 (1951): 48.

9. Trinterud, "Origins of Puritanism," p. 44, has dated it during the reign of Edward VI.

posited one basic covenant — the covenant of grace between God and the elect. In this covenant God promised salvation through Christ to believing sinners. Soon this was supplemented by the notion of a prior covenant of works, which required perfect and unaided obedience to the law as a condition for receiving God's blessings. However, as Richard Sibbes explained, "this fellowship being placed in man's own freedom, and having so weak a foundation, he lost both himself and it, so that now by the first covenant of works, Adam and all his posterity are under a curse."[10] In this light the covenant of grace was seen as a subsequent divine remedy, so that the sinner might "recover again his communion and fellowship with God." This "new and better covenant" was restricted to the elect. However, the covenant of works continued to govern God's dealings with all of humanity. In its federal form, as a covenant between God and individual nations, it was an extremely powerful instrument of social control both within and without the church. The covenant of works "provided a theological basis for a moral, civil, and religious obligation binding upon all men."[11] English Puritans passed on a tradition of covenant theology to their counterparts in New England, where it provided the governing assumptions for ecclesiastical and civil life in the colonial period.

Like Calvin and Bullinger, English Puritans exhibited differences in emphasis over the meaning of the covenantal relationship between God and humanity. These differences were transplanted to New England, where they intensified in the decades after the Antinomian Controversy. While it is important to remember what Brooks Holifield has termed the "ambidexterity" of Puritan theologians, Janice Knight notes that

> The Intellectual Fathers and Spiritual Brethren did not frame the question of human responsibility and divine prevenience in the same way. Though both groups spoke of the covenant, they came to different conclusions about the relative importance of absolute or conditional promises in that relationship.[12]

10. Sibbes, *Complete Works,* 6, p. 3.
11. Trinterud, "Origins of Puritanism," p. 44.
12. Janice Knight, *Orthodoxies in Massachusetts: Rereading American Puritanism* (Cambridge, Mass.: Harvard University Press, 1994), p. 92.

Without denying the role of human faith, Boston's John Cotton emphasized God's free grace that indwells sinners and unites them to God in faith. "Give me Christ," he declared, "and I claim my right to the promise and to all the comforts and blessings thereof."[13] By contrast, his contemporary Peter Bulkeley in nearby Concord upheld divine grace but accented the role of human obligation in the covenant: human faith is "not a condition only consequent, but antecedent to our actuall justification."[14]

An important gauge of these differences in theological accent on the nature of the covenantal union was the role given to the covenant of redemption. When the trinitarian covenant of redemption supplies the terms of the covenant of grace, as it arguably did for Sibbes, Cotton, and other Spiritual Brethren, the covenantal emphasis is on prevenient divine grace.[15] In this case the covenant of grace is a temporal realization of God's eternal gracious plan for saving sinners through Christ. Despite temporal human failings, salvation remains part of the eternal, immutable purposes of God. "It is a comfortable consideration," Sibbes declared, "to see how our salvation . . . stands upon the unity of the three glorious persons in the Trinity, that all join in one for the making of man happy."[16] Thomas Goodwin reassured his readers that human salvation was secured by an eternal agreement "struck Dialogue-wise" between God and Christ. Christ undertook the saving work of the cross, and "God undertakes to Christ again, to justifie, adopt and forgive, sanctifie and glorifie those he gives him."[17] Westminster divine Samuel Rutherford and David Dickson in Scotland like-

13. David D. Hall, ed., *The Antinomian Controversy, 1636-1638: A Documentary History* (Middletown, Conn.: Wesleyan University Press, 1968), pp. 98-99.

14. Bulkeley, *The Gospel-Covenant; or The Covenant of Grace Opened* (London, 1651), p. 358.

15. Even among the Spiritual Brethren, there was still hesitancy to pursue the trinitarian implications of the covenant of redemption. John Preston, for example, in *The New Covenant or The Saints Portion,* a widely read series of sermons on the differences between the covenant of grace and the covenant of works, made no mention of the covenant of redemption. This hesitancy was understandable, given the adherence to the traditions of *sola Scriptura* and divine simplicity examined in previous chapters. Lack of scriptural precedent and the strongly unified view of the immanent Trinity required by divine simplicity discouraged the notion of an eternal "consultation among the persons of the Trinity."

16. Sibbes, *Complete Works,* 4, p. 294.

17. Goodwin, *Works,* 3, pp. 26, 138.

wise presented the covenant of redemption as a distinct covenant of "surety," and contended eloquently for its role in assuring believers of God's steadfast grace to them. The covenant of redemption was founded "in the old and eternall design of love in the heart of God toward his Son, . . . the bosome darling and beloved of the Father."[18] As Perry Miller noted, in the covenant of redemption "God was not merely bound by His pledge to the creature, but still more firmly tied by a compact with Himself."[19] In this way, what originated as an elaboration of the covenant of grace came to be seen as its foundation. The eternal intratrinitarian covenant was, in Rutherford's words, "the cause of the stability and firmnesse of the Covenant of Grace."[20]

The idea of an eternal covenant of redemption alongside or within the covenant of grace was a "comfortable consideration" for another reason. It not only made the salvation promises more sure, but also relieved some of the uneasiness, especially among the Spiritual Brethren, about a bilateral covenant between God and humanity concerning human redemption. Too much emphasis on personal response of faith to the covenant offer as "antecedent to our actuall justification"[21] seemed to threaten the sufficiency of divine grace.[22] Did the efficacy of the redemptive goodness of God depend on an appropriate human response? Formulators of the covenant of grace who were sensitive to the dangers of preparationism stressed that faith itself is a divine gift. As Sibbes declared, "all our grace that we have to answer the covenant, is by reflection from God."[23] The covenant of redemption served as an additional hedge against any tendencies to a synergistic view of human salvation, by emphasizing the gracious, eternal work of God in redemption.

In particular, the covenant of redemption made clear that the link

18. Samuel Rutherford, *The Covenant of Life Opened* (Edinburgh, 1655), p. 326.

19. Perry Miller, *The New England Mind: The Seventeenth Century* (Cambridge, Mass.: Harvard University Press, 1954), p. 405.

20. Rutherford, *Covenant of Life Opened,* p. 309.

21. Bulkeley, *The Gospel-Covenant,* p. 358.

22. See William K. B. Stoever, *'A Faire and Easie Way to Heaven': Covenant Theology and Antinomianism in Early Massachusetts* (Middletown, Conn.: Wesleyan University Press, 1978), ch. 1, for a helpful account of how the Puritan emphasis on human activity in conversion need not be seen as a violation of God's sovereignty, but rather as a way to preserve the Reformed dialectic between divine grace and created nature.

23. Sibbes, *Complete Works,* 6, p. 19.

between God's grace and human redemption was to be found in Christ, not in human faith or preparation.[24] In Sibbes's words, the covenant of grace is

> a sure covenant, because it is established in the Messiah, Christ, God-man. And Christ being God and man, is fit to be the foundation of the covenant between God and man, for he is a friend to both parties . . . he brings God and man together comfortably and sweetly, and keepeth them together in a sure and firm agreement.[25]

"O what happinesse," Rutherford exclaimed, "that I am not mine own keeper, but that . . . the Father and Son have Covenant-wise closed and stricken hands, the one having given, and the other received me a-keeping."[26] Letting the covenant of redemption supply the "terms and form" of the covenant of grace provided a hedge against any temptation to exalt the role of human works in salvation.

By contrast, for the traditional Massachusetts "orthodoxy" of Thomas Hooker, Thomas Shepard, and Peter Bulkeley, "the terms and the form of God's dealings with mankind for salvation are established in the covenant of works."[27] This perspective lends a restorationist, contractual tone to the covenant of grace. Christ's role in the new covenant is to fulfill the conditions posited in the covenant of works and apply them to believers. Believers enter into the covenant of grace by fulfilling their new obligation, namely faith. Their sanctification be-

24. Much recent scholarship on Puritanism has rejected Perry Miller's argument for a "preparationist" group in Puritanism who held that acts of obedience to the law placed an obligation on God for a gracious reponse. The difference in theological nuance between the Intellectual Fathers and the Cambridge Brethren on the issue of preparationism is interesting, but should not be overplayed. For a summary of this scholarship, see David D. Hall, "On Common Ground: The Coherence of American Puritan Studies," *William and Mary Quarterly* 3, no. 44 (1987).

25. Sibbes, *Complete Works*, 6, p. 19.

26. Rutherford, *The Covenant of Life Opened*, p. 294.

27. Stoever, *'A Faire and Easie Way to Heaven,'* p. 96. Stoever sees the covenant of works as "paradigmatic in both form and content of God's redemptive activity." While he finds in general a strong continuity between the two covenants in early American Puritanism, he acknowledges John Cotton as an exception. For Cotton, there was more a disjunction between the two, with the covenant of works serving as a foil to highlight God's great mercy in Christ. In my reading, Sibbes and other Spiritual Brethren generally share Cotton's approach.

comes important evidence for their inclusion in the covenant of grace. As Peter Bulkeley noted, "our sanctification is more manifest to us then [sic] our justification. It is easier discerned."[28] While Bulkeley admitted that "The whole businesse of our salvation was first transacted between the Father and Christ, before it was revealed to us," his first concern was to argue that "the same promise" made to Christ "is afterwards in time made to us also," and requires our response of faith and holy obedience.[29] In his sizable treatise on "the Gospel-Covenant," he devoted a scant three pages to explicating the covenant of redemption. Even here, the trinitarian relations took on a markedly different tone than in the Sibbesian treatments. Instead of being the sweet agreement of the "three glorious persons of the Trinity" for extending their shared happiness outward, Bulkeley's covenant was "a commandment from the Father to the Son, which he must submit to, and obey."[30] This trinitarian rhetoric of command and obedience echoed the covenant of works, not the covenant of grace.

The extraordinary subordination of the Son to the Father in covenant schemes raised theological difficulties, in that it threatened the orthodox confession of the immanent parity of the persons of the Trinity. Versions of covenant theology that downplayed the eternal covenant of redemption and lifted up the submissive obedience of Christ seemed particularly susceptible to Arian interpretation. In Edwards's day, the Arian solution to this tension between the immanent parity of the members of the Trinity and the economic subordination of the Son to the Father was to surrender claims for the equal status of the Son: the subordination evident in the work of redemption became a reflection of the eternal subordination of the Son to the Father in the Godhead.

In the context of new Arian challenges, eighteenth-century defenders of orthodoxy proposed some innovative alternatives for explaining the submission of the Son to the Father in the work of redemption. Thomas Ridgley, whose concern "not to think or speak of God in such a way as tends to overthrow the simplicity of the divine nature"[31] was noted in

28. Bulkeley, *The Gospel-Covenant*, p. 263.
29. Bulkeley, *The Gospel-Covenant*, pp. 31, 43.
30. Bulkeley, *The Gospel-Covenant*, p. 31.
31. Ridgley, *A Body of Divinity: Lectures on the Assembly's Larger Catechism* (London: 1731-33; reprint, Philadelphia: William Woodward, 1814), I, p. 203.

the previous chapter, came up with an innovative defense against the Arian threat. He conceded with the Arians that the Scriptures portrayed the Son "as dependent on the Father, inferior and obedient to him." His solution was to redefine the referent of *Son*. This term had traditionally designated the second person of the Trinity, eternally generated by the Father. But after reviewing some traditional ways of explaining eternal generation, Ridgley complained: "The Arians are ready to insult us upon such modes of speaking, and suppose that we conclude that the Son receives his divine perfections, and therefore cannot be God equal with the Father."[32] Ridgley concluded that *Father* and *Son* do not properly designate eternal, immanent distinctions within the simple Godhead. However, he was unwilling to side with the Arians in assigning the role of Son entirely to the human Jesus. Ridgley offered a compromise position: Christ is God's Son in his role as the divine-human mediator. Upholding Christ's status as Son on the basis of his mediatorial role in human salvation, rather than his eternal subsistence with God provided a way to explain the Son's subordinate status: only the *incarnate* Christ was subordinate to the Father. Thus the biblical texts regarding the Son's generation by the Father "respect him as God-man, Mediator"; likewise those that speak of the Spirit's procession "respect the subserviency of his acting as a divine Person to the Mediator's glory, in applying the work of redemption."[33]

Ridgley's compromise solution only widened the gap between the immanent and economic Trinity and, as we shall see, Edwards emphatically rejected it. Nor was he impressed with yet another variation on the Son's role in the work of redemption, put forth by the renowned hymn writer Isaac Watts. Watts puzzled over the Trinity for more than twenty years, confessing in the end that he had only "learned more of my own ignorance."[34] His distinctive solution was to posit the preexistence of Christ's human soul. In this way he could retain the assur-

32. Ridgley, *A Body of Divinity*, 1, p. 263.
33. Ridgley, *A Body of Divinity*, 1, p. 267.
34. See D. Jennings and P. Doddridge, eds., *The Works of the Late Reverend and Learned Isaac Watts* (London, 1753), vol. 6, for his writings on the Trinity between 1722 and 1746. In his 1722 treatise *The Christian Doctrine of the Trinity . . . Asserted and Prov'd, [and] . . . Vindicated by Plain Evidence of Scripture, without the Aid or Incumbrance of Human Schemes,* Watts condemned going beyond the express words of Scripture in formulating trinitarian doctrine.

ance of an eternal covenant of redemption between the Father and the Son, while still appealing to the Son's humanity to explain his covenant subordination, as Ridgley had done.

"The Supreme Harmony of All"

Edwards inherited the entire Reformed covenant tradition, and used it to great advantage in his theological reflections and sermons.[35] Like other covenant theologians, Edwards posited three covenants — those of works, grace, and redemption. His treatment of the covenant of works was quite traditional in its neglect of the Trinity. However, Edwards's treatments of the covenants of grace and redemption were distinctive in their elaboration of trinitarian roles. Edwards perceived a complex harmony between the internal, loving consent of the Trinity and order of acting agreed upon by the divine persons in their eternal "consultation" regarding human redemption. This trinitarian harmony helped him combat both the Arminian temptation "to depend on our own righteousness" and the growing theological challenges to Christ's divinity.

This focus on the society of the Trinity helped the young Edwards articulate his deep uneasiness with the notion that "faith is the proper condition of the covenant of grace." "Talking thus," he declared flatly, "is doubtless the foundation of Arminianism and neonomianism, and tends very much to make men value themselves for their own righteousness." The root of "all this confusion," in Edwards's mind, was "the wrong distinction men made between the covenant of grace and the covenant of redemption."[36] The covenant of grace was not to be

---

35. In an influential interpretation of Edwards, Perry Miller, *Errand into the Wilderness* (Cambridge, Mass.: Belknap Press, 1956), p. 98, charged that he "threw over the whole covenant scheme" and "declared God unfettered by any agreement or obligation." Conrad Cherry disagreed in part, showing the role of the covenant of grace in Edwards's theology. See "The Puritan Notion of the Covenant in Jonathan Edwards' Doctrine of Faith," *Church History* 34 (1965): 328-41. Harry S. Stout has argued for the importance of the "national" covenant in Edwards's thought. See "The Puritans and Edwards," in Nathan Hatch and Harry Stout, eds., *Jonathan Edwards and the American Experience* (New York: Oxford University Press, 1988), pp. 142-59.

36. Works, 13, p. 198 (no. 2).

thought of as a distinct covenant between God the Father and believers, with its own conditions and obligations: "The covenant that God the Father makes with believers is indeed the very same with the covenant of redemption made with Christ before the foundation of the world, or at least is entirely included in it."[37] The covenant between the Father and believers was only an expression of the eternal covenant of redemption between the Father and the Son. The condition of this covenant is Christ's righteousness alone — human faith has no role to play in it. Echoing the distinction of the Spiritual Brethren between a conditional covenant and a free testament, Edwards insisted that "there is vast difference between a free offer and a covenant . . . ; that which is commonly called the covenant of grace is only Christ's open and free offer of life, whereby he holds it out in his hand to sinners and offers it without any condition."[38] Rather than being the antecedent condition for salvation, "faith is the soul's *active* uniting with Christ, or is itself the very act of unition, *on their part*."[39] If people "will call the receiving of life the 'condition' of receiving of life, they are at their liberty," Edwards declared. "But I believe it is much the more hard to think right, for speaking so wrong."[40]

Often Edwards followed Rutherford and the Sibbesians in seeing the covenant of redemption, not as an analogical extrapolation from the more basic covenant of grace, but as the very foundation of it. All of the Father's "acts of friendship and favour" towards the redeemed were made directly with Christ in the eternal covenant of redemption. There were not two separate covenants — "one covenant that was made with Christ, and another, that Christ had nothing to do with, with believers." Rather, there was a profound harmony between the eternal and temporal covenants: both were made by God with Christ, the temporal covenant of grace respecting Christ in his capacity as "a common head and representative of believers."[41] Even before the creation and incarnation, the redeemed were included "virtually" in the Father's promises to the Son, because they were already viewed as members of Christ's

37. *Misc.*, no. 1091.

38. Works, 13, p. 199 (no. 2).

39. Sereno E. Dwight, ed., *The Works of President Edwards with a Memoir of His Life*, 10 vols. (New York: S. Converse, 1829-30), 5, p. 364.

40. Works, 13, p. 199 (no. 2).

41. Works, 13, p. 198 (no. 2).

body. In the eternal consultation between the Father and the Son, the conditions of human redemption had already been secured, and "God acted on the ground of that transaction, justifying and saving sinners, as if the things undertaken had been actually performed long before they were performed indeed."[42] The aim of the "consultation among the persons of the Trinity" in the covenant of redemption was the extension of the loving union of the Godhead to include the elect. It was "God's design" in the work of redemption "to admit the church into the divine family as his son's wife."[43]

However, Edwards was also an "ambidextrous" theologian, and, as his disillusionment over the spiritual state of his congregation grew, the harmony between the two covenants modulated to accent better the centrality of "Christ's open and free offer of life" in the covenant of grace and the importance of human response. In an entry written in the late 1740s, Edwards posited God the Son, not the Father or God in general, as the first party in the temporal covenant of grace. Within this scheme, the covenant of grace, "by which Christ himself and believers are united one with another, is properly a different covenant" from the covenant of redemption.[44] In this entry, Edwards picked up the conditional language he had expressed discomfort with in the 1720s:

> . . . the covenant of grace, if thereby we understand the covenant between Christ himself and his church or his members, is conditional as to us: the proper condition of it, which is a yielding to Christ's wooings and accepting his offers and closing with him as a Redeemer and spiritual Husband, is to be performed by us.

In Edwards's 1749 treatise *An Humble Inquiry,* written during the nadir of his relations with Northampton, his emphasis was again on "compliance and conformity to . . . the conditions of the covenant of grace," not the covenant's manifestation of eternal divine grace.[45] When it was pastorally advantageous, Edwards ignored the connections between the covenant of grace and the covenant of redemption.

42. Dwight, *The Works of President Edwards,* 5, pp. 400-401.
43. Works, 18, p. 367 (no. 741).
44. *Misc.,* no. 1091.
45. Works, 12, p. 485.

Edwards did employ the covenant of redemption strategically against the Arians of his day. The beautiful harmony of the immanent Trinity required the ontological equality of its members — if the persons are not of the same essence, they "don't infinitely consent."[46] Relations of cordial consent were the basis of the harmony of the triune society. Despite the Father's eternal priority as the "fountain of deity," it would not be fitting for the Father to find supreme happiness in loving a person of inferior metaphysical status; and so the Father and Son must be ontological peers. While the work of redemption required a temporary economic subordination, it did not threaten the Son's eternal equality with the Father within the divine society.

Not as concerned as Ridgley was to uphold divine simplicity, Edwards posited a perfect fittingness and harmony between the structures of the immanent and economic Trinity. The immanent Trinity is the foundation of the economic; it is both the source and pattern for all God's works *ad extra*. And the work of redemption, which is the focal point of the economic Trinity, is "the greatest and supreme work of God," because it illustrates the eternal distinctions among the divine persons:

> . . . in this work, though in no other, God doth distinctly manifest himself in each of the persons of the Godhead, in their mutual relations one to another and in that economy there is established amongst them, and in their distinct persons appearing in the eternal agreement and covenant these divine persons entered into about this work, and in the several offices and parts which each one bears in it, and how they are therein concerned one with another.[47]

Because of the fittingness he perceived between the immanent Trinity and God's work of redemption, Edwards refused to follow Ridgley in locating the Son's subordination to the Father in the temporal reality of the incarnation. There had to be an eternal fittingness to the Son's role in the work of redemption, yet one that did not compromise his "equal essential glory."[48]

46. Works, 13, p. 283 (no. 117).
47. Works, 18, p. 308 (no. 702).
48. Works, 14, p. 434.

No. 1062 in the "Miscellanies," known as *Observations Concerning the Scripture Oeconomy of the Trinity and the Covenant of Redemption*,[49] is a small treatise on the covenant of redemption in which Edwards systematically explored its trinitarian implications. Edwards's trinitarian covenant logic led him to reject alternative christological positions, such as those of Ridgley and Watts. He argued instead that the only way to secure the Son's dignity in the work of redemption was to posit a general pattern of trinitarian action within the immanent Godhead that was in harmony with its economic work.[50] The theme of trinitarian consent governs the entire structure of *Observations*, revealing another facet of Edwards's relational ontology.

Edwards's analysis of this consent was complex, revealing three interconnected levels of trinitarian relationship. At the base was the ontological relation of the persons. Within the immanent Trinity there is a quasi-genetic order of subsistence — the Father is in some ineffable sense the head of the Trinity, "the deity in its direct existence." The Son and Spirit are "of" and "from" the Father, and thus are in some sense dependent. As Edwards explained in an earlier manuscript, "that the divine essence should be, and should be what it is, is not in any respect in any dependence or by derivation," yet it is appropriate to affirm that "the Son derived the divine essence from the Father, and the Holy Spirit derives the divine essence from the Father and Son."[51] Edwards stressed that the Father's position "is more properly called priority than superiority, as we ordinarily use such terms."[52] The Son and Holy Ghost do not depend for their "being or well-being" on the Father's will: "for it is no voluntary, but a necessary proceeding, and therefore infers no proper subjection of one to

49. Miscellany 1062 was first published in 1880 by Egbert C. Smyth as part of the controversy, begun by Horace Bushnell in 1854, surrounding Edwards's supposed heterodoxy on the Trinity. It is reproduced in Helm, *Trinity*, pp. 77-94.

50. In some notes to himself about his plans to write "A Rational Account of the Main Doctrines of the Christian Religion," Edwards saw the need not only "To explain the doctrine of the Trinity before I begin to treat of the work of redemption; and of their equality, their equal honor in their manner of subsisting and acting, and virtue"; but also "to speak of their equal honor in their concern in the affair of redemption afterwards" (Works, 6, p. 396).

51. *Fragment on the Trinity*, Boston Public Library. Used by permission of The Works of Jonathan Edwards, Yale University.

52. *Misc.*, no. 1062.

the will of another."[53] Furthermore, the three persons each partake of the same divine perfections. As Edwards asserted in an early sermon: "all the Persons of the Trinity are in Exact Equality as we are taught in the Catechism those three are the same in substance Equal in Power and Glory."[54] At the ground level of the trinitarian structure, there was a profound equality among the divine persons, despite their differences in order of subsistence. "That which infinitely and perfectly agrees is the very same essence."[55]

The next level Edwards called the "oeconomical," though strictly speaking it is still within the immanent Trinity.[56] Edwards described it as a general "order of acting" established in eternity by the mutual consent of the trinitarian persons for all their works *ad extra*. Yet the triune decision as to the economic patterning of their action was not "merely arbitrary," nor was it simply a utilitarian strategy to achieve certain ends. In establishing the economical order of acting, the persons of the Trinity "all naturally delight in what is in itself fit, suitable and beautiful."[57] Thus the order of acting within the divine economy must be "agreeable" to the order of subsistence of the previous level:

> . . . tho there be no difference of degree of Glory or excellency, yet there is order in the Trinity. The three persons of the Trinity may be looked upon as a kind of family, so there is Oeconomical order. Thus the Father, tho he be no Greater than the son or the Holy Ghost, yet he is first in order, and the son next, and the Holy Ghost last.[58]

There was a harmony between the order of subsistence in the immanent Trinity and the economical patterning of their actions *ad extra:* "that as the Father is first in the order of subsisting, so he should be first in the order of acting." Likewise the Son and Spirit, who origi-

---

53. *Misc.,* no. 1062. By contrast, in his "The Scripture-Doctrine of the Trinity," Samuel Clarke had argued that the Son, while divine and having existence prior to his taking human form, is "none the less dependent on the Father for that existence and for the power he exercises by delegation."

54. Ms sermon on John 15:10 (May-June 1731). Beinecke Library, Yale University.

55. Works, 13, p. 283 (no. 117).

56. I modernize Edwards's spelling throughout this discussion.

57. *Misc.,* no. 1062.

58. Ms sermon on John 15:10, Beinecke Library, Yale University.

nate from the Father, also "act from Him and in a dependence on Him."[59]

The third level was the covenant of redemption, the intratrinitarian plan regarding exactly which actions *ad extra* the Trinity would undertake to accomplish their end of glorifying themselves through human salvation. As Edwards stated in a sermon on Ephesians 3:10, "In this work every distinct person has his distinct parts and offices assigned him. Each one has his particular and distinct concern in it, agreeable to their distinct, personal properties, relations, and economical offices."[60] Edwards referred to this as a divine counsel, "which the persons of the Trinity came into from eternity as it were by mutual consultation and covenant."[61]

In the covenant of redemption, both the equality and hierarchical ordering of the previous two levels are again reflected. The Father's headship and the Son's abject humiliation must be viewed as the result of a prior agreement among the three persons. In the covenant transactions, the Father does not arrogate power for himself; instead, consonant with his authority in the immanent and economical Trinity, he is appointed by the Son and Spirit to act as head in the plan of redemption as well. Nor are the Son and Holy Spirit compelled by the Father into subordinate roles. In contrast to Bulkeley, Edwards did not portray the covenant as "a commandment from the Father to the Son, which he must submit to, and obey."[62] The Son and Spirit undertake their roles as agreed upon in the economy, and as a fitting reflection of their order of subsistence in the immanent Trinity.

Edwards was adamant that the economical pattern be viewed as logically prior to the covenant agreement among the trinitarian persons; this is the main argument of *Observations*. His theological motivation was his concern to protect the equality of the Father and Son, while asserting the Father's priority. The subordination of the Son in the work of redemption was not an indication of an inferior ontological status,

---

59. *Misc.,* no. 1062. Rowan Williams has written of "a derived or responsive creativity" in the case of the Son and Holy Spirit that is both contrasted and in continuity with the Father's "absolute creativity which is the source and context of all things." *On Christian Theology* (Oxford: Blackwell, 2000), pp. 140-41.

60. Dwight, *The Works of President Edwards,* 7, p. 77.

61. *Misc.,* no. 993.

62. Bulkeley, *The Gospel-Covenant,* p. 31.

but the result of the mutual decision within the Trinity to reflect the immanent order of subsistence.

Edwards rejected Ridgley's compromise, according to which the Father's priority "is voluntarily established in the covenant of redemption," as contrary to "the whole tenor of the gospel": "it appears to be unreasonable to suppose, as some do, that the Sonship of the second person of the Trinity consists only *in the relation he bears to the Father in his mediatorial character.*"[63] By contrast, Edwards insisted that this "Sonship," and thus the priority of the Father to the Son, preceded Christ's role of mediator, being grounded "in the order of nature" of the immanent Trinity. The representations of the "wondrous love and grace of God" in giving the Son for human salvation would be "absurd, if he were not God's Son, till after he was appointed to be our Mediator."[64] The logic of the covenant appointment of Christ as mediator required the antecedent priority of the Father within the immanent Trinity.

A corollary of the Father's eternal priority is that the Son be "a distinct Person from Eternity." Here Edwards's insistence on "distinct personal agency" within the Trinity reappeared. On this point Edwards opposed Watts's notion of the pre-existence of Christ's human nature.

> According to what seems to be Dr. Watts' scheme, the Son of God is no distinct divine person from the Father. So far as he is a divine person, he is the same person as the Father. So that in the covenant of redemption the Father covenants with himself.[65]

This made no sense to Edwards, nor did the possibility that "the two natures in the same person covenanted together." "How does this confound our minds," Edwards complained, "instead of helping our ideas and making them more easy and intelligible!"[66] Just as his notion of consent required genuine plurality within the immanent Trinity, the logic of the eternal covenant clearly required two distinct personal agents within the Godhead.

In view of the Arian challenges, there were special theological difficulties associated with the third level of Edwards's analysis, which pos-

63. *Misc.,* no. 1062, emphasis added.
64. *Misc.,* no. 1062.
65. *Misc.,* no. 1174.
66. *Misc.,* no. 1174.

COVENANTAL HARMONIES

ited the covenant of redemption. The outworking of human redemption required a humiliation and condescension of the Son far below that of his economical status. Taking on human flesh and suffering the horrible agony of rejection on the cross were not roles the Father could simply *appoint* him to, lest the Son be viewed as ontologically inferior. This is why the third level required a covenant. The Father has the prerogative, as head of the plan of redemption, to propose the matter to the Son. But the Son, as a divine person equal to the Father, undertakes this role voluntarily — it cannot be forced upon him. Here Edwards again faulted Watts's notion of an eternal covenant with the human person Jesus Christ:

> On this scheme it will follow that the covenant of redemption was made with a person that was not *sui juris,* and not at liberty to act his own mere good pleasure, with respect to undertaking to die for sinners; but was obliged to comply.[67]

Watts's scheme violated the nature of the covenant as a voluntary transaction. And this put human salvation at risk, because "He that is a servant, and that can do no more than he is bound to do, cannot merit."[68] The efficacy of the atoning work of Christ depended on his free consent to die for sinners.

According to Edwards, the covenant of redemption entailed a special "rule and authority" for the Son as well as a new subjection. The second, or "economical," order posits the Father as "the King of heaven and earth, Lawgiver and Judge of all."[69] But the trinitarian covenant vests the Son with this kingly role until the completion of the work of redemption at the end of the world. Edwards noted that, "things are not thus fixed to be thus ultimately and eternally, for that would amount even to an overthrowing the economy of the persons of the Trinity."[70] The exigencies of the work of redemption render this special temporary authority fitting, both to reward the Son's obedient subjection and "to put him under greater advantages to obtain the success of his labors."[71]

67. *Misc.,* no. 1174.
68. Dwight, *Works of President Edwards,* 7, p. 69.
69. *Misc.,* no. 1062.
70. Works, 18, p. 373 (no. 742).
71. *Misc.,* no. 1062.

109

In another way the great work of redemption did effect a permanent alteration in the structure of the divine economy: by trinitarian agreement, the Son continues for all eternity as the "Husband and vital Head of the church."[72] As Edwards declared in a sermon series on John 16:8, "The holy Trinity saw it meet that he that had been at so great cost to purchase salvation should also have the disposal of it."[73] God's special aim in the covenant of redemption "was to procure a spouse or a mystical body for his Son."[74] Having given his life to present the church to God as his perfect and unblemished bride, Christ is for eternity the head of the redeemed, "that they might be united to God and glorified in him."[75]

Edwards was quick to see that the Son's new authority implied an unusual subordination of the Holy Spirit. In exploring these implications he confronted a Reformed ambivalence regarding the role of the Holy Spirit in the work of redemption. While Reformed Christians were wont to extol "the equality of each person's concern in the work of redemption,"[76] Edwards pointed out their artifice:

> If we suppose no more than used to be supposed about the Holy Ghost, the honour of the Holy Ghost in the work of redemption is not equal in any sense to the Father and the Son's; nor is there an equal part of the glory of this work belonging to Him.[77]

If the Holy Spirit only applies the benefits of the covenant agreement between the Father and Son, the Spirit's participation in the work of redemption is less than theirs.[78] Edwards's response to the problem was twofold. He explained why the logic of the covenant does not permit the Spirit to be a proper partner in it; and he developed an alternative way to give the Spirit an equal role in the work of redemption.

In his sermon series on John 16:8, Edwards gave careful attention to

---

72. *Misc.,* no. 1062.

73. Works, 14, p. 380.

74. *Misc.,* no. 1245.

75. Works, 18, p. 416 (no. 769).

76. Helm, *Trinity,* p. 123.

77. Helm, *Trinity,* pp. 68-69.

78. Thomas Goodwin also noted this slighting of the Holy Spirit: we "do not hold and pursue after fellowship with him as a distinct person; nor is his love in what he hath done for us, set on as a seal upon our hearts." Works, 6, p. 39.

the role of the Holy Spirit. He began by arguing the ontological equality between the Holy Ghost and the Son: "Though in the Trinity there is such a thing as prior and latter in order, yet there is no such thing as degrees of dignity or excellency."[79] Edwards's next step was to show how "'tis agreeable to the order of persons in the Trinity and their manner of subsisting" that the Holy Spirit apply Christ's work. Yet Edwards upheld the divine majesty of the Spirit as well, advising that, "We ought to be filled with gratitude to the Spirit of God for his wonderful condescension and beneficence in coming to take up his abode in such [poor creatures], and so honoring of us as to make us his temple."[80] The Spirit's economic role fittingly reflects both the mutuality and subordination within the immanent Trinity.

In *Observations* Edwards developed the implications of the Spirit's subordinate role in redemption for the covenant. He concluded that the twofold authority given the Son in the covenant of redemption entailed a twofold subjection of the Spirit not present in the original economical order. First, the Spirit was required to give the Son "that subjection that is economically due to the Father."[81] This authority of the Son over the Spirit will be resigned when the work of redemption is finished. Second, the Spirit was called to obey the incarnate Christ in the same way that he obeyed the Son in the divine economy. This subjection is permanent, because Christ will be the head of the church forever.

Although the Son's subordination in the work of redemption demanded a special covenant, the Spirit's does not because "There is no humiliation or abasement in this new subjection of the Spirit to the Son."[82] The Spirit's subordination in the work of redemption is only "circumstantially" different from that of the economical order. As Edwards concluded, "The Holy Spirit is not thus subject to the Son by any abasement he submits to, by any special covenant, but by the gift of the Father, exercising his prerogative as Head of the Trinity, as he is by his economical character."[83] The practical significance of this distinction between the subjection of the Son and Spirit is that the Spirit's obedience is in no way "meritorious" for sinners. Edwards asserted on the

79. Works, 14, p. 378.
80. Works, 14, p. 436.
81. *Misc.*, no. 1062.
82. *Misc.*, no. 1062.
83. *Misc.*, no. 1062.

basis of this analysis that the covenant of redemption was only between the first and second persons of the Trinity, and that there is no other covenant made by either the first or second person with the Holy Spirit. Though "his concern in the covenant is not that of a party covenanting,"[84] nevertheless the Holy Spirit's role in the covenant of redemption was "equally honorable" with that of the others. As Edwards insisted, ". . . whatsoever is done by each person is done by the consent and concurrence of all."[85]

Thomas Goodwin complained in a similar way about the lack of honor given the Holy Spirit in the work of redemption. His remedy for the neglect of the Spirit within covenant theology was to emphasize the Spirit's distinct personhood:

> If we believe he is a person in the Trinity, let us treat with him as a person, apply ourselves to him as a person, glorify him in our hearts as a person, dart forth beams of special and peculiar love to, and converse with him as with a person.[86]

Here Goodwin reflected a particular emphasis in the trinitarian piety of the Spiritual Brethren, according to which Christian believers have "distinct communion" with each person of the Godhead. There was an intimate connection between "distinct communion" and the believer's full assurance of salvation:

> In assurance . . . a man's communion and converse is . . . sometimes with the Father, then with the Son, and then with the Holy Ghost; . . . and so a man goes from one witness to another distinctly, which, I say, is the communion that John would have us to have. . . . till all three persons lie level in us, and all make their abode with us, and we sit as it were in the midst of them, while they all manifest their love unto us.[87]

The notion that "the believer communes with God not in general but with His revealed nature as three Persons, and that he communes with

84. *Misc.*, no. 1062.
85. Works, 14, p. 380.
86. Goodwin, *Works*, 6, p. 39.
87. Goodwin, *Works*, 8, p. 379. Quoted in Joel R. Beeke, *Assurance of Faith: Calvin, English Puritanism, and the Dutch Second Reformation* (New York: Peter Lang, 1991), p. 221.

each Person distinctly," is also explicit in the title of a treatise by Goodwin's colleague John Owen, called *Of Communion with God the Father, Son, and Holy Ghost, Each Person Distinctly, in Love, Grace and Consolation.*[88] The emphasis on "distinct communion" is another indication of the openness of the Spiritual Brethren to social conceptions of the Trinity.

This trinitarian construal of "distinct communion" in the writings of the Spiritual Brethren resonated with Edwards's ongoing concern for balance and consent in the intricate workings of the economic Trinity. But Edwards's best efforts to delineate an equal role for the Holy Spirit within the social trinitarian framework of covenant theology did not satisfy him. In order to guarantee a fitting place for the Spirit in the work of redemption, Edwards turned instead to the trinitarian depiction of the Holy Spirit as divine love. The confluence between the notion of "distinct communion" and this depiction of the Holy Spirit is clear in Edwards's famous sermon "God Glorified in Man's Dependence," in which he elaborated "our dependence on each person in the Trinity for all our good," and insisted that the Holy Spirit "*is* all our good."[89] This role for the Holy Spirit will be explored in the next two chapters.

The issue Edwards saw clearly — how to articulate both unity and irreducible difference within the immanent and economic Godhead and its theological consequences for Christian community — remains. Some contemporary theologians simply evade the issue by putting Jesus Christ firmly on the human side, a bearer of knowledge about God, but not himself a redeemer from sin. On this view, there is no irreducible difference within the Godhead to worry about.[90] For those unwilling to cede trinitarian conceptions of God, this is not an option. Other theologians tolerate a large disjunction between the immanent and economic Trinity. They carry on the long theological tradition, articulated within the framework of divine simplicity, that insists that all of God's economic works are undivided — they are the works of all three members of the Trinity. Since the Godhead is simple, it would be im-

88. See Beeke, *Assurance of Faith,* p. 220.

89. Works, 17, pp. 201, 207.

90. See, e.g., John Hick, "Jesus and the World Religions," in John Hick, ed., *The Myth of God Incarnate* (Philadelphia: Westminster Press, 1977).

possible for one of the divine persons to do one thing and another of the divine persons to do another. Particular works might be "appropriated" to a particular member of the Trinity, but, as William Placher points out, "this was just a kind of heuristic fiction: all the works of the Trinity *ad extra* were equally the works of the whole triune God." Placher (quoting Karl Rahner) notes the incarnation as a dramatic refutation of this traditional approach: only the Word takes on human flesh. Thus it is not true that "there is nothing in salvation history, in the economy of salvation, which cannot equally be said of the triune God as a whole and of each person in particular."[91] There must be some correspondence, however mysterious and indirect, between God's life in movement and relation to itself and God's self-revelation to the world in the work of redemption.

Edwards's articulation of the covenant of redemption protected both irreducible difference within the Godhead and the correspondence between the immanent and economic Trinity. Yet its theological defects seem obvious. An unnuanced social model of the Trinity risks succumbing to tritheism, in which the persons of the Trinity appear as "three distinct Gods, friends one to another."[92] As Hans von Balthasar has noted,

> . . . it is mistaken to take a naïve construction of the divine mystery after the pattern of human relationships (as Richard of St. Victor attempted by way of a counterblast to Augustine) and make it absolute; for it fails to take into account the crude anthropomorphism involved in a plurality of beings.[93]

Nowhere is this risk greater than in the trinitarian covenant of redemption, which takes on the appearance of salvation-by-committee. For all the endearing quaintness of Goodwin's notion of an eternal agreement "struck Dialogue-wise" between the Father and the Son, the anthropo-

91. William C. Placher, *Narratives of a Vulnerable God: Christ, Theology, and Scripture* (Louisville: Westminster/John Knox, 1994), pp. 56-57. The Rahner quotation is from *The Trinity*, trans. J. Donceel (New York: Herder & Herder, 1970), p. 23.

92. Edwards rejected this locution in Works, 18, p. 84 (no. 539).

93. Hans Urs von Balthasar, *Theo-Drama: Theological Dramatic Theory*, Vol. III, *The Dramatis Personae: The Person in Christ*, trans. Graham Harrison (San Francisco: Ignatius Press, 1992), pp. 526-27.

morphism of the covenant of redemption creates serious theological problems.

Edwards's development of the covenant of redemption is alarmingly reminiscent of classical social contract theory, in which a person is a self endowed with an indissoluble right to self-determination. In describing the Son's covenant dealings with the Father, Edwards insisted that the Son must be *sui juris,* at liberty to act his own mere good pleasure,[94] because a contract made with a "person" lacking this liberty would be invalid. Anthropomorphism does not get much cruder than this!

Karl Barth rightly criticized the anthropomorphic notion of "a special intertrinitarian arrangement and contract . . . between the persons of the Father and the Son":

> Can we really think of the first and second persons of the triune Godhead as two divine subjects and therefore as two legal subjects who can have dealings and enter into obligations one with another? This is mythology, for which there is no place in a right understanding of the doctrine of the Trinity. . . .[95]

Barth therefore emphatically rejected the notion of "a purely intertrinitarian decision as the eternal basis of the covenant of grace." While he conceded that it may seem "sublime and uplifting," he considered the covenant of redemption "much too uplifting and sublime to be a Christian thought"![96]

A related problem in covenant imagery is the exacerbation of subordinationist trinitarian themes. There is already a stubbornly subordinationist tendency in the classical trinitarian vocabulary's appeals to human generation and familial roles. Mary Rose D'Angelo points out that Christian use of the terms *Father* and *Son* has never been fully successful in excluding notions of subordination and temporal priority from trini-

94. *Misc.,* no. 1174.

95. Karl Barth, *Church Dogmatics* IV/1 (Edinburgh: T. & T. Clark, 1956), pp. 64-65. Yet Barth shared the uneasiness of the Spiritual Brethren about a "bilateral" covenant of grace between God and humanity. His appeal to a "primal history" underlying all of God's relationships *ad extra* functions in a way similar to the covenant of redemption in Puritan thought.

96. Barth, *Church Dogmatics* IV/1, p. 66.

tarian doctrine. This defect of the metaphor was recognized early on in the development of the doctrine, as was the need to supplement both biblical language and technical terms such as *ingenerate, generated* and *proceeding* with other analogies.[97] The anthropomorphism of covenant of redemption imagery heightens this difficulty, because it so clearly reinscribes the patterns of the deferential society of Edwards's time. The notions of a son agreeing, at great personal cost, to a father's plan, and of another member of the society being excluded from the covenant altogether, mirrored familiar social arrangements. Feminist theologians have been alert to the ways in which subordinationist language and narratives within the Godhead tend to shore up subordinationist schemes within human communities. In societies still battling the injustices of deferential and exclusive social arrangements, the social presuppositions of Edwards's covenantal scheme are deeply troubling.

Here Barth is less helpful. Though he avoided the "mythology" of the covenant of redemption, he did not elude its subordinationism or its tendency to neglect the Spirit. Barth shared the uneasiness of the Spiritual Brethren about a "bilateral" covenant of grace between God and humanity, and made an appeal to a "primal history" underlying all of God's relationships *ad extra* that functioned in a way similar to the covenant of redemption in Puritan thought. In that primal history, an eternal decision concerning human redemption takes place. But the Godhead does not "remain alone" at "the origin of the covenant." Humanity "must be present as the second partner at the institution of the covenant to make it a real covenant." In a mysterious way,

> . . . there is already present, and presumed, and assumed into unity with His own existence as God, the existence of the man whom He intends and loves from the very first and in whom He intends and loves all other men, of the man in whom He wills to bind Himself with all other men and all other men with Himself.[98]

The eternal presence of the humanity of Christ introduces subordinationist themes into Barth's trinitarianism, leading him to posit "the of-

---

97. Mary Rose D'Angelo, "Beyond Father and Son," in *Justice as Mission: An Agenda for the Church,* ed. Christopher Lind and Terry Brown (Burlington, Ontario: Trinity Press, 1985), p. 110.

98. Barth, *Church Dogmatics* IV/1, p. 66.

fensive fact that there is in God himself a superiority and a subordination — that it belongs to the inner life of God that there should take place within it obedience." As Kathryn Tanner has noted, Barth here draws "too close a parallel between the relationship of Son and Father and the obedience and humility of the Word incarnate before the Father." The difference between the humanity of Jesus and the divinity of the Father becomes an eternal difference within the Godhead.[99]

Like Richard Sibbes, Barth could not resist making the Trinity "the pattern of our unity."[100] He thus compounded his theological mistake by finding a mirror of this hierarchy of "God in relationship" in "a structural and functional" subordination of women to men.[101] Social trinitarians like Jürgen Moltmann draw much more egalitarian conclusions about human social arrangements from their vision of trinitarian relations between the Father and the Son.[102] But whether they are reinscribing present or hoped-for social arrangements, both Barth and Moltmann illustrate the dangers of drawing too close a parallel between trinitarian relations and human relations. As Kathryn Tanner asserts, "by modeling human relations directly on trinitarian ones, theologians tend either to downplay the difference between social relations and trinitarian ones, or lose a realistic sense of human relationships."[103] This is not utterly to reject the Trinity as "a pattern for our unity": we are called to live out an account of the hope that sustains us (1 Peter 3:15) by rejoicing in God's gifts, and finding ourselves in losing ourselves. But as the next chapters show, Edwards's tendency to assimilate the Spirit's role in the divine life too closely to the Spirit's presence in the humanity of Jesus and of the church led to both theological and pastoral problems.

A plea for theological modesty seems to be in order. Edwards's bridge-building projects between the immanent and economic Trinity

---

99. Kathryn Tanner, *Jesus, Humanity and the Trinity: A Brief Systematic Theology* (Minneapolis: Fortress Press, 2001), p. 52. See also p. 76.

100. Sibbes, *Complete Works,* 3, p. 194.

101. Karl Barth, *Church Dogmatics* III/4 (Edinburgh: T. & T. Clark, 1961), p. 117.

102. In my view, Moltmann's social trinitarianism runs the same risks of anthropomorphism and the subordination of the Spirit to the Son that we have seen in articulations of the covenant of redemption. See Jürgen Moltmann, *The Spirit of Life: A Universal Affirmation,* trans. Margaret Kohl (Minneapolis: Fortress Press, 1992).

103. Tanner, *Jesus, Humanity and the Trinity,* p. 82.

and between the Godhead and human communities still beckon. As stated above, human assurance of salvation demands that there be a deep coherence between God's eternal being and the temporal work of redemption. And Christians naturally look to the triune God of redemption for clues to the shape of their corporate life together. But the theological spans required in each case are too large and mysterious to inspire architectural confidence. While the divine work of human redemption is not at all alien to God's eternal being, it is not simply identical with it. Much less can frail and fallible human communities held together by the forgiveness of sins lay claim to the immanent Trinity as their "social program" in any but the most formal and indirect sense. As Rowan Williams notes, the economic drama "puts to us the question how God can be if this is how he is historically," and leaves us "with only the most austere account of God's life as such."[104] Edwards's flamboyant use of the covenant of redemption schema needs to be tempered by his admission elsewhere that "I am far from pretending to explaining the Trinity so as to render it no longer a mystery."[105]

104. Rowan Williams, *On Christian Theology*, pp. 160-61.
105. Helm, *Trinity*, pp. 121-22.

Chapter 4

THE GRAND DESIGN OF REDEMPTION

"Now I think it can hardly be said which of the persons in the Trinity has the greatest share in this work of redemption: it's all from every one of them."

EDWARDS, Sermon on John 16:8

The work of redemption formed the centerpiece of Jonathan Edwards's reflections on God's relation to the created world. Ordained from eternity, the work of human redemption "may be looked upon as the great end and drift of all God's works and dispensations from the beginning." "All other works of providence may be looked upon as *appendages* to this great work, or *things* which God does to subserve that grand design."[1] Even "the world itself seems to have been created in order to it."[2] While punishment of sins and the eternal rejection of some sinners were integral parts of Edwards's theology, he was clear that judgment is God's "strange work," executed "for the sake of something else," not for its own sake.[3] The work of redemption reveals the depth and ultimate triumph of God's love. Its aim is intimate, eternal fellowship between God and human creatures, and their mutual glory and happiness: "the

1. Works, 18, p. 284 (no. 702).
2. Works, 9, p. 118.
3. *Misc.,* no. 1081. Even hell serves to "heighten in the eyes of the saints the value of [Christ's] love and gentleness" to them (*Misc.,* no. 957).

happiness of the deity, as all other true happiness, consists in love and society."[4]

The "supreme harmony" of the Trinity was more in evidence in the complex work of redemption than anywhere else. This work concerns "not only what Christ the mediator has done, but also what the Father and the Holy Ghost have done as united or confederated in this design of redeeming sinful men."[5] As Edwards declared, "Now I think it can hardly be said which of the persons in the Trinity has the greatest share in this work of redemption: it's all from every one of them."[6] Where the "supreme harmony" of the Trinity was lost from view, Edwards's account of the work of redemption faltered. In this way, his trinitarian vision of the work of redemption shows up the inconsistencies and problems in his thought as a whole.

For Edwards, at the root of both the inner life of the Trinity and its great work of human redemption was the notion of union. Union was for him an important theological correlate of his relational ontology. Ultimate reality concerned the dynamics of union — within God, between God and creatures, and among creatures themselves. Union was both the end and the means of God's work of redemption. By uniting with human nature in "its mean, defaced, broken, infirm, ruined state,"[7] Christ through the power of the Spirit brings the saints to progressively intimate union with God and other creatures. The union begun on earth, and heightened during the millennium, culminates in the bliss of everlasting heavenly union with God, saints, and angels.

The Christian tradition has affirmed three fundamental unions: the union of the persons of the Trinity, the union of God and humanity in the incarnate Christ, and the union of human believers with God and with each other. However, these three unions have often been affirmed in very different ways, often without any strong connections between them. One result has been the perceived irrelevance of the Trinity for understanding the incarnation or for assuring the saints' union with God. By contrast Edwards treated these three unions in a remarkably

4. Helm, *Trinity*, p. 64.
5. Works, 9, pp. 117-18.
6. Works, 14, p. 435. As Sibbes affirmed, "the blessed Trinity, as they have a perfect unity in themselves in nature, for they are all one God, so they have a most perfect unity in their love, and care, and respect to mankind." *Complete Works*, 4, p. 294.
7. Works, 18, p. 208 (no. 664b).

parallel fashion: in his mind, they were all spiritual unions, unions of love and consent. In a notebook entry he grouped the three together, declaring that

> What insight I have of the nature of minds, I am convinced that there is no guessing what kind of union and mixtion, by consciousness or otherwise, there may be between them. So that all difficulty is removed in believing what the Scripture declares about spiritual unions — of the persons of the Trinity, of the two natures of Christ, of Christ and the minds of saints.[8]

In Edwards's thought the union of the immanent Trinity had direct relevance for the unions his Northampton congregation was more immediately concerned about: the union of Christ with sinful human nature, the heavenly union of the elect with God, and the union of saints in a rapidly changing society.

In describing the perfect unity of the Trinity in human redemption, Edwards was particularly concerned to highlight the contribution of the Holy Spirit, for he thought that Reformed covenant theology had diminished the Spirit's role in the work of redemption. Not a proper partner in the trinitarian covenant of redemption, the Spirit's role of applying Christ's benefits was "but a little thing" compared to the Father's giving up "his infinitely dear Son" and the Son's "offering up Himself a sacrifice" for our salvation.[9] The economic role posited by covenant theology did not befit the Spirit's immanent dignity and equality with the other members of the trinitarian society.

Edwards's remedy for this defect was to transcend the bounds of covenant theology, with its implicitly social view of the Trinity, and extrapolate a new economic office based on the Spirit's role in the psychological model as God's love. Just as the Holy Spirit was the bond of union within the Trinity, so the Holy Spirit was the bond of union be-

---

8. Works, 13, p. 330 (no. 184). Edwards's emphasis on spiritual union renders implausible R. C. De Prospo's definition of theism as "a discursive pattern that is based on the ultimate duality between Creator and Creation and that continues indefinitely to generate hierarchical duplicities." *Theism in the Discourse of Jonathan Edwards* (Newark, Del.: University of Delaware Press; Cranbury, N.J.: Associated University Presses, 1985), p. 12. In Edwards's theology it is precisely God's union with creation that is the basis for creaturely difference.

9. Helm, *Trinity*, p. 69.

tween God and humanity in the incarnation. And just as the Holy Spirit was the mutual love of the Father and Son in the immanent Godhead, so in the economic Trinity the Spirit was "that love of the Father and the Son to the world."[10] It was only fitting that "As the persons of the Trinity are equal among themselves, so there seems to [be] an exact equality in each person's concern in the work of redemption, and in our concern with them in that great affair." To any suggestions "that more glory belongs to the Father and the Son because they manifested a more wonderful love," Edwards replied that "the Holy Ghost *is* that wonderful love."[11] By this approach, Edwards assured that the persons of the Trinity

> should all of them have their particular glory manifested with a brightness and luster answerable to their equal, essential glory; that not only the perfections of the divine essence common to all might be manifested therein, but that glory of God be shown which consists in the deity's subsistence in three persons and their particular manner of subsistence.[12]

As he further explained it, "the personal glory of each of the persons in the Trinity is equal, though each one, as they have a distinct personality, have a distinct glory, and so one has a peculiar glory that another has not." The peculiar glory of the Spirit is to be "the end of the Father in electing" and "the end of the Son in all his suffering." The Spirit "was the great precious thing to which all the other two do is subordinated."[13]

Edwards drew out the "particular" glory of the Holy Spirit in human redemption using the motif of the emanation and remanation of God's knowledge and love. In the work of redemption the internal divine glory of the Trinity emanates toward intelligent creatures in an abundant communication of knowledge, love, and delight. Human beings in turn glorify God by reflecting back to God in a mode appropriate to creatures the wisdom, love, and joy that God is. Edwards typically ex-

10. Helm, *Trinity,* p. 123.
11. Works, 13, p. 467 (no. 402).
12. Works, 14, p. 434.
13. *Fragment on the Trinity,* Boston Public Library. Used by permission of the Works of Jonathan Edwards, Yale University.

pressed this divine glorifying by means of the distinctions of the psychological analogy:

> God glorifies himself towards the creatures also two ways: (1) by appearing to them, being manifested to their understandings; (2) in communicating himself to their hearts, and in their rejoicing and delighting in, and enjoying the manifestations which he makes of himself.[14]

While the role of the Son is to communicate divine wisdom, the distictive work of the Spirit is to communicate God's love, evoking joy and delight in the redeemed.

Yet the parallelism in Edwards's formal pronouncements concerning the economic roles of the Son and Spirit within the framework of the psychological image is misleading. The Son's role as Wisdom or Word was not nearly as central to his economic trinitarian reflections as the Spirit's role of Love. In describing the redeeming work of the Son, Edwards relied principally on the social conception of the Trinity, in its depiction of the Son as a distinct personal agent, capable of entering human history as a helpless infant and atoning for human sin on the cross. Redemption is a matter of intimate social union: God's grand design in this work is to expand the "divine family" so that the perfect consent between the Father and Son will embrace the redeemed as well. "Though many individual persons were chosen, yet they were chosen to receive God's infinite and peculiar love in union as one body, one spouse, all united in one Head."[15] In a "restricted" sense, the work of redemption "was begun with Christ's incarnation and carried on through Christ's life and finished with his death."[16] Covenant theology, with its emphasis on love and union with God through Christ, remained the main linguistic currency for Edwards's development of the Son's economic work. This social theme of fellowship with God through Christ governed Edwards's treatment of election and incarnation.

The psychological image of the Son as God's Word still retained an important role in Edwards's theology of preaching and revelation. All saving human knowledge of God attained through Scripture, proph-

14. Works, 13, p. 495 (no. 448).
15. *Misc.*, no. 1245.
16. Works, 9, p. 117.

ecy, and preaching depends ultimately on the Son, who is the internal act of God's own self-knowledge. Through the external repetition of God's disposition to self-knowledge, the saving knowledge conveyed to the saints is not a bare "notional" knowledge of the things of religion: it is truly "Christ's being in the creature in the name, idea or knowledge of God being in them."[17] The Son's role as the Father's Word or Idea likewise had a secure place in Edwards's reflections on ministry. As a perfect revealer of divine things, Christ is the prototype for prophets, apostles, and ministers, who are all shadows of God's eternal "personal Word." In their partial and imperfect way, they too are "words of God." However, Edwards used the psychological model principally to highlight the economic role of the Holy Spirit as God's love. As will be seen in the next chapter, Edwards employed it in developing his views of conversion and sanctification, and it permeated his explorations of true sainthood during the Great Awakening period.

Edwards's use of two contrasting motifs to describe the trinitarian work of redemption and the various works "subserving" it sometimes inspired creative combinations and adaptations. What the two images had in common was an emphasis on the glory of God manifested in the loving bestowal of gifts; fittingly, in his reflections on heaven, that eternal "world of love," true harmony between the images was finally achieved. In describing the earthly work of redemption, the fit between the two trinitarian models was often awkward, and most of the time Edwards developed one model largely to the exclusion of the other. Yet each stage of God's work of redemption — creation, election, incarnation, sanctification, and glorification — reflects Edwards's broad vision of the significance of the Trinity for Christian life and practice.

Creation and the Fall into Sin

Since the rise of the Enlightenment, influential continental theologians had begun to view the doctrine of the Trinity as problematic

17. *Misc.*, no. 1084. In the imaginative trinitarian theology of Henry Vane, one of the Cambridge Brethren, the emphasis on Christ as trinitarian communicator is considerably more prominent. See his *Retired Mans Meditation, Or The Mysterie and Power of Godliness Shining forth in the Living Word, to the Unmasking the Mysterie of Iniquity in the Most Refined and Purest Forms* (London, 1655).

based on the deliverances of human reason, and increasingly shifted theological weight to the notion of God as the creator of the universe and the basis of moral law.[18] As Robert Jenson has remarked, Edwards could sound like "the unchastened rationalists of his period,"[19] and we will be looking at some of the problems a rationalist approach generated for Edwards's doctrine of creation a bit later. But when the triune God was at the center of his theological reflection, it was clear to Edwards that the true puzzle was not the Trinity but the creation of a finite world. Why would the God who is already perfect union desire union with what is not God? The creation cannot add anything to God who is already the perfection of love and wisdom. There is within the Godhead already a perfect, harmonious society; the Father "hath in his Son an adequate object for all the desires of this kind that are in his heart, and in his infinite happiness he sees as much happiness as can be."[20] If "God stands in no need of creatures and . . . neither can his happiness be said to be added to by the creature,"[21] what is God's end in creation?

The intrinsic beauty of the world does not justify God's creation of it. In an implied critique of the secular moralists of his day, Edwards remarked sardonically that it was not enough

> that the world was made to have all the parts of it nicely hanging together, and sweetly harmonizing and corresponding; that is, that the world was nicely contrived, that when it was done it might be a nicely contrived world.[22]

Edwards was by no means aloof to the beauties of the visible world, and remarked frequently on how in creating it "God does purposely make

18. For an account of this shift, see William C. Placher, *The Domestication of Transcendence: How Modern Thinking about God Went Wrong* (Louisville: Westminster/John Knox Press, 1996).

19. Robert W. Jenson, *America's Theologian: A Recommendation of Jonathan Edwards* (Oxford: Oxford University Press, 1988), p. 22. It should be noted that rationalist pressures also fueled certain sorts of trinitarian arguments in Edwards's theology, for example his appeals to "ancient heathen" knowledge of the Trinity.

20. *Misc.*, no. 1218. "The Father, Son and Holy Ghost were happy in themselves, and enjoyed one another before the world was." Sibbes, *Complete Works*, 6, p. 113.

21. Works, 18, p. 237 (no. 679).

22. Works, 13, pp. 189-90 (no. tt).

and order one thing to be in agreeableness and harmony with another."[23] But according to Edwards's exemplarist conception of the universe, material things are "images or shadows" of more basic spiritual realities. Thus the physical world cannot be an end in itself, for in creating the world God "makes the inferior in imitation of the superior." The preservation of the whole material universe "by gravity or attraction, or the mutual tendency of all bodies to each other," was for Edwards "a type of love or charity in the spiritual world."[24] As we have seen, the agreeableness and harmony of the material universe is derivative: "the sweetest and most charming beauty" of the physical creation is "its resemblance of spiritual beauties."

But even the intrinsic beauty of the spiritual world cannot be God's sole end in creation. Charles Taylor has described the deist picture, current in Edwards's time, "of the universe as a vast interlocking order of beings, mutually subserving each other's flourishing, for whose design the architect of nature deserves our praise and thanks and admiration."[25] Even a "nicely contrived" world of intelligent creatures did not satisfy Edwards, because the end of creation of the physical and spiritual world would still be self-contained. On the deist view God remains external to the world as its designer, rather than being the paradigm of its beauty and the goal of its consents. Edwards acknowledged that "God has so made and constituted the world of mankind, that he has made it natural and necessary, that they should be concerned one with another, and their inclination to society."[26] But human society in itself is a shadowy and incomplete reality, always pointing beyond itself to heavenly unions. The "sweet mutual consents" of finite earthly spirits are an image of heavenly communion with God and finally of the perfect consent within the Trinity.

To find God's end in creating the world, Edwards had to start at the beginning, with God's intrinsically relational and communicative nature. Edwards agreed with Richard Sibbes that "God's goodness is a

23. *Works*, 11, p. 53. See Clyde A. Holbrook, *Jonathan Edwards; The Valley and Nature: An Interpretive Essay* (Lewisburg, Pa.: Bucknell University Press, 1987), for both an appreciation and a critique of Edwards's view of the natural world.

24. *Works*, 11, p. 81.

25. Charles Taylor, *Sources of the Self: The Making of the Modern Identity* (Cambridge, Mass.: Harvard University Press, 1989), p. 244.

26. *Misc.*, no. 864.

communicative, spreading goodness"; were that not the case, "there never had been a creation nor a redemption."[27] God is perfectly "happy in himself," and yet "has a natural propensity and inclination to communicate happiness to some other beings."[28] There is in God an eternal desire to radiate outwards in emanations of understanding and love towards creatures who are able to receive these gifts. This desire could not remain unfulfilled, for "God would be less happy" if "it were possible for him to be hindered in exercising his own goodness, or to be hindered from glorifying himself."[29] In Sibbes's more explicit metaphors, "Such a goodness is in God as is in a fountain, or in the breast that loves to ease itself of milk."[30] The perfect love and delight of God *ad intra* has a centrifugal force that naturally seeks external expression towards creatures. In the words of Maximus the Confessor, "God, full beyond all fulness, brought creatures in being . . . so that they might participate in Him in proportion to their capacity and He Himself might rejoice in His works . . . through seeing them joyful and ever filled to overflowing with His inexhaustible gifts."[31]

The union established in creation was a first step toward the ultimate creaturely union with God accomplished by the work of redemption. Edwards equated God's purpose in creation with

> the creature's glory and happiness during the whole of the designed eternal duration of the world he was about to create: which is in greater and greater nearness and strictness of union with himself, and greater and greater communion and participation with him in his own glory and happiness, in constant progression, throughout all eternity.[32]

Redemption is not God's response to a creation gone wrong. It is rather the culmination of God's desire for union with creatures that was the

27. Works, 6, p. 113.
28. Works, 14, p. 153.
29. Works, 18, p. 238 (no. 679).
30. Works, 6, p. 113.
31. Maximus the Confessor, "Third Century of Love," trans. G. Palmer, P. Sherrard, and K. Ware, in *The Philokalia*, vol. 2 (London: Faber & Faber, 1981), section 46. Cited in Kathryn Tanner, *Jesus, Humanity and the Trinity: A Brief Systematic Theology* (Minneapolis: Fortress Press, 2001), p. 36.
32. Works, 8, p. 459.

divine aim in creating them in the first place.[33] According to Kathryn Tanner, "God who is already abundant fullness, freely wishes to replicate to every degree possible this fullness of life, light, and love outward in what is not God; this is possible in its fullness only to the extent the world is united by God to Godself over the course of the world's time."[34] Creation thus belonged to the basic soteriological story line narrated by Edwards's two trinitarian idioms.

On the psychological model, creation is "the everlasting process of God's repetition of God's prior actuality now in time and space."[35] Corresponding to God's emanation of internal glory in knowledge, virtue, and happiness is the remanation of this glory in the saints' knowledge of God, "high esteem of God, love to God, and complacence and joy in God; and the proper exercises and expression of these."[36] Creatures are brought into existence to know and love God, and to rejoice in God's glorious excellency. God's being is glorified and enlarged by endowing creatures with the forms of God's own perfect knowledge, holiness, and love, so that they can then respond to their Creator in praise. God does not create the world in order to receive something God lacks:

> What God has in view in neither of them, neither in his manifesting his glory to the understanding nor communication to the heart, is not that he may receive, but that he [may] go forth: the main end of his shining forth is not that he may have his rays reflected back to himself, but that the rays may go forth.[37]

---

33. This understanding of the relationship between creation and redemption is called supralapsarianism, a distinctly minority viewpoint in the Reformed tradition. For example, Francis Turretin, one of Edwards's favorite Reformed scholastics, complained that, on the supralapsarian view, "God's plan for humanity's salvation or damnation would have been formed before he decreed its being and fall, which would be absurd." *Institutio,* IV.ix.12. (Deus consilium inivisset de homine salvando, vel perdendo, antequam quicquam decrevisset de ejus futuritione et lapsu, quod absurdum.) In the contemporary period, Karl Barth has been the standard bearer for supralapsarianism, albeit in a revised form.

34. Tanner, *Jesus, Humanity and the Trinity,* p. 2.

35. Sang Hyun Lee, "Edwards on God and Nature: Resources for Contemporary Theology," in *Edwards in Our Time: Jonathan Edwards and the Shaping of American Religion,* ed. Sang Hyun Lee and Allen C. Guelzo (Grand Rapids: Eerdmans, 1999), p. 17.

36. Works, 8, p. 527.

37. Works, 13, p. 496 (no. 448).

Thus God's delight in the happiness of the creatures "is not distinct from the delight that he has in himself, for 'tis to be resolved into the delight that he has in his own goodness."[38]

According to the social analogy for the Trinity, the "eternal society or family in the Godhead" is not self-contained; it seeks spiritual union beyond its bounds in the eternal happiness between the Son and his spouse, the church. In an early notebook entry, Edwards began quite predictably with the assertion that "the Father's begetting of the Son is a complete communication of all his happiness, and so an eternal, adequate and infinite exercise of perfect goodness." But this left unresolved the question posed earlier: "Why then, did God incline further to communicate himself, seeing he had done it infinitely and completely?" In a surprising move, Edwards insisted that "the Son has also an inclination to communicate himself in an image of his person that may partake of his happiness," and that "this was the end of creation."[39] As the Son is the perfect image of the Father, so the world is an image of the Son. Edwards even found in this a new

> trinity, an image of the eternal Trinity; wherein the Christ is the everlasting father, and believers are his seed, and the Holy Spirit, or Comforter, is the third person in Christ, being his delight and love flowing out towards the church.[40]

In this idiosyncratic move, Edwards reinforced the links among the Trinity, the incarnation, and the work of redemption as different variations of his fundamental theme of spiritual union.

Occasionally Edwards attempted to bring the two trinitarian idioms together in his theology of creation, as in this tortuously argued passage in his *Discourse on the Trinity:*

> the creation of the world is to gratify Divine love as that is exercised by divine wisdom. But Christ is Divine wisdom, so that the world is

---

38. Works, 18, p. 238 (no. 679).

39. Works, 13, p. 272 (no. 104).

40. Works, 13, p. 273 (no. 104). Cf. John Cotton's claim that just as the persons of the Trinity "nourished, delighted and solaced each other," so "God ordained Christ to be a nourisher, and solacer of his Church." *First John Generall,* p. 12.

made to gratify Divine love as exercised by Christ or to gratify the love that is in Christ's heart to provide a spouse for Christ.[41]

Tensions clearly remain, but this passage shows how both trinitarian models of creation centered on notions of God's overflowing love to creatures and desire for spiritual union with them. The world is made not principally as a display of divine power but to gratify divine love.

Creation and redemption are progressive movements in God's aim for union with creaturely reality. Since God "makes the inferior in imitation of the superior," creation can be seen as a type of redemption: "the creation of man in particular seems to have been in such a manner, as it was that it might shadow the manner of his greater creation, viz. his new creation."[42] In no. 702 of the "Miscellanies," Edwards illustrated this by drawing elaborate parallels between creation and redemption, highlighting the distinct economic roles of the members of the Trinity. Both creation and redemption required "a consultation of the persons of the Trinity." Just as God took Adam from the dust, so Christ takes the redeemed from their vile condition. Just as God breathed in Adam the breath of life, so the Holy Spirit infuses the redeemed with holiness. Just as Adam and Eve were exalted to earthly dominion, so the redeemed are exalted to membership in Christ's body. Both creation and redemption, in Edwards's view, are ultimately undertaken by the Father for the sake of the Son, who is "the end of all God's works *ad extra*." "God created the world for his Son, that he might prepare a spouse or bride for him to bestow his love upon; so that the mutual joys between this bride and bridegroom are the end of creation."[43] Creation is in order to redemption — the enlargement of the fellowship of the trinitarian family by making room for "the exceeding expressions of Christ's love to his spouse and for her exceeding close and intimate union with, and high and glorious enjoyment of, him."[44]

There seems to be a universalist logic at work in Edwards's trinitarian theology of creation. The ultimate end of creation is "God's glorifying his love and communicating his goodness." Within Edwards's

41. Helm, *Trinity*, p. 131.
42. Works, 18, p. 286 (no. 702).
43. Works, 13, p. 374 (no. 271).
44. Works, 18, p. 298 (no. 702).

supralapsarian scheme, this was prior in God's plan "to the very being of the subject, and to everything but mere possibility."[45] In his trinitarian treatise on the *End of Creation*, Edwards argued that divine glory and human happiness in fact coincide in God's purposes in creation. "According to Scripture, communicating good to creatures is what is in itself pleasing to God: and that this is not merely subordinately agreeable, and esteemed valuable on account of its relation to a further end."[46] God's glory naturally overflows in the communication of good to creatures, so that divine glory and creaturely happiness may together be looked upon as God's one ultimate end in creating the world. Since divine love and goodness are in infinite abundance, there would seem to be no hindrance to God's achieving this ultimate end of happiness for all persons. There is no scarcity of gifts in God, no sense in which creatures are in competition with each other for God's limited redemptive resources. As Robert Adams argues, "This does not imply that we all (or any of us) deserve to be loved by God," or, I would add, that no creaturely resistance to God's love could ever be ultimately successful, "but rather that loving all is most fitting to God's magnificence."[47]

One could even argue that this universalist logic embraces the whole creation, not just the human race. "God made all things," Edwards declared, "and the end for which all things are made, and for which they are disposed, . . . is that God's glory may shine forth and be received."[48] Sang Hyun Lee has made a good case within Edwards's theology for understanding "the entire created realm as God's repetition of God's own glory."[49] On this reading, the "world then would have to have a dependent and yet real integrity of its own. That is to say, the created existence would have to be a beautiful system or network of relations which

---

45. Works, 18, p. 317 (no. 704). Edwards is clear in this entry about the asymmetry between God's decrees of redemption and damnation. His account of the decree of damnation is clearly infralapsarian: "sinfulness is necessarily supposed *or already put* in the decree of punishing sinfulness."

46. Works, 8, p. 503.

47. Robert Merrihew Adams, *Finite and Infinite Goods: A Framework for Ethics* (New York: Oxford University Press, 1999), p. 175. There are intriguing resemblances between Edwards's theological vision and Adams's beautiful contemporary rendition of a Platonic worldview.

48. Works, 13, p. 496 (no. 448).

49. Lee, "Edwards on God and Nature," p. 17.

repeats God's inner-trinitarian glory."[50] Indeed, on this reading, the role of "every created entity is to be a repetition or image of God's beauty."[51] Edwards's conception of God's trinitarian union with creation could have funded a deep and expansive theology of cosmic redemption that embraced the groanings of all creation for liberation from its bondage to decay.[52]

Yet it did not, and we find instead a drastic truncation of the moral and theological significance of the creaturely world within Edwards's thought. Instead of a cosmic redemption, there is a cosmic holocaust: the earth created by God is annihilated in a paroxysm of apocalyptic violence, and the vast majority of God's creatures are eternally bereft of the communications of God's goodness and love that were God's end in creation. Edwards's treatment of sin, exacerbated by the idealist and rationalist impulses of his theology, is largely to blame for the failures of his doctrine of creation.

In Edwards's theology, human and angelic sin strikes a blow from which God's gracious end in creating the world never recovers: creaturely sin occasions the eternal destruction of the earth and most of its creatures. In God's final judgment on sin, "the world of men is to be destroyed, and therefore elect men are taken out of it and carried into the world of angels, and reprobate men are left in it to perish and sink with it."[53] Severed from the Father's gift-giving, most of the creation does not benefit from the redemptive work of Christ and the Holy Spirit. Though the suffering of Christ "was great enough to lay the foundation for an universal refreshing, . . . that all spiritual and external should be immensely exalted in perfection, beauty and glory,"[54] this "universal refreshing" of Christ's work is confined to "elect things." Likewise, the Spirit's gifts of faith and holiness abundantly supply what sinful creatures lack: delight in the beauty and grace of God. But these

---

50. Lee, "Edwards on God and Nature," p. 39.

51. Lee, "Edwards on God and Nature," p. 40.

52. Cf. Romans 8:20-22. Contemporary ecotheologies have developed relational themes in this direction. See, e.g., Richard Fragomeni and John Pawlikowski, O.S.M., *The Ecological Challenge: Ethical, Liturgical, and Spiritual Responses* (Collegeville, Minn.: Liturgical Press, 1995); H. Paul Santmire, *The Travail of Nature: The Ambiguous Ecological Promise of Christian Theology* (Philadelphia: Fortress Press, 1985).

53. *Misc.*, no. 936.

54. *Misc.*, no. 952.

special gifts of the Spirit are poured out only on the elect few. Reprobate humanity fails to receive these gifts of Christ and the Spirit; thus they fail to participate in God's end for creation. And with their eternal punishment and separation from God comes the destruction of the earth that was created to display "images and shadows of divine things."

The trinitarian harmony noted in Edwards's discussion of creation and redemption faltered in much of his treatment of sin, marked by his repeated appeals to an undifferentiated "God." The agency of the Holy Spirit as the love and happiness of God drops out almost completely. When the "communicative, spreading goodness" of the Holy Spirit is no longer the definitive manifestation of divine glory, then the divine glory can appear in destruction of the world and the "eternal flame, that the bodies of the wicked are to be tormented in," just as well as in the happiness of creatures and "the eternal light" of God's love.[55] Union with God through the power of the Spirit is no longer "the great end and drift of all God's works and dispensations from the beginning."[56]

In Edwards's treatment of sin, Christ's redemptive agency frequently appears in opposition to that of the Father, as mercifully shielding human sinners from the divine wrath.[57] At other times the second person of the Trinity undergoes a transmogrification from Christ the slain Lamb to Christ the slayer on a white horse (Rev. 19:11-16): "the same glorious person that is the Savior of believers is the person that 'treads the winepress of the fierceness and wrath of almighty God' (Rev. 19:15). The same that is the sweet refreshing light of Israel is the consuming fire of the wicked."[58] In justifying the fate of the damned, Edwards's interpretation of the crucifixion shifted from Christ's supreme act of self-dispossessing mercy to a violent human act that required equally violent divine avenging, with devastating consequences for the whole earth:

---

55. *Misc.*, no. 926.

56. Works, 18, p. 284 (no. 702).

57. For example, Edwards found in "the pillar of cloud defend[ing] the children of Israel from the sunbeams in that parched wilderness, where they beat with great vehemence," a type of "Christ's defending his church from the wrath of God." *Misc.*, no. 931.

58. *Misc.*, no. 930. See, among many examples, Edwards's "Day of Judgment" sermon on Acts 17:31 (December 1729), in Works, 14, pp. 514-41. I am in basic agreement with the Barthian critique of Edwards advanced by Stephen Holmes, *God of Grace and God of Glory: An Account of the Theology of Jonathan Edwards* (Grand Rapids: Eerdmans, 2001): Christ the Judge is not the one "judged in our place."

The great Creator that made all these stars, and is the Creator of this great system of bodies, has been murdered, and his blood has been wickedly shed in this system, and on this earth; and no wonder that this breaks down the whole frame, and fetches all down in vengeance and in fury on this earth.[59]

As a result of human sin, the Lord of all creation now consigns the earth "to fall and be ruined, and . . . to be the eternal seat of those creatures that fall and are ruined."[60] In much of Edwards's treatment of sin, God's original end for creation seems nowhere in view.

Though Edwards's idealism was formed within his relational ontology, as was argued in Chapter 2, it threatened to dissolve God's relations to the physical creation. Within Edwards's idealist framework, non-perceiving being was radically subordinated to perceiving being. Edwards found it evident "that the moral part is the end of all the rest of the creation. The inanimate, unintelligent part is made for the rational as much as a house is prepared for the inhabitant."[61] In fact, "the world would be altogether good for nothing without intelligent beings."[62] As Sang Hyun Lee argues, non-perceiving beings are created by God to be "images or shadows of divine things," but achieving this destiny requires "the regenerate person's imaginative perception of them as images or shadows of divine things."[63] This would presumably involve delight in the material world as well as knowledge of it, as Edwards's own *Personal Narrative* illustrates.[64] Even still, Edwards's idealism calls into question the integrity of the material creation, its abiding worth before God apart from the actions of human creatures.[65]

---

59. *Misc.*, no. 930.

60. *Misc.*, no. 952.

61. Works, 8, pp. 470-71.

62. Works, 13, p. 186 (no. kk).

63. Lee, "Edwards on God and Nature," p. 32.

64. See Works, 16, pp. 790-804. See also *Works*, 13, pp. 278-80 (no. 108).

65. Edwards's idealism even threatened the integrity of the intelligent creation. Thomas Schafer notes the danger that Edwards's "doctrine of perception could destroy the perceiving soul," and worries that, "instead of guaranteeing the value and immortality of intelligent creatures, Edwards' doctrine of perception leaves God finally alone, talking to a reflection of himself in a mirror" (Works, 13, p. 49). Despite its deeply relational themes, Edwards's idealism always threatened to evolve into monism.

THE GRAND DESIGN OF REDEMPTION

Edwards's philosophical idealism exacerbated the prevalent theological anthropocentrism of his day. At times his writings exhibit a marked human disdain for the rest of creation: "These intelligent, voluntary creatures are the highest above other things, have 'em in possession and at command, and have power to order the inferior creatures, and to destroy them at their pleasure."[66] The material world functions as a beautiful and elaborate backdrop for the drama of human redemption, but humanity remains "the end of the rest of the creatures in this lower world, . . . for which the rest are made, and to whose use they are subordinated."[67] Therefore it did not trouble Edwards that at the day of judgment "all the visible universe shall be turned into a great furnace,"[68] because humanity, "the end of all, is equivalent to the whole. Therefore, there is no need of anything else to be preserved; nothing is lost, no part is in vain, if the end of all be preserved."[69] While ecological sensibility is not altogether absent in Edwards's theology, his idealism strongly works against a valuing of all creation.

At the beginning of this section we noted the rationalist shift in Edwards's day from God as Trinity to God as creator and moral lawgiver, and this shift is reflected in long notebook passages in which Edwards appeared content to present God as "First Cause" and "moral governor" of the world without any reference to the Trinity.[70] This rationalist strain in Edwards's thought tended to sever the theological connections we have noted between creation and redemption. It is not surprising that, in the passage quoted above about intelligent creatures having the "power to order the inferior creatures, and to destroy them at their pleasure," Edwards went on to remark that intelligent creatures thereby demonstrate that they are "next to the First Cause," who like-

---

66. *Misc.,* no. 896. On the basis of passages like this, I dispute Lee's contention that "The uniqueness or superiority of intelligent beings, therefore, does not give them any right to dominate over other parts of the universe. Any element of anthropocentrism in Edwards is thoroughly subordinated to his theocentric outlook. In their ultimate responsibility toward God, therefore, nature and humanity are equal partners." Lee, "Edwards on God and Nature," p. 30.

67. *Misc.,* no. 865.

68. *Misc.,* no. 952. Edwards tended to revert to materialist images in his treatment of judgment and hell.

69. *Misc.,* no. 865.

70. See, e.g., *Misc.,* no. 864.

wise has the power to order and destroy inferior creatures at will.[71] Creation is not ordered to redemption here: the First Cause of the universe has no necessary connection to the God of the gospel narratives whose end in all things is "the making happy sinful men in Christ."[72] Whereas the creativity of "the Father" of Jesus Christ "loves and does not negate, frustrate or destroy," the absolute power of the First Cause may well show itself to be "alien to love, to mercy and gift":[73] "As God has shown his power in building the world, and now shows his power in upholding it, so he will show his power by dashing it in pieces in his wrath."[74]

Edwards's treatment of sin, aggravated by his idealist and rationalist impulses, was disastrous for his doctrine of creation. But this theological disaster could have been avoided, because there are trinitarian strands within Edwards's view of sin that preserve a strong connection between God's work in creation and redemption. If redemption is a matter of spiritual union with God, sin for Edwards was spiritual alienation from God, manifested as lack of love for God. Sin defies God's desire for union; it resists incorporation into the triune life of God through Christ. At its root, sin is the creaturely attempt to reject God's gifts of love and union, and to refuse to be ministers of these gifts to others.[75] Thus salvation and damnation, eternal union with God and eternal separation from God, were not theologically parallel for Edwards. Only salvation is "the great end and drift" of all of God's work, a perfect reflection of the love and union of God's internal being. Damnation is alien to the eternal trinitarian life of God. The central figure in the story of salvation is "a God that delights in mercy," and who "has no pleasure in the Destruction or Calamity of persons or people."[76] God's punishment of sinners is grounded in human sinfulness, not in God's eternal desire to execute "vindictive justice." And God's eternal punishment of sin is not an extrinsic response to creaturely fallenness;

71. *Misc.*, no. 896.

72. Works, 18, p. 295 (no. 702).

73. Rowan Williams, *On Christian Theology* (Oxford: Blackwell, 2000), p. 141.

74. *Misc.*, no. 933.

75. Kathryn Tanner uses similar language to describe sin. See *Jesus, Humanity and the Trinity*, p. 2.

76. Ms sermon on Jonah 3:10 (21 December 1727), quoted in Gerald R. McDermott, *One Holy and Happy Society: The Public Theology of Jonathan Edwards* (University Park, Pa.: Pennsylvania State University Press, 1992), p. 27.

it is simply what human sin desires and effects, namely, separation from God.[77] Redemption, not damnation, remains "the main great work of power, wisdom and grace that is the hinge of all" God's relations to creatures.[78]

Sin is creaturely resistance to the aims of God's great work of redemption. This essentially privative notion of sin served as the basis for Edwards's frequent discussions of the sin against the Holy Spirit. According to Edwards, the reason why the New Testament designates sin against the Holy Spirit as unpardonably grievous[79] is that it is specifically aimed against God's *love*. It involves a deliberate rejection of the Spirit's acts "wherein consists his nature and office, viz. divine love, either expressing the love of God, or breathing love to God."[80] The unpardonable sin is to "willfully and maliciously reproach . . . that [which] should attract our love and win our hearts, viz. the beauty and grace of God."[81] The "grace and love of the Father in electing and in sending his Son" as well as "the holiness, grace and love of the Son in all that he did, and suffered, and now does" consist in the Holy Spirit.[82] Because the Holy Spirit "is the sum of all those benefits" bestowed by the work of redemption, the rejection of the Holy Spirit is in effect the rejection of the end for which God created them: joy in the love and knowledge of God. Though great effort was expended in the Reformed tradition to make the unpardonable sin against the Holy Spirit distinctive (and hence avoidable),[83] for Edwards it reflects what was the essence of all human sin.

---

77. As Kathryn Tanner notes, "punishment for sin is the sin itself as punishment, namely, the separation itself." *Jesus, Humanity and the Trinity*, p. 87.

78. Works, 18, p. 402 (no. 752). For the asymmetry between God's decrees of redemption and damnation, see *Works*, 18, pp. 314-21 (no. 704).

79. See Matt. 12:31-32; Mark 3:29; Luke 12:10; Acts 7:51.

80. Works, 13, p. 517 (no. 475).

81. Works, 13, p. 521 (no. 475).

82. Works, 18, pp. 328-29 (no. 706).

83. As Edwards (approvingly) paraphrased Francis Turretin's argument: "so that he that has violated the laws of the Father may have a remedy in the satisfaction of the Son. He that injures the person of the Son, and casts contempt on his satisfaction, there remains hope for him in the grace of the Spirit. . . . But he that does avowedly reject and trample on the Spirit and declare war against him, there remains nothing else whence any hope can arise to him. There remains never another divine person to appear for his help." Works, 18, pp. 326-27 (no. 706).

If sin is at its root a creaturely attempt to reject union with God, the work of redemption is not going to be a smooth, placid affair, devoid of struggle or bitter disappointment. Like any good story, it is going to involve a fight, in which the wisdom and determination of the protagonist are displayed. Humanity's calamitous fall into sin might seem to thwart God's intentions for union with creatures. But Edwards delighted in showing God's unsearchable wisdom in using the devastation of human sin to establish an even closer relation with God than obtained before the fall:

> If man had never fallen, God would have remained man's friend; he would . . . have had the favor of all the persons of the Trinity. But now Christ becoming our surety and Saviour, and having taken on him our nature, occasions . . . a nearer relation than otherwise would have been. . . . The sin and misery of man, by this contrivance, are made an occasion of his being more happy, not only than he was before the fall, but than he would have been, if he never had fallen.[84]

The work of redemption is a more glorious manifestation of the love by each person of the Trinity to human creatures than would have been possible without the fall into sin. The Father "so loves that He gave His only begotten Son"; the Son "so loved the world as to give up Himself"; and the Holy Spirit "is that love of the Father and the Son to the world."[85] Redemption from sin gives the saints greater motive to love and depend on God, thereby increasing their happiness and union with God: "So much the greater and more absolute dependence we have on the divine perfections, as belonging to the several persons of the Trinity, so much the greater occasion have we to observe and own the divine glory of each of them."[86] In short, Edwards could portray the work of overcoming sin as an intensification of God's commitment to union with the creaturely world. In this way, he preserved a strong connection between God's trinitarian work in creation and redemption.

84. Sereno E. Dwight, ed., *The Works of President Edwards with a Memoir of His Life*, 10 vols. (New York: S. Converse, 1829-30), 7, p. 94.

85. Helm, *Trinity*, p. 123.

86. Dwight, *Works of President Edwards*, 7, p. 158.

Election and Incarnation

Edwards was a staunch double predestinarian in an age when the notion of a particular election of some to salvation and some to eternal damnation was increasingly repudiated as unworthy of a just and benevolent deity.[87] This repudiation was linked with antitrinitarianism in rejecting the popular concept of an angry and just Father glorifying himself in the damnation of sinners, and sparing the elect on account of the suffering intercessions of a loving, merciful Son.[88] Edwards's theological reflections at times fell prey to this trinitarian dichotomizing, portraying Christ's mediatorial work as a merciful attempt to wrest at least a portion of fallen humanity from the punishment decreed by a just and angry God. For example, Edwards could declare that Christ "loved man and so greatly desired his salvation," yet he had "so great respect to the majesty and holiness of God, that he had rather die than that salvation should be any injury or dishonor unto those attributes."[89] This discord within the "supreme harmony" of the Trinity encouraged viewing Christ's reconciling work "mainly as an external transference of penalty between sinners and God."[90] Indeed, Edwards's most common metaphors for the atonement were transactional and financial: by his suffering, Christ pays off the debt of sin and purchases the benefits of salvation for the elect. Paying off the debt satisfies the demands of God's "majesty and holiness," while Christ's purchase of benefits merits the eternal happiness of the elect.[91] The language of the

---

87. Samuel Johnson, in *A Letter from Aristocles to Authades concerning the Sovereignty and Promises of God* (Boston, 1745), 2, found that God's election of individuals "without any consideration of their good and ill behaviour, is contrary to the nature and attributes of God." Cf. Edwards's nemesis Charles Chauncy, *Salvation for all men illustrated and vindicated as a scripture doctrine* (Boston, 1782). For an acute analysis, see Norman S. Fiering, "Irresistible Compassion: An Aspect of Eighteenth-Century Sympathy and Humanitarianism," in Frank Shuffelton, ed., *The American Enlightenment*, vol. 11, Library of the History of Ideas, ed. John W. Yolton (Rochester, N.Y.: University of Rochester Press, 1993), pp. 73-96.

88. Claude Welch, *In This Name: The Doctrine of the Trinity in Contemporary Theology* (New York: Scribner, 1952), pp. 23-24.

89. Works, 13, p. 497 (no. 449).

90. Thomas F. Torrance, *Karl Barth, Biblical and Evangelical Theologian* (Edinburgh: T. & T. Clark, 1990), p. 231.

91. Stephen Holmes, *God of Grace and God of Glory*, p. 142, notes these two sorts of images in Edwards's theology of atonement.

cross becomes that of acquisition, not dispossession. These metaphors for atonement were common in the Reformed tradition Edwards knew, but did not harmonize well with his themes of overflowing love and union.

This transactional imagery for the atonement also had implications for Edwards's understanding of election and incarnation. In order to "purchase sanctification," the humanity Christ assumed had to be pure and undefiled. Christ's conception by the power of the Holy Spirit guaranteed that, from the moment of conception on, "the man Jesus was not one of the corrupt race of mankind."[92] Edwards's reliance on external forensic metaphors for the atonement encouraged a sharp differentiation between Christ's humanity and that of the sinners he redeemed. Similarly, under the influence of Edwards's theory of limited atonement, the treatment of election retreats from images of God's overflowing abundance and delight to notions of scarcity, of a grace that is all the "more wonderful" for being so "rare": "'Election' seems to denote a choosing out one or a few out of many, a choosing a portion out of the common mass; but if the multitude or mass itself was taken, and only a few distinguished ones left, this could hardly be called an election."[93] Edwards's quotation from Thomas Shepard in this entry suggests that mercy, not judgment, is God's "strange work."

However, there are other strands within Edwards's Christology that weave election and incarnation into the center of his basic soteriological story line, stretching from God's eternal disposition to be united with creatures in communications of joy and goodness to the culmination of that union in heaven. In election and incarnation, the dramatic action of the story of redemption peaks. God has chosen in Jesus Christ

> to unite himself to a created nature, and to become one of the creatures, and to gather together in one all elect creatures in that creature he assumed into a personal union with himself, and to manifest to them and maintain intercourse with them through him.[94]

Union embraces Edwards's understanding of both Christ's person and work. By means of "a personal union," the incarnate Christ gratifies

92. Works, 18, pp. 416-17 (no. 769).
93. Works, 18, p. 65 (no. 520).
94. Works, 18, p. 389 (no. 744).

God's love for creation by bringing sinful creatures into union with God. The union between God and humanity that Christ embodies in the incarnation is also what he mediates to sinful creatures. "He embodies what he mediates in himself, for what he mediates and what he is are one and the same."[95]

Christ is "the head of election, and the pattern of all other election."[96] In electing Christ, God graciously chose one of the human "species" to "have the most transcendent union with the eternal Logos even so as to be one person."[97] (Although the Son "was not actually incarnate" when elected by God in eternity, "yet he was so in design.")[98] It is therefore in his human nature that Christ "more especially is called the Elect of God" and receives the glory of election: "he was as it were the first elect and the head of election. All are elected only as his members, that in all things he might have preeminence."[99]

God's end in electing Jesus Christ for the glory of incarnate union is the extension and enlargement of that glorious union in the election of the saints. In the election of Christ, God exalted

> one of the creatures so high that he should be one person with God, and should have communion with God, and glory in all respects answerable, and so should be the head of all other elect creatures, that they might be united to God and glorified in him.[100]

Here the transactional language of atonement falls away. Atoning reconciliation is "accomplished *within* the incarnate constitution of the Mediator and not in some *external* transactional way between himself and mankind."[101] As Ava Chamberlain notes, "the primary focus of Edwards's analysis of the doctrine of justification is not the forensic transaction that occurs by means of justification but the ontological

---

95. Torrance, *Karl Barth,* p. 230. Though Torrance is describing Karl Barth's theology, the parallels with Edwards are obvious.

96. Works, 18, p. 418 (no. 769). As Robert Jenson notes, "Edwards' doctrine of election anticipates at most points the justly praised 'christological' doctrine of election developed by Karl Barth." *America's Theologian,* p. 106.

97. *Misc.,* no. 1245.

98. Dwight, *Works of President Edwards,* 6, p. 389.

99. *Misc.,* no. 1245.

100. Works, 18, p. 416 (no. 769).

101. Torrance, *Karl Barth,* p. 230.

transformation that occurs by means of union with Christ."[102] In Edwards's words, "What is real in the union between Christ and his people is the foundation of what is legal."[103] The redemptive benefits of Christ are never separable from union with him. Believers have salvation in Christ only as they "remain one with Christ in faith and love by the gracious workings of the Holy Spirit."[104]

In a startling passage, Edwards made the social goal of Christ's union with believers explicit. Christ's aim for his followers was that

> he and his Father and they should be as it were one society, one family; that his people should be in a sort admitted into that society of three persons in the Godhead.[105]

Here the New Testament theme, prominent in Puritan writings, of the Father's adoption of the saints as his children was combined with an explicitly social analogy for the Trinity. In Chapter 1 we saw Edwards take notice of van Mastricht's representation of how God, the "Paterfamilias," brings the church into the "communion" and "society" of the trinitarian family.[106] But Edwards's unnerving suggestion of an expansion of the trinitarian family is also reminiscent of a minority strand found in Christian mystical writings of the believers' intimate incorporation into the life of the Trinity.[107]

The notion of believers being "in a sort admitted into that society" of the Trinity, underscores the strong links in Edwards's thought between the transformation of Christ's human nature through the spiritual union of the incarnation and the transformative union that is the ultimate end of the work of redemption — the union of saints with

---

102. Works, 18, p. 39.

103. Works, 18, p. 105 (no. 568).

104. Tanner, *Jesus, Humanity and the Trinity*, p. 90.

105. Works, 18, p. 110 (no. 571).

106. Works, 13, p. 524 (no. 482). I am paraphrasing Schafer's description of van Mastricht.

107. The sixteenth-century Carmelite mystics Teresa of Avila and St. John of the Cross asserted a transforming union of the soul with Christ leading to incorporation into the life of the Trinity. In *The Spiritual Canticle*, John asserted that "the soul can actually breathe with the 'very breath' of the Spirit that moves between the Father and the Son." The soul is actually now knit into the life of God. Sarah Coakley, "Deepening Practices: Perspectives from Ascetical and Mystical Theology," in *Practicing Theology: Beliefs and Practices in Christian Life*, ed. Miroslav Volf and Dorothy C. Bass (Grand Rapids: Eerdmans, 2002), p. 89.

God. By emphasizing the communal aspects of election, Edwards muted the emphasis, prominent in Calvin as well as in the later Reformed tradition, on the election of individuals. The union with Christ in election is inescapably social: it is becoming part of the society of believers who as one body are chosen for fellowship with the divine society of the Trinity. As the next chapter will show, this emphasis on the intrinsically social nature of human redemption also provided a check on the individual, experiential focus of the revivals of Edwards's day.

There are also strong resonances, once again, between Edwards's Christology and that of the Spiritual Brethren. Like the fifth-century christological school in Alexandria, the Spiritual Brethren tended to emphasize the unity of Christ's person and affirm the divine Logos as the subject of all that Christ did and suffered. Richard Sibbes declared that

> when he died, God died; when he was crucified, God was crucified. If he had been two persons, he had died but in one person, and the other had not died. Now, being but one person, though two natures, whatsoever was done in the [one] nature, the person did it according to the other nature.[108]

Sibbes boldly entreated his readers to "think of God born of a virgin, of God lying in the cradle, sucking the breast!"[109] The Sibbesians' practical concern that Christians "may go securely to God our brother, to him that is of one nature with us" overrode worries about theological precision. It was clear that the center of their faith was the Christ "who took our flesh upon him for that purpose, that he might have experimental knowledge of our infirmities and weaknesses, and from that he might be the more sweet, and kind, and gentle to us."[110]

Likewise, the centrality of the notion of union in Edwards's theology as a whole encouraged the development of strongly Alexandrian themes in his Christology. The Son of God so loved the human nature that he desired "a most near and close union with it, something like the union in the persons of the Trinity, nearer than there can be between any two distinct [beings]."[111] In his sermon on "The Excellency of

108. Sibbes, *Complete Works,* 5, p. 481.
109. Sibbes, *Complete Works,* 5, p. 484.
110. Sibbes, *Complete Works,* 5, p. 480.
111. Works, 13, p. 329 (no. 183).

Christ," he marveled at how "the divine majesty and holiness . . . are attributes of one in our nature," and how the "human excellencies of Christ . . . are in so great a person as the eternal Son of God."[112] In a sermon on Romans 2:10 Edwards averred that "one end of God's assuming a human body" is

> that the saints might see God with bodily eyes; that they might see him, not only in the understanding, but in every way of seeing of which the human nature is capable; that we might see God as a divine person as we see one another.[113]

As "a divine person," Christ answers the human inclination to have "complacence in someone as a friend, to love and delight in someone that may be conversed with as a companion."[114] God constitutes in Jesus a life that makes possible a new degree of union between God and humanity.

Christ was for Edwards not only the main actor in the divine work of human redemption. He is also the perfect instantiation of the divine goal in this work: consenting union between God and humanity. Edwards's relational ontology encouraged an understanding of union that was based on affective as well as ontological ties. In the union of the Trinity, "The Son is one with the Father in nature and also in love."[115] Edwards then drew an explicit parallel between the union of the immanent Trinity and that of the incarnation: "This union of Christ to us, in like manner, consists in two things, viz. union of nature, and love, as his union with God did."[116] In fact, within Edwards's non-substantialist ontology, a union "of love" is constitutive of the ontological reality of a union "of nature." Christ's unique existence in two natures is not an example of "possessive individualism," so that his divine and human natures should be understood "on the model of the ownership of property."[117] Rather, the union of natures in him is dis-

112. Works, 19, p. 590.
113. Dwight, *Works of President Edwards*, 8, p. 265.
114. Works, 19, p. 589.
115. Works, 14, p. 402.
116. Works, 14, p. 403.
117. Taylor, *Sources of the Self*, p. 196. Taylor credits Brough Macpherson for the term *possessive individualism*. Edwards used the metaphor of possession to great effect, however, in describing the results of the believer's union with Christ. See Works, 13, pp. 183-84 (no. ff).

played in relations of perfect love both to God and to humanity. As Stephen Daniel points out,

> the Christ that Edwards describes is not properly an individual —
> at least not in the way that modernity defines an individual as the
> subject of predication. Both divine and human, Christ subverts
> ontologies (including emanationist theories) in which substan-
> tialistic individuality becomes the mark of existential legitimacy.
> Christ's existence emphasizes his deference to others, instead of
> his own individuality. That act of self-displacement is at the heart
> of the ontology of supposition that permeates all of Edwards' phi-
> losophy.[118]

The incarnation is the supreme "act of self-displacement," in which God's love for humanity forms the basis of their "thorough union": "there is no other way of different spirits' being thus united, but by love."[119] Christ "so dearly loved [sinners] that they were looked upon by God as one and the same with him."[120]

Since the incarnation was for Edwards the perfect instantiation of loving consent between God and humanity, it is not surprising that he gave the Holy Spirit a central role in bringing about this incarnate union:

> As the union of believers with Christ be by the indwelling of the
> Spirit of Christ in them, so it may be worthy to be considered,
> whether or no the union of the divine with the human nature of
> Christ ben't by the Spirit of the Logos dwelling in him after a pecu-
> liar manner and without measure. Perhaps there is no other way of
> God's dwelling in a creature but by his Spirit.[121]

Proposing this distinctive role for the Spirit in the incarnation strengthened the correspondences Edwards discerned among the three types of spiritual union. Within the life of the Trinity, the Holy Spirit is the bond of loving union between the Father and Son. Similarly, in the

---

118. Stephen H. Daniel, *The Philosophy of Jonathan Edwards: A Study in Divine Semiotics* (Bloomington: University of Indiana Press, 1994), p. 197.

119. Works, 13, p. 463 (no. 398).

120. Works, 13, p. 165 (no. b).

121. Works, 13, p. 528 (no. 487).

incarnation, the human Jesus "hath communion with the Logos in the love which the Father hath to him as his only begotten Son."[122] Thus "the Holy Spirit is the bond of union by which the human nature of Christ is united to the divine, so as to be one person."[123] Edwards protected Jesus' uniqueness by insisting that

> The Spirit of God never dwelt in any other creature in anywise as it dwells in the man Christ Jesus; for in him he dwells without measure, on which account also he is called Christ, or Anointed.[124]

The Holy Spirit is also the foundation of the union between God and the saints. All "the communion of the creatures with God or with one another in God, seems to be by the Holy Ghost. 'Tis by this that believers have communion with Christ."[125] In sum, the Holy Spirit is "the bond of perfectness by which God, Jesus Christ and the church are united together."[126] As both the means of incarnation and the means of the ontological transformation of the saints, the agency of the Holy Spirit is at the center of the work of redemption.

Like John Owen, one of the Spiritual Brethren, Edwards saw Christ's incarnate life "as continually empowered, comforted, and sanctified by the Holy Spirit."[127] As Edwards declared, "all that was divine in the man Christ Jesus is from the Spirit of God — divine power, and divine knowledge, and divine will, and divine acts."[128] In Owen's theology, this emphasis on the role of the Spirit helped protect the genuine humanity of Jesus Christ: by the power of the Spirit, Jesus' humanity was

122. Works, 13, p. 529 (no. 487).

123. Works, 18, p. 411 (no. 764b).

124. Dwight, *Works of President Edwards*, 9, p. 261.

125. Works, 13, p. 529 (no. 487). Cf. John Cotton's conviction that the Holy Ghost gives "such an offer as all the World cannot give, he out-bids the World, and even promises Fellowship with the Father and the Son, or Eternal Life." *First John Generall*, p. 189.

126. Works, 13, pp. 529-30 (no. 487).

127. Alan Spence, "Christ's Humanity and Ours: John Owen," in C. Schwöbel and C. E. Gunton, eds., *Persons Divine and Human* (Edinburgh: T. & T. Clark, 1991), p. 75. This article is cited in Stephen Holmes, *God of Grace and God of Glory*, p. 136. Though both Owen and Edwards gave a large place to the Holy Spirit in their Christologies, Holmes overplays the similarities between them.

128. Works, 18, p. 413 (no. 766). Edwards cited Owen's work on the Holy Spirit in *Misc.*, no. 1047.

gradually perfected over the course of his earthly life. As Owen declared, Christ's "growth in grace and wisdom was the peculiar work of the Holy Ghost; for as the faculties of his mind were gradually enlarged, he was filled with grace for actual obedience."[129] In Owen's Christology, "the act of the Son in assuming the human nature into personal union with himself"[130] is the immediate cause of the incarnation. But the historical unfolding of Christ's life in ever increasing union with God was the work of the Holy Spirit. "In the representation of things new to his human nature, the wisdom of it was objectively increased; and in new trials he learned experimentally the new exercise of grace. And this was the constant work of the Spirit, who dwelt in him fully and without measure."[131] As in the case of ordinary believers, the effect on Christ of the Spirit's indwelling was gradual and progressive.

By contrast, in Edwards's Christology the work of the Holy Spirit was conformed to the example of the immanent Trinity, more than to the experience of believers. The Holy Spirit is the immediate agent of the incarnation: as in the case of the union between the Father and the Son, the Spirit is the "person that acted as the principle of union between the manhood of Christ and the person of the Son."[132] This distinctive role for the Spirit fueled a tendency to describe the incarnate union in ahistorical ways, with the result that the humanity assumed by the Word seems to have no need for growth in wisdom or stature (Luke 2:40). Christ's conception by the Holy Spirit guaranteed Christ's perfect holiness from the start: "seeing it was the immediate work of infinite, omnipotent, holiness itself, the thing wrought must needs be perfectly holy, without any unholiness." "Christ was conceived in the womb, and of the substance of a mother that was one of the corrupt

---

129. John Owen, *The Holy Spirit, His Gifts and Power: Exposition of the Spirit's Name, Nature, Personality, Dispensation, Operations and Effects*, abridged by George Burder (Grand Rapids: Kregel Publications, 1960), p. 96.

130. Owen, *The Holy Spirit*, p. 93. Owen, unlike Edwards, stopped short of attributing the incarnation itself to the work of the Holy Spirit.

131. Owen, *The Holy Spirit*, p. 96. Cf. Kathryn Tanner, *Jesus, Humanity and the Trinity*, p. 27: "God's making the humanity of Jesus God's own is an all or nothing affair, but what is assumed and its effects on human life are not. . . . The purification and elevation of the human in Christ is a historical process because the humanity assumed by the Word is historical."

132. *Works*, 18, p. 334 (no. 709).

race of mankind," but "the Holy Ghost, which is the omnipotent holiness of God itself . . . prevail[ed] over any ill influence, that the nature of the mother might be supposed to have."[133] Though "the immediate seed of Mary, a mean person," was "liable to the guilt and pollution, and so to the misery and damnation, that comes by the fall," the power of the Holy Spirit prevented "the man Jesus" from becoming "one of the corrupt race of mankind."[134] Edwards occasionally hinted that the humanity assumed by the Word was in "its mean, defaced, broken, infirm, ruined state,"[135] but the distinctive role of the Spirit in the incarnation encouraged modeling Christ's holiness on the already perfect holiness of the Trinity: "The Holy Ghost is not called the Holy Ghost or Holy Spirit so often in Scripture merely because the creature's holiness is from him, but chiefly because God's holiness consists in him."[136] Christ, in whom the Spirit dwells "without measure" (John 3:34), seems to possess a perfect holiness from the start. There is little in Edwards's treatment of the incarnation to suggest that Christ was "made perfect" over the course of his life "through what he suffered" (Heb. 5:8-9).

Likewise, the Holy Spirit protected the incarnate Christ from the limitations of human ignorance. As "a bond of union between . . . the divine Logos and . . . the human nature of Christ," the Holy Spirit ensures that "the knowledge of the one is the knowledge of the other."[137] The "communion of understanding" between the Logos and the human nature of Christ "is such that there is the same consciousness."[138] Thus "the man Christ Jesus was conscious of the glory and blessedness the Logos had in the knowledge and enjoyment of the Father before the world was as remembering of it."[139] Even on the cross, Christ's di-

133. Works, 18, p. 414 (no. 767).

134. Works, 18, pp. 416-17 (no. 769). See Ava Chamberlain, "The Immaculate Ovum: Jonathan Edwards and the Construction of the Female Body," *William and Mary Quarterly* 3rd Series, 57, no. 2 (April 2000): 289-322.

135. Works, 18, p. 208 (no. 664b).

136. *Misc.*, no. 1047.

137. Works, 18, p. 413 (no. 766).

138. Works, 13, p. 529 (no. 487).

139. Works, 13, p. 529 (no. 487). Though Edwards elsewhere acknowledged that "'twas impossible that the man Christ Jesus should remember this as it was in the Deity," since human understanding cannot comprehend the ideas of "the Infinite Mind." Works, 13, p. 341 (no. 205).

vine knowledge rendered it "impossible that Christ should have this sense, that God was really angry with him and that he was the object of his hatred, and it was impossible that he should utterly despair of ever being delivered from that doleful state."[140] Rather than dramatizing God's continuing, gracious involvement in creaturely existence, the role of the Spirit in much of Edwards's treatment of the incarnation served to exempt the incarnate Christ from the full frailties of the human condition.

The presence of God in the frailties of the human condition is much more in evidence in Edwards's account of the Spirit's work in the lives of the saints. Through the power of the Spirit, "Christ brings God and man to each other, and actually unites them together." But this is done "by various steps and degrees, which terminate in the highest step, in that consummation of actual union, which he will accomplish at the end of the world."[141] The ultimate benefit of the work of redemption is saints' participation in "the infinite intimacy between the Father and the Son."[142] But as the next chapter will indicate, the road to that perfect communion is a bumpy one, marked by "recurring patterns of spiritual declension and revival, of backsliding and reformation."[143]

Despite its problems, Edwards's trinitarian treatment of election and incarnation concatenated what were for him the three fundamental "spiritual unions — of the persons of the Trinity, of the two natures of Christ, of Christ and the minds of saints."[144] Edwards's thought reveals *union* to be an extremely elastic and adaptable term in Christian theology. While Edwards found its paradigm within the immanent Godhead, the term ranged widely across his theological reflections. *Union* informed his understanding of Christ's unique existence, and the significance of his suffering. It provided a framework for portraying the devastation of sin beyond the Reformed mainstay of disobedience to divine law. It helped Edwards articulate the process and ultimate goal of human redemption and the centrality of the Spirit's role in it. It guided his vision of communal life in the church and in heaven.

140. Works, 13, p. 402 (no. 321b).

141. Works, 18, p. 422 (no. 773).

142. Works, 18, p. 109 (no. 571).

143. Helen P. Westra, "Divinity's Design: Edwards and the History of the Work of Revival," in *Edwards in Our Time,* p. 137.

144. Works, 13, p. 330 (no. 184).

The term *union* summed up for Edwards the dynamic, relational beauty of God's being and work.

Together, the union within the Godhead, the union of God and humanity in the incarnate Christ, and the union of human believers with God and with each other provide an irenic and capacious précis of Christian theology. Whether the Godhead is portrayed in terms of different persons or relations or modes of being, it is about the union of irreducible distinctness within God. Whether incarnation is described as a metaphysical junction of distinct natures or the transformation of a human life by the indwelling of the Spirit, it is about the union between God and humanity in Jesus Christ. Whether Christ's atonement is seen as God's solidarity with a hurting world, or God's reconciliation with alienated creatures, or God's redeeming humanity from the bondage of evil,[145] it is about the restoration and reaffirmation of creation's union with God. Despite the varying institutional recipes for ecclesial community, church is about Christians in union with God, with each other, and with creation.

Agreeing on a general term will not obviate the need for theological arguments about the best way to construe *union* in each of these cases. In human communities, calls for union can be a cover for oppressive hegemony. In the theological realm, too much stress on union raises questions about divine freedom and creaturely integrity. But *union,* at least in an Edwardsean sense, rules out strictly individualist understandings of salvation and monist understandings of God, by affirming the excellence of irreducible difference-in-communion. The continuing role of the Spirit in establishing this communion in the "one holy and happy society" of believers will be the focus of the next chapter.

145. William Placher has described the cross of Christ in these three ways. See "The Cross of Jesus Christ as Solidarity, Reconciliation, and Redemption," in W. Brueggemann and G. Stroup, eds., *Many Voices, One God: Being Faithful in a Pluralistic World* (Louisville: Westminster/John Knox, 1998), pp. 155-66.

Chapter 5

THE TRINITY AND PASTORAL PERPLEXITIES

There is scarce anything that can be conceived or expressed about the degree of the happiness of the saints in heaven, the degree of intimacy of union and communion with Christ and fullness of enjoyment of God, but what the consideration of the nature and circumstances of our redemption by Christ do allow us and encourage us to hope for.

EDWARDS, "Miscellanies," no. 741

The Spirit of God in Northampton

Unlike those that preceded it, this chapter is concerned primarily, not with the Trinity's eternal nature or past actions, but with the phase of God's great work of redemption that was contemporaneous with Edwards's life, the conversion and sanctification of human sinners. This chronological shift is also reflected in the trinitarian economy: while creation highlighted the role of the Father, and election and incarnation that of the Son, the work of conversion and sanctification was especially attributed to the Holy Spirit. The spiritual fruits of conversion and sanctification were a wellspring for Edwards's deepest hopes: in them he found adumbrations of millennial harmonies, and of the saints' final glorification in heaven, that perfect "world of love." The perplexities of discerning the Spirit's presence in actual sinners also revealed a painful divide between his theological vision of harmonious spiritual union and his own pastoral experiences of bitterness, distrust, and ultimately disunion. The centrality of the Trinity for Edwards's understanding of conversion and sanctification illumines both his great hopes and deep discouragements regarding the progress of re-demption in his own day.

As is characteristic of Edwards's published writings, his extended re-flections on true sainthood — beginning with *A Faithful Narrative, Dis-tinguishing Marks* and *Some Thoughts on the Revival,* and culminating in *Religious Affections* and *The Nature of True Virtue* — do not abound with explicit references to the Trinity. What marks them as trinitarian is the persistent identification of the Holy Spirit with divine love and the pervasiveness of the core trinitarian vocabulary of love, consent, and union. Conversion, justification, sanctification, and glorification for Edwards, like creation, election, and incarnation, had their roots in the eternal consent and excellency of the immanent Trinity and the loving counsels of the Trinity regarding human redemption. In all these phases of the great work of redemption, God's love and desire for spiri-tual union flow outward, emanating beyond the boundaries of the Godhead. But conversion and sanctification also mark the point of remanation, where the love infused in the saints flows back to God and each other, a process that reaches its culmination in glorification.[1]

Though he used a variety of metaphors to portray the Spirit's re-demptive work, love was the touchstone. For Edwards, this love simply *is* the Holy Spirit: "'tis in our partaking of the Holy Ghost that we have communion with the Father and Son and with Christians: this is the common excellency and delight in which they all [are] united."[2] Within the immanent Trinity, the "Holy Spirit is the act of God between the Father and the Son, infinitely loving and delighting in each other."[3] When this disposition to acts of love and delight in God is infused in human persons by the indwelling of the Holy Spirit, they are enabled

---

1. C. C. Goen, ed., *The Great Awakening,* The Works of Jonathan Edwards, vol. 4 (New Haven: Yale University Press, 1972), p. 293. Cf. Sibbes, "The Holy Ghost . . . breeds love to God again, shewing the love of God to us, and thereupon he is called the Spirit of love." Geoffrey F. Nuttall, *The Holy Spirit in Puritan Faith and Experience* (Oxford: Blackwell, 1946), p. 14, has contended that "a large influence in directing the Puritans' attention to the doctrine of the Holy Spirit was the preaching of Richard Sibbes."

2. Works, 13, p. 448 (no. 376).

3. Works, 13, p. 260 (no. 94).

to partake of God's own "excellence and beauty; that is of holiness, which consists in love."[4] As the culminating chapters in Edwards's larger trinitarian story of redemption, the work of the Spirit in conversion, sanctification, and glorification is to unite saints to God and to each other with the same love that unites the Father and Son.[5]

The infusion of the Holy Spirit produces true virtue in the saints. In his great treatise by this name, Edwards defined the nature of true virtue within the Godhead in an explicitly trinitarian way as "the mutual love and friendship which subsists eternally and necessarily between the several persons in the Godhead, or that infinitely strong propensity there is in these divine persons one to another."[6] With the Trinity as a paradigm, Edwards emphatically rejected any notion of virtue that neglected love of God or subscribed to some narrow, private system of affection. The sanctifying work of the Spirit is to increase "benevolent affection or propensity of heart towards Being in general."[7] Just as the "mutual love and friendship" within the Trinity flow out to creatures, so the "universal benevolence" in the saint flows out to "particular beings," so that he "delights in the appearance of union with his fellow creatures."[8] The disordered, narrow love of sinners is transformed by the work of the Spirit into a delight in the loveliness of God that spills over into love for fellow creatures. As Sibbes noted, "those that are led with the Spirit of God . . . are like him; they have a communicative diffusive goodness that loves to spread itself."[9]

Before their infusion by the Holy Spirit, the saints are empty vessels waiting to be filled. In his retrospective account of his own conversion, Edwards wrote of his experience of being filled with the Spirit:

4. Works, 6, p. 364. Cf. John Preston: the Holy Spirit "shewes you the beauty and excellency of Christ, it shewes you what grace is, and makes you love it." *The Breast-Plate of Faith and Love* (London, 1637), p. 197.

5. Works, 2, p. 201: "The Spirit of God so dwells in the hearts of the saints, that he there, as a seed or spring of life, exerts and communicates himself, in this his sweet and divine nature, making the soul a partaker of God's beauty and Christ's joy, so that the saint has truly fellowship with the Father, and with his Son Jesus Christ, in thus having the communion or participation of the Holy Ghost."

6. Works, 8, p. 557.

7. Works, 8, p. 557.

8. Works, 4, p. 422.

9. Sibbes, *Complete Works*, 6, p. 113.

> God in the communications of his Holy Spirit, has appeared as an
> infinite fountain of divine glory and sweetness; being full and suf-
> ficient to fill and satisfy the soul: pouring forth itself in sweet com-
> munications, like the sun in its glory, sweetly and pleasantly diffus-
> ing light and Life.[10]

With the infusion of "divine glory and sweetness" come a new desire
and aptitude for union with God. The love and esteem between Christ
and believers becomes *mutual,* for true consent requires "a mutual act
of both, that each should receive the other, as actively joining themselves one to another."[11] In his own enduring love for Sarah Pierpont,
Edwards found the closest analogy to the intimacy and beauty of the
mutual consent between Christ and the saints. In a notebook entry
written while they were courting, Edwards noted, "Therefore when we
feel love to anyone of the other sex, 'tis a good way to think of the love
of Christ to an holy and beautiful soul."[12] Like the union between lovers, Christ's union with believers, though still marked by deference, is
forged through mutual love, not domination:

> he don't force them, but sweetly inclines their wills to the most ex-
> cellent things and to their own happiness. He overcomes them by
> his love; he governs them by infusing his love into them, and so in-
> clining them to obedience. His dominion over his people is by mu-
> tual love and esteem.[13]

Believers' active consent to their union with Christ, begun at conversion, increases in intensity and constancy with spiritual maturity. In
redescribing Sarah's exemplary spiritual experience Edwards wrote of
her being "swallowed up in a kind of glow of Christ's love, coming
down from Christ's heart in heaven," and her heart "all flowing out in
love to him; so that there seemed to be a constant flowing and

10. Works, 16, p. 801.

11. Sereno E. Dwight, ed., *The Works of President Edwards with a Memoir of His Life,* 10
vols. (New York: S. Converse, 1829-30), 5, p. 364.

12. Works, 13, p. 333 (no. 189). Cf. John Cotton, "If the Creature can fill and ravish us
with servile delights, how much more can the Persons of the blessed Trinity one another, yea and us also?" *First John Generall,* p. 11.

13. Works, 14, p. 427.

reflowing from heart to heart."[14] The Holy Spirit is the agent both of the pouring forth of God's "sweet communications" to the soul, and of their remanation to God in the soul's active consent. As Thomas Schafer has noted, the love that converted and sanctified persons display towards God "is simply his own love reflected and returned to him."[15]

Because the affections were for Edwards "the very life and soul of all true religion,"[16] he gave the will primacy over the intellect in conversion and sanctification.

> Divine love, or charity, is represented as the sum of all the religion of heaven, and that wherein mainly the religion of the church in its more perfect state on earth shall consist . . . ; and therefore the higher this holy affection is raised in the church of God, or in a gracious soul, the more excellent and perfect is the state of the church, or a particular soul.[17]

His voluntarist understanding of conversion and sanctification was a fitting reflection of the role of the Spirit within the Godhead: God possesses "understanding and will, which will is the same with the Holy Ghost."[18] The focus of the Spirit's operation in human persons made in God's image is likewise the will, and so works traditionally ascribed to the Spirit, such as conversion and sanctification, would on the terms of Edwards's trinitarian logic be a matter of the will more than the intellect.

The redemptive work of the Spirit is to indwell the soul and create a new habit of love and holiness. As a new active principle seated in the will, the Holy Spirit elicits holy love for God and acts of love toward others, culminating in the saint's glorification. Using an argument parallel to the one he would later employ in *The Nature of True Virtue,* Edwards asked how

14. Works, 4, p. 332.

15. Thomas A. Schafer, "Jonathan Edwards and Justification by Faith," *Church History* 20 (December 1951): 62. See also Sang Hyun Lee, *The Philosophical Theology of Jonathan Edwards* (Princeton: Princeton University Press, 1988), pp. 231-41.

16. Works, 4, p. 297.

17. Works, 2, p. 299.

18. Works, 18, p. 359 (no. 732).

a man that has no true grace within him shall begin to exercise it: before he begins to exercise it, he must have some of it. How shall [he] act virtuously the first time? how came he by that virtue which he then acted?[19]

His conclusion was that true virtue cannot be acquired through the exercise of natural principles. The springs of all outward acts lie in inner dispositions, and so those with "no true grace within" cannot perform truly gracious acts. The only remedy is an infusion of grace by the Holy Spirit. "Those that deny infusion by the Holy Spirit," declared Edwards, "must necessarily deny the Spirit to do anything at all."[20] This includes even the work of assisting "the natural powers," which was traditionally seen as an alternative to the view of infusion. According to Edwards, "the part that the Spirit doth, how little soever that be, is infused."[21] The Spirit dwells as a vital principle in the human heart, bestowing an inner disposition to loving consent to "Being in general."

Edwards's frequent assertion in *Religious Affections* that the Holy Spirit "communicates himself to the soul in his own proper nature"[22] evidently raised some eyebrows in the theological community. In an unpublished letter, he responded to criticisms that his view implied a communication of God's *essence* to the elect, thus deifying them. For one steeped in the theological tradition of divine simplicity, this would be an obvious conclusion. For if God is simple, there is no distinction to be made between God's being or essence, and God's mode of being, or nature. Edwards's response to this criticism once again reveals his distance from that tradition:

19. Works, 13, p. 242 (no. 73).

20. Works, 13, p. 171 (no. p). Van Mastricht and Turretin set an example for Edwards in their use of the notion of infusion. Turretin described sanctification as "a moral and internal infusion" of the Spirit, *Institutio,* XVI.iii.6 (morali ac interna infusione); similarly, van Mastricht viewed regeneration as "a physical act powerfully infusing spiritual life in the soul." *Treatise on Regeneration* (New Haven, n.d.), p. 21.

21. Works, 13, p. 171 (no. p). Cf. John Owen: the work of the Holy Spirit is "a real, internal, powerful, physical work. . . . He doth not make us holy only by persuading us so to be." Owen, *The Holy Spirit, His Gifts and Power: Exposition of the Spirit's Name, Nature, Personality, Dispensation, Operations and Effects,* abridged by George Burder (Grand Rapids: Kregel Publications, 1960), p. 387.

22. See e.g., Works, 2, pp. 201, 233, 236, 237, 392.

I confess, my skill in the English tongue does not extend so far as to discern the great impropriety of the word as I have used it. The word "nature" is not used only to signify the essence of a thing, but is used very variously.[23]

In referring to the Holy Spirit's nature, Edwards claimed that he was not intending to denote the being of the entire Godhead, but the Spirit's "peculiar beauty and glory," namely that love and holiness which is "eminently his character."[24] He denied outright that the saints partake of God's essence so as to be "'Godded' with God, and 'Christed' with Christ, according to the abominable and blasphemous language and notions of some heretics."[25] Yet Edwards's rhetoric concerning the Holy Spirit frequently muddied this nice distinction between nature and essence: the Holy Spirit is "the spirit of divine love, in whom the very essence of God, as it were, all flows out or is breathed forth in love."[26] For Edwards, there was no final distinction between the person of the Holy Spirit and "the good, the holiness, the love, the excellency which is in God."

While there appears to be a distinction in Edwards's thought between the Father's primordial knowledge of the divine essence and the "reflex act of knowledge" by which the Son is generated, there is no

---

23. Works, 8, p. 639.

24. Works, 8, p. 639. In Works, 13, p. 462 (no. 396), Edwards posited a distinction between nature and essence. The word *spirit* can signify either "the divine essence (as sometimes it is, as when we read that God is a Spirit)" or the holy "temper and disposition or affection of God," which for Edwards "is no other than infinite love." He insisted that the "divine nature spoken of, II Pet. 1:4, that we are made partakers of through the gospel," is "the divine temper and affection," rather than the divine essence.

25. Works, 2, p. 203. The leader of the familists, Henrik Niclaes, claimed that the true believer "is godded with God and co-deified with him, and that God is hominified with him." Quoted in William K. B. Stoever, 'A Faire and Easie Way to Heaven': Covenant Theology and Antinomianism in Early Massachusetts (Middletown, Conn.: Wesleyan University Press, 1978), pp. 162-63.

26. Works, 8, p. 370. Turretin and van Mastricht were careful not to suggest that the Holy Spirit becomes the immediate possession of the saints. In this connection, van Mastricht distinguished between "the Spirit giving" (Spiritum dantem) and "the spirit given" (spiritum datum). Treatise on Regeneration, p. 23. What is infused in conversion and sanctification is the gift of "spiritual power," not the third person of the Trinity. Edwards's identification of the Holy Spirit with love made it difficult for him to observe this distinction.

such distinction regarding the Holy Spirit: "God loves Himself only in a reflex act."[27] Edwards identified God's eternal disposition to love the primordial divine essence with the external expression of this disposition in the Godhead, namely the breathing forth of the Holy Spirit. In this breathing forth, the boundaries between the actions of the Godhead *ad intra* and *ad extra* are blurred: "the excellent brightness and fullness of God" is "spread abroad, diffused and as it were enlarged"[28] both within the Godhead and outside it. God's reflexive self-love

> is the eternal and most perfect and essential act of the divine nature, wherein the Godhead acts to an infinite degree and in the most perfect manner possible. The deity becomes all act, and the divine essence itself flows out & is as it were breathed forth in Love & Joy.[29]

The abiding principle of love in the saints is, despite Edwards's disclaimers, "the divine essence flowing out and breathed forth in God's infinite love to and delight in Himself."[30]

Where Edwards's portrayal of the Godhead loses its intratrinitarian sociality, there is a tendency to describe the Spirit's work of union between the elect and God in monistic rather than social categories:

> God's respect to the creature, in the whole, unites with his respect to himself. Both regards are like two lines which seem at the beginning to be separate, but aim finally to meet in one, both being directed to the same center. And as to the good of the creature itself, if viewed in its whole duration, and infinite progression, it must be viewed as infinite; and so not only being some communication of God's glory, but as coming nearer and nearer to the same thing in its infinite fullness. The nearer anything comes to infinite, *the nearer it comes to an identity with God.*[31]

---

27. Helm, *Trinity*, p. 130.

28. *Misc.*, no. 1082. Though later in this entry Edwards treated in a more parallel fashion "the proceeding and generation of the Son and the proceeding and breathing forth of the Holy Spirit," both *ad intra* and *ad extra*.

29. Helm, *Trinity*, p. 108.

30. Helm, *Trinity*, p. 118.

31. Works, 8, p. 459, emphasis added.

Here Edwards appeared to forget his youthful insight that "there must be more than a unity in infinite and eternal essence, otherwise the goodness of God can have no perfect exercise."[32] In this passage, his vision of the union effected by the Holy Spirit between the saints and God sounds perilously close to being "Godded with God."[33]

Despite his theological imprecisions and inconsistencies, Edwards's vision of the elect's spiritual union with God did finally elude the threat of monism by emphasis on the social analogy for the Trinity: the saint's union with God comes "nearer and nearer to that strictness and perfection of union which there is between the Father and the Son."[34] By letting the two trinitarian models complement each other, Edwards was able to show that the union with God forged by the Spirit's indwelling love is a *social* union, in which the identities of the saints and the members of the divine Trinity are preserved.

Conversion and Holy Practice

"This town never was so full of love, nor so full of joy, nor so full of distress as it has lately been," Edwards exclaimed, regarding the 1734 awakening in Northampton. Though in distress over their sinful ways, the new converts had "their hearts filled with love to God and Christ," and seemed "to be united in dear love and affection one to another, and to have a love to all mankind."[35] This love for God and each other was the work of the Holy Spirit, the agent and exemplification of divine love.

32. Works, 13, p. 263 (no. 96).

33. Paul Ramsey, ed., *Ethical Writings*, The Works of Jonathan Edwards, vol. 8 (New Haven: Yale University Press, 1989), p. 640, attempts to come to Edwards's rescue by interpreting this assertion of the saints' "identity with God" so as to deny a metaphysical identity: "the creature comes forever nearer and nearer to the good, the holiness, the love, the excellency which is in God. This is not the same thing as approach to metaphysical or personal identity of nature in the sense of essences or being. . . . The Holy Spirit acts in creatures in his own proper nature as he acts *ad intra;* i.e. he kindles the same love, the same good, in human hearts. Progress in heaven can be [only] asymptotic; monism will never be." Yet Ramsey's interpretation does not take account of the extraordinary power of the psychological analogy in Edwards's trinitarian thought. For Edwards, the Holy Spirit simply is "the good, the holiness, the love, the excellency which is in God."

34. Works, 8, p. 443.

35. Works, 4, p. 104.

The fruits of the Spirit's work were in Edwards's view profoundly relational: conversion is more than the bestowal of a private religious experience; sanctification is more than the restoration of personal holiness. The Spirit's principal soteriological role was the outpouring of love, consent, and union.

Given the profoundly social dimensions of his view of the Spirit, for Edwards experience of redemption could not be chiefly a matter of intuition or individual perception. His well-known appeals to Locke's "new simple idea" and his analogy between having a "new kind of perception or spiritual sensation" and enjoying "the sweet taste of honey,"[36] should not be overplayed. As Wayne Proudfoot notes, "The new sensation, and the analogy with the deliverances of the other senses, plays no epistemic role in Edwards's criteria for distinguishing genuine from spurious affections." Given the impressive human capacity for self-deception, there is no guarantee that "sincere first-person reports of a new sensation or perception" are authentic evidence of the Spirit's work.[37] Instead, ardent worship and ardent Christian practice are the truest indications of the Spirit's presence, and the standard by which Edwards judged the New England revivals.

On this side of the eschaton, even the saints are still sinners, reflecting and returning God's perfect love in only a dim and fragmented way. In his roles as pastor and religious psychologist, Edwards probed this remanation of love in all its human ambiguities. Within the triune life, the Spirit is a perfect, continuous stream of joy and love. On earth, the outpouring of the Spirit is instead a "surprising work of God" that refreshes particular places and seasons. Therefore the saving work of the Holy Spirit in Christian persons and communities does not exhibit a smooth progression to holy love. Both in human individuals and in the church universal the Spirit moves by fits and starts. The periods of doubt and spiritual deadness afflicting individual believers and particular churches are a microcosm of the declines and setbacks in the history of the work of redemption as a whole. Discerning the movements of the Spirit thus requires ongoing attentiveness to both one's own

36. Works, 2, pp. 205-6.
37. Wayne Proudfoot, "Perception and Love in *Religious Affections*," in *Jonathan Edwards's Writings: Text, Context, Interpretation,* ed. Stephen J. Stein (Bloomington: Indiana University Press, 1996), pp. 122-23.

heart and the larger social and political events of the day. The revival-declension-revival pattern[38] that Edwards witnessed in the Connecticut River valley in the 1730s and 1740s was only a notable instance of the more general *modus operandi* of the Spirit. As Michael Crawford notes, Edwards "made the phenomenon of the revival the key element in the drama of redemption. He conceived of revivals as the engine that drives redemption history."[39]

Of course, the centrality of revivals in the work of redemption also implies the centrality of gospel ministers to God's redemptive design. Edwards supposed that

> the deliverance of the Christian church will be preceded by God's raising up a number of eminent ministers that shall more plainly and fervently and effectually preach the gospel than it had been before, and reprove his own church, and show her her errors, and also shall convince gainsayers, and shall thoroughly detect the errors of the false church.[40]

This was clearly a role to which Edwards considered himself divinely appointed. Being a channel of the Spirit's work in "sweetly and pleasantly diffusing light and Life" called for pastoral harshness at times. As preacher, according to Helen Westra, "Edwards was by turns brusque, benevolent, belittling, bold, and beseeching toward his listeners as he variously delivered exhortations, jeremiads, and hell-fire sermons." In his sermons, Edwards consciously aimed to serve as an agent of the Spirit to "open his parishioners' eyes and ears and move them individually and collectively."[41]

Edwards did not eschew a modified preparationism, in which, "except in very extraordinary cases," God prepared the heart of the sinner "for the receiving of Christ by a sense of his sin and misery, and a despair of help in himself and in all others."[42] While conversion could be

38. Helen P. Westra, "Divinity's Design: Edwards and the History of the Work of Revival," in *Edwards in Our Time: Jonathan Edwards and the Shaping of American Religion,* ed. Sang Hyun Lee and Allen C. Guelzo (Grand Rapids: Eerdmans, 1999), p. 138.

39. Michael J. Crawford, *Seasons of Grace: Colonial New England's Revival Tradition in Its British Context* (New York: Oxford University Press, 1991), p. 132.

40. Works, 18, p. 518 (no. 810).

41. Westra, "Divinity's Design," p. 132.

42. Works, 13, p. 400 (no. 317).

"wrought in a moment," it involved "preparatory circumstances to introduce it,"[43] especially the means of grace provided by structured life in Christian community. Means such as attending worship, praying privately, or studying Scripture were not in themselves gracious, but they "cause those effects in our souls whereby there is an opportunity for grace to act. . . . God don't see meet to infuse grace, where there is no opportunity for it to act."[44] Means of grace are to be used gratefully, but Edwards refused to ascribe to a fixed morphology for the Spirit's work or its human response. Recognizing that "The methods of grace are as obscure as those of nature,"[45] he insisted that "The goodness of [a] person's state is not chiefly to be judged of by any exactness of steps, and method of experiences."[46]

Edwards's sense of the complexity and ambiguity of the Spirit's presence seems to have grown with pastoral experience. While as a young pastor in the early 1730s Edwards could argue that "A false notion gives no opportunity for grace to act,"[47] another decade of ministry convinced him that "there may be true exercises of grace . . . that may be founded on an error, that which is not agreeable to the truth, and that the erroneous practice founded on that error may be the occasion of those true and holy exercises which are from the Spirit of God."[48] In a notebook Edwards began in the 1740s on "things to be particularly enquired into and written upon," he signaled his interest in how "the Exercises of Holiness & obedience in this world prepare Persons for Heaven," but immediately followed with the observation that "This is not absolutely necessary because God bestows Heaven on Elect Infants. They are united to an Head that has had a Trial & to a Body that has had a Trial."[49] The Spirit's work of union is finally not dependent on correct doctrinal knowledge or moral exercises. There is a

43. Works, 13, p. 173 (no. r).

44. Works, 18, p. 84 (no. 539). Cf. John Cotton, "Be careful to nourish him; do not starve this Guest, neglect not the Word, and Ordinances, which are the food of the Spirit." *First John Generall*, p. 196.

45. *Misc.*, no. 899; the entry is a quotation from Stephen Charnock (1628-80).

46. Works, 4, p. 556.

47. Works, 18, p. 86 (no. 539). Edwards includes here the false notion of "Father, Son and Holy Ghost as three distinct gods, friends one to another."

48. *Miscellanies*, no. 999.

49. "Subjects of Enquiry," Beinecke Library, Yale University.

freedom in the "surprising work" of the Spirit that eludes human comprehension and control.

Ever alert to the beauty of spiritual consents, Edwards took special notice of the new unities created by the New England revivals of the 1740s. On the local level, Edwards noted with delight the "surprising" power of the Spirit's presence "to destroy old grudges, and make up long continued breaches, and to bring those that seemed to be in a confirmed irreconcilable alienation, to embrace each other in a sincere and entire amity."[50] Across the colonies, the Great Awakening encouraged an unprecedented fellowship among American evangelicals that transcended denominational and theological differences.[51] As George Whitefield, the leading revival preacher of his day and center of a transatlantic "Calvinist connexion," exclaimed:

> What a divine sympathy and attraction is there between all those who by one spirit are made members of that mystical body, whereof Jesus Christ is the head! . . . Blessed be God that his love is so far shed abroad in our hearts, as to cause us to love one another, though we a little differ as to externals.[52]

Through Whitefield's and Edwards's connections with evangelicals in Scotland in the midst of similar revival movements, this fellowship became, in the years following the Great Awakening, transatlantic as well.[53] In this international community "not only all united in one Head, but in great affection and in more mutual correspondence," Edwards saw foreshadowings of millennial blessings.[54]

Yet faction and conflict scarred the face of the revivals from the beginning, and pressures within the revival paradigm toward individualism worked against loving Christian fellowship. In the anonymity of mass outdoor revivals, the significance of the congregational setting receded, and the notion of religious experience was radically individu-

50. Works, 4, p. 327.

51. Sydney E. Ahlstrom, *A Religious History of the American People*, 2 vols. (Garden City, N.Y.: Doubleday, 1975), I, p. 361.

52. Letter CXXXV (Philadelphia, Nov. 28, 1739), in *Letters of George Whitefield* (Edinburgh: Banner of Truth Trust, 1976), p. 126.

53. See Harold P. Simonson, "Jonathan Edwards and His Scottish Connections," *Journal of American Studies* 21, no. 3 (1987): 353-76.

54. Works, 5, p. 446.

alized; the self replaced the gathered faithful as the primary authority for discerning the Spirit's presence. Even within congregations, the mixture of "high discoveries and great transports of joy" with spiritual pride was deadly, disposing "persons to affect separation, to stand at a distance from others, as better than they."[55] In fact, Edwards lamented, some supporters of the revival almost seemed to follow the maxim "that the more division and strife, the better sign; which naturally leads persons to seek it and provoke it."[56]

How can the revivals be the work of the Holy Spirit, demanded Edwards's arch opponent Charles Chauncy, seeing that they are marked by "Faction and Contention," by Christians "openly and scandalously separated from one another"?[57] Mere "impulses and impressions" in individual souls are not a reliable mark of the Holy Spirit's presence. "In vain may any pretend to be under the extraordinary guidance of the Spirit," he exclaimed, "while in their practice they trample upon this law of Christian love."[58] In Edwards's view, this was a much more serious strike against the authenticity of the revivals than Old Light quibbles about the extraordinary means used to effect conversions. For at this one point in their reflections on the revivals, Edwards and Chauncy were in firm agreement: "Charity or divine love, is in Scripture represented as the sum of all the religion of heaven, and that wherein mainly the religion of the church in its more perfect state on earth shall consist."[59] The "law of the Spirit" (Rom. 8:2) is faith active through love, and no one claiming the genuine presence of the Holy Spirit can lack this. Despite his continuing support for the revivals, Edwards's preoccupation with love as the genuine manifestation of the converted and sanctified life led him to protest vigorously against their factionalism and censoriousness.

Mourning the "most harsh, severe and terrible language" with

55. Works, 4, p. 422.

56. Works, 4, p. 447.

57. Letter to Mr. George Wishart, August 4, 1742, in Richard L. Bushman, ed., *The Great Awakening: Documents on the Revival of Religion, 1740-1745* (New York: Atheneum, 1970), p. 120.

58. "Enthusiasm Described and Caution'd Against," in Alan Heimert and Perry Miller, eds., *The Great Awakening: Documents Illustrating the Crisis and Its Consequences* (Indianapolis: Bobbs-Merrill, 1967), p. 238.

59. Works, 4, p. 299.

which some "speak of almost everything that they see amiss in others,"[60] Edwards chastised his supporters:

> If we proceed in such a manner, on such principles as these, what a face will be introduced upon the church of Christ, the little beloved flock of that gentle Shepherd, the Lamb of God? What a sound shall we bring into the house of God, into the family of his dear little children? How far off shall we soon banish that lovely appearance of humility, sweetness, gentleness, mutual honor, benevolence, complacence, and an esteem of others above themselves, which ought to clothe the children of God all over?[61]

The revival's exaltation of inner religious experience, with its tendency towards spiritual pride and uncharitableness, was for Edwards a mark of a satanic infiltration of the Spirit's work. Loving union was the true mark of the Holy Spirit's influence, and inevitably this worked against prideful pretensions and divisive claims to special spiritual perception.

As, in Edwards's judgment at least, the vigorous piety of the revivals degenerated into self-affirming emotionalism, he gradually developed a hermeneutic of suspicion regarding accounts of individual conversions. "I am far from saying that it is not requisite that persons should give any sort of account of their experiences to their brethren," insisted Edwards in *Religious Affections,* his consummate reflections on the revival. He even conceded that this may assist "others in forming a judgment of their state."[62] But there was more than a tinge of sarcasm in Edwards's rejection of accounts of private religious experiences as a measure of a true Christian:

> Christ nowhere says, Ye shall know the tree by its leaves or flowers, or ye shall know men by their talk, or ye shall know them by the good story they tell of their experiences, or ye shall know them by the manner and air of their speaking, and emphasis and pathos of expression, or by their speaking feelingly, or by making a very great show by abundance of talk, or by many tears and affectionate expressions.[63]

60. Works, 4, p. 419.
61. Works, 4, p. 420.
62. Works, 2, pp. 416-17.
63. Works, 2, p. 407.

The richness of life together in the Spirit depended on more than the community's discernment that an individual "talked like one that felt what he said."[64] If the essence of saving religion is in personal spiritual perception, then the Christian community plays a distinctly secondary role as a disengaged observer who has no unmediated access to the experiences themselves. If the Spirit's work principally concerns inner religious experience, directly accessible only to the individual, the role of the community becomes limited to making external judgments on accounts of personal religious perception. Instead, Edwards cut against the individualist and introspective tendencies of the revivals by denying that the individual has privileged access to her own spiritual states. His observations of Christian susceptibility to religious self-deception drove him to deny the primacy of the individual as the locus of spiritual insight and to reemphasize the role of the community in discerning the Spirit's presence.

Just as the Spirit's love binds believers together in community, so its presence in the individual must be manifest to the community. Regeneration and sanctification are not only relational in nature, he observed — they are relationally discerned. It is the Christian community as a whole that discerns the "sincerity of a professing Christian." Believers lack "such a spirit of discerning" as to determine *with certainty* "who are godly, and who are not," and Edwards thought that "no graces have more counterfeits than love and humility."[65] And yet love is the virtue "wherein the beauty of a true Christian does especially appear," and the preeminence of love in a Christian's life must be visible "to the eye of his neighbors and brethren."[66] Earthly community in the church is a preparation for heavenly community with God and the saints, and in heaven, religious experience in its highest form was for Edwards a practical, communal affair. The heavenly vision of God was not an inward, private rapture, but a cooperative social effort: "They shall delight to assist each other in their contemplations, communicating their glorious contemplations one to another."[67] Likewise on earth, love and knowledge of God was a communal endeavor.

64. Works, 2, pp. 408-9.
65. Works, 2, pp. 181, 146.
66. Works, 2, pp. 147, 407.
67. Dwight, *Works of President Edwards*, 8, p. 258.

Whereas regeneration, "the first work" of the Holy Spirit, infused a new sense of the sweetness of God's loving mercy in Christ,[68] Edwards as pastor was more concerned about the soul's continuing growth in true virtue. To those in his congregation swept up in George Whitefield's message of the immediate experience of spiritual rebirth, Edwards countered with the requirement for a lifelong course of spiritual obedience. "The whole work of sanctification" should be considered part of God's regeneration of the sinner. "And therefore the new birth is not finished till the soul is fully restored, and till the corruption and death that came by Adam and the first birth is wholly removed."[69] His view of the redemptive work of the Holy Spirit tilted away from a conventionally Protestant emphasis on God's sovereign grace in saving sinners towards a typically Catholic stress on the abiding reality of salvation in human persons.[70]

During his years as pastor in Northampton, Edwards continually returned to the connection between justification and works of obedience, or practice. Whereas Reformed scholastics had traditionally made a firm distinction between justification, the forensic act by which the believing sinner is counted righteous before God, and the sanctification that followed, wherein the believer is actually made righteous or holy by the grace of God,[71] Edwards's concern for holy practice encouraged a blurring of the lines between the two. His notebooks during the revival period contained numerous arguments about "how works jus-

68. "The first effect of the power of God in the heart in Regeneration, is to give the heart a Divine taste or sense; to cause it to have relish of the loveliness and sweetness of the supreme excellency of the Divine nature." Helm, *Trinity*, p. 49. Cf. Richard Sibbes, "God giveth knowledge *per modum gustus.* When things are to us as in themselves, then things have a sweet relish." Sibbes, *Complete Works,* 4, pp. 334, 363.

69. *Misc.,* no. 847. This entry was written shortly after Whitefield's visit to Northampton in 1740. For further discussion of Edwards's pastoral concern for holy practice, see the "Editor's Introduction" in Works, 20.

70. Anri Morimoto describes the difference between the "Protestant concern" and the "Catholic concern" in salvation in these terms, and gives an account of previous efforts to emphasize the Protestant features of Edwards's soteriology. See *Jonathan Edwards and the Catholic Vision of Salvation* (University Park, Pa.: Pennsylvania State University Press, 1995). However, the difference between Protestant and Catholic theology on this point should not be overdrawn.

71. Richard A. Muller, *Dictionary of Latin and Greek Theological Terms, Drawn Principally from Protestant Scholastic Theology* (Grand Rapids: Baker, 1985), p. 163.

tify" that stressed ongoing holy practice as integral to faith's acceptance of Christ. "Our act of closing with and accepting of Christ is not
in all respects completed by our accepting him with our hearts till we
have done it practically too, and so have accepted him with the whole
man: soul, spirit and body."[72] In his polemic against the enthusiasts'
overemphasis on the initial conversion of the heart, Edwards skated
close to the edge of denying the once-for-all sufficiency of the gift of
faith. "Even after conversion," he asserted, "the sentence of justification in a sense remains still to be passed, and the man remains still in a
state of probation for heaven," until his faith produces fruits of obedience.[73] Fruits of obedience are intrinsic to saving faith, not merely external evidence for its existence: "Scripture is plain concerning faith,"
Edwards insisted, "that the operative or practical nature of it is the life
and soul of it."[74]

In a retrospective letter to his Scottish friend Thomas Gillespie, a
tired and disillusioned Edwards lamented the tendency of his
Northampton congregation

> to lay almost all the stress of their hopes on the particular steps
> and methods of . . . the first work of the Spirit of God on their
> hearts in their convictions and conversion, and to look but little at
> the abiding sense and temper of their hearts, and the course of
> their exercises, and fruits of grace.[75]

A firmer hope of the Spirit's indwelling presence was to be found in the
convert's abiding sense of love for God and, even more, in the fruits of
love springing from this new temper of heart in sanctification. Perse-
verance in holy practice was for Edwards the most definitive sign of the
Spirit's presence. The Holy Spirit's presence in the heart is most clearly
displayed by outward acts of love. "To speak of Christian experience
and practice as if they were two things, properly and entirely distinct, is
to make a distinction without consideration or reason." As we have already noted, religious experience was not for Edwards primarily a matter of intuition or private perception. Instead, holy love visibly exer-

72. *Misc.*, no. 951.
73. *Misc.*, no. 847.
74. *Misc.*, no. 868.
75. Works, 4, p. 564.

cised in the Christian community was at the heart of religious experience. "Christian practice is the sign of signs, in this sense that it is the great evidence which confirms and crowns all other signs of godliness."[76] Loving practice is not only "one kind or part of Christian experience" — "both reason and Scripture represent it as the chief and most important and most distinguishing part of it."[77] Here Edwards's thought again resonates with the mystical theology of Teresa of Avila, for whom "the criteria of authenticity" of a particular religious experience "do not lie in the character of the experience itself but in how it is related to a pattern of concrete behaviour, the development of dispositions and decisions. There is no one kind of experience that declares itself at once to be an experience of God." The true test rather is whether the love of God is manifest in the pattern of a human life as a whole.[78]

"The harmony and beauty of society consists very much in the good that one member of society does another."[79] Edwards explicitly noted that the love marking the Spirit's presence among true Christians was not merely "the immanent workings of affection which men feel one to another"; rather, it is love "as exercised and expressed in practice."[80] The hearts of true Christians "are united to the people of Jesus Christ as their people, to cleave to them and love them as their brethren, and worship and serve God and follow Christ in union and fellowship with them."[81] Holy practice, even more than inward sentiment, was the cause of deeper union and love among Christians. The earthly fruits of the Spirit must be discerned and visibly shared within the community of saints.

One fruit of the Spirit to which Edwards drew special attention in his *Faithful Narrative* of the 1734-35 revivals was how "it immediately puts an end to differences between ministers and people." He noted

76. Works, 2, p. 444.

77. Works, 2, pp. 450-51.

78. Rowan Williams, *Teresa of Avila* (Harrisburg, Pa.: Morehouse Publishing, 1991), pp. 145, 147.

79. Ms sermon on Gen. 12:3, Beinecke Library, Yale University.

80. Works, 2, p. 357. Cf. John Cotton, "Our joy cannot be full, except we enjoy union with him, and communion with his Children." *First John Generall,* p. 3.

81. Works, 2, p. 417. Cf. Sibbes, "As we are knit to Christ by faith, so we must be knit to the communion of saints by love. That which we have of the Spirit is had in the communion of saints." *Complete Works,* 3, p. 432.

that while there was "considerable uneasiness at New Hadley between some of the people and their minister," since the revival "the people are now universally united to their minister." Likewise,

> There was an exceeding alienation at Sunderland, between the minister and many of the people; but when this concern came amongst them it all vanished at once, and the people are universally united in hearty affection to their minister.[82]

In his glowing account of David Brainerd's ministry Edwards noted several times the "sweet union of soul" he shared with his "dear Christian Indians."[83] In Edwards's view, this "hearty affection" and "sweet union" would be outwardly marked by the people's attentiveness to their minister's counsel, and deference to his authority.

While he too enjoyed times of sweet union early on, hearty affection was not to characterize Edwards's pastoral relationships at Northampton. The growing bitterness and wrangling were evidence for Edwards that the Holy Spirit had withdrawn from his congregation. The blame for this disaffection did not belong only to his congregation, though the self-righteous tone of his *Humble Inquiry* and farewell sermon certainly leaves this impression. Kenneth Minkema has described Edwards as a "fair-weather friend to his congregation."[84] When his ministerial presence in Northampton was associated with spiritual revival, Edwards was quick to see the town as "full of the presence of God, full of love and joy as never before." But when this love and joy languished, Edwards's unforgiving and unrelenting criticism of his parishioners only increased their bitterness and divisions. Edwards's vision of communal love within the Trinity set an impossible standard for his Northampton congregation. When the people failed to attain it, Edwards's trinitarianism could inscribe a narrow moralism, in which the gracious, self-dispossessing love of God towards sinners was overshadowed by harsh judgments and stringent demands for visible holiness. Ironically, as his national and international stature as an expert on "re-

---

82. Works, 4, p. 103.

83. Norman Pettit, ed., *Life of David Brainerd*, The Works of Jonathan Edwards, vol. 7 (New Haven: Yale University Press, 1985), p. 380.

84. Kenneth P. Minkema, "The Edwardses: A Ministerial Family in Eighteenth-Century New England," Ph.D. Dissertation, University of Connecticut, 1988, p. 238.

ligious affections" grew, so did the mutual resentment and disaffection between Edwards and his congregation. Loving union came to easier expression in Edwards's private notebooks and published treatises than in his actual intercourse with parishioners.

Edwards's trinitarian reflection figured indirectly into the issue precipitating his dismissal from Northampton: his changing policies on admission to the Lord's Supper. For twenty years he followed the example of his grandfather, Solomon Stoddard, in refusing to link access to the sacrament with assurance of salvation. Stoddard had viewed the Supper as a source of the Spirit's life-giving nurture, a means of grace for sinners, not a vehicle for exclusion and judgment. The Lord's Supper is nourishment for the spiritually weak, and hence all sincere and morally upright Christians are invited. Edwards's growing uneasiness with this policy came to a head in February 1749, when he announced to his Northampton congregation that he would henceforth admit to full communion only those who were "in profession, and in the eye of the church's Christian judgment, godly or gracious persons." Edwards was now asserting an explicit linkage between profession, outward manifestations of godliness, and actual sainthood. Only those who have been truly converted by the Spirit can make a sincere profession. And only those whose profession is judged sincere should be admitted to full church membership, which includes the privileges of the Lord's Supper and baptism for their children.

Within Edwards's new eucharistic understanding, the Lord's Supper was no longer a means of grace by which the Spirit brought sinners into union with God; it became an expression of union already realized. Edwards now portrayed the Lord's Supper as an anticipation of the great eschatological banquet, in which the saints who have been "in a sort admitted to that society of three persons in the Godhead"[85] will feast together with the Father, Son, and Holy Spirit. Communion privileges in the earthly church belong to those who can already declare themselves "by profession and in visibility a part of that heavenly and divine family."[86] The Lord's Supper, Edwards declared, is

---

85. Works, 18, p. 110 (no. 571).
86. Works, 12, p. 321. I am indebted to David D. Hall's interpretation of Edwards's "ecclesiastical writings" in this volume.

the Christian church's great feast of love; wherein Christ's people sit together as brethren in the family of God, at their father's table, to feast on the love of their Redeemer, . . . sealing their love to him and one another.[87]

There is no place at the table for those who have not, "in the eye of the church's Christian judgment," already been infused with the love of Christ by the Holy Spirit. Ironically, Edwards's own lack of charity towards those whose reflections of the Trinity's love remained dim and uncertain barred a majority of his congregation from the sacrament that was supposed to communicate that self-giving love of the Trinity to them. The eucharist as a medium of God's grace was turned into an instrument of pastoral judgment and control. Edwards's abrupt reversal on sacramental practice brought on an "uncommon degree of rage and madness" among the members of his congregation.[88] Sixteen months later, he was dismissed.

The nadir of Edwards's relations with Northampton coincided with the 1749 publication of his not very *Humble Inquiry* into new requirements for congregational participation in the Lord's Supper. A little-noticed feature of this painfully strident treatise is his repeated appeal to the Trinity. After noting that his opponents "suppose it to be requisite, that communicants should believe the fundamental doctrines of religion with all their heart, the doctrine of three persons and one God, in particular,"[89] Edwards countered that the opportunities for spiritual pretense were just as great in this requirement of doctrinal orthodoxy, as in his own insistence on a sincere affirmation of grace-inspired love for God. Edwards found it easy to imagine how "a man who secretly in his mind give no credit to the commonly received doctrine of the Trinity, yet may, by pretending an assent to it, and in hypocrisy making a public profession of it, get into the church."[90] More fundamentally, Edwards found it artificial, even hypocritical, to separate people's "right speculative notions" of God from "a proper respect to him in their hearts." What could it mean, he asked, for those without "the least spark of true love to God in their hearts, to say, publicly and solemnly,

87. Works, 12, p. 255.
88. Works, 12, p. 17.
89. Works, 12, p. 295.
90. Works, 12, p. 313.

that 'They avouch God the Father, Son, and Holy Ghost to be their God'"?[91] For Edwards, God's love for us and our love for God were so inextricably bound up with the doctrine of the Trinity that he could not imagine how one could sincerely hold "a true notion" of the triune God without having a concomitant love for God. Yet in this treatise Edwards's own "true notion" of the Trinity as a fount of overflowing love toward sinners seems strangely absent.

Reformed theology has characteristically portrayed the Lord's Supper as *both* nourishment for the spiritually weak and as love feast for none but the truly faithful. The tension between the acknowledgment of sinners' need for grace and the anticipation of the saints' eschatological transformation has proved pastorally and theologically fruitful.[92] In refusing sacramental access to "a middle sort of persons with a moral sincerity,"[93] Edwards absolutized the eschatological image of the Supper as love feast for the truly faithful. The love feast became an idealized model for understanding the earthly church: when the church is truly itself, it is free from "lukewarmness" of faith and is completely caught up in the love of the Trinity. In losing the Reformed sacramental tension between the Supper as both food for sinners and a feast for saints, Edwards portrayed the "church's abiding fundamental reality" in a way that ignored the "confusions and stupidities" of its sinful concrete existence. His new view of the sacrament failed to "make a sufficient distinction between the church militant and the church triumphant."[94]

Edwards's changing sacramental policies also revealed the ecclesiological danger of Richard Sibbes's exclamation that "the Trinity should be the pattern of our unity."[95] In the case of Edwards's "love

---

91. Works, 12, p. 211.

92. These two sacramental visions can be correlated, respectively, with images of church as mother and as bride. See Amy Plantinga Pauw, "The Church as Mother and Bride in the Reformed Tradition: Challenge and Promise," in W. Brueggemann and G. Stroup, eds., *Many Voices, One God: Being Faithful in a Pluralistic World* (Louisville: Westminster/John Knox, 1998), pp. 122-36.

93. Works, 12, p. 220.

94. I am borrowing language from Nicholas M. Healy, *Church, World and the Christian Life: Practical-Prophetic Ecclesiology* (Cambridge: Cambridge University Press, 2000), pp. 8, 37. Healy is addressing problems in modern ecclesiologies.

95. Sibbes, *Complete Works*, 3, p. 194.

feast" model, the role of the Holy Spirit in the earthly church was too closely assimilated to the perfect, continuous outflowing of love between the Father and the Son. Among human sinners, the Spirit's work of loving union remains. But it takes place in the midst of chronic human disorder and imperfection, and so aims not at a smug fellowship of the righteous but at the gathering of sinners for common repentance and common praise.[96] Within this arena of the Spirit's work, the heat of judgmentalism is at least as spiritually dangerous as the "lukewarmness" of religious doubt. Edwards's new policy on the Lord's Supper attempted to anticipate the final separation between lovers of God and haters of God. But the Spirit's earthly work of regeneration is a protracted, ambiguous, and messy business, of which God alone is judge. Though there is much to praise in Edwards's emphasis on communal discernment and on holy practice as the definitive mark of the Spirit's presence in the church, his sacramental exclusivism undercut his insistence elsewhere on the mystery and graciousness of the Spirit's work.

Glorification

Edwards found some refuge from ministerial disaffection in his extended reflections on the millennium, that "future promised glorious day of the church's prosperity" on earth.[97] When that blessed era dawned, Christian faith would be everything it was not in Northampton: "Religion shall not be an empty profession as it now mostly is, but holiness of heart and life shall abundantly prevail."[98] The

96. Rowan Williams has described the pilgrim church's holiness in these terms. See *A Ray of Darkness: Sermons and Reflections* (London: Cowley Publications, 1995), pp. 114-15.

97. Works, 5, p. 340. This ardent millennialism also has resonances with the Cambridge Brethren: "the Brethren read the signs of the times, prayed for the millennial dawn, and worked on its behalf. . . . both in England and America, Cotton and Davenport, following Sibbes and Preston, preached the coming of a middle kingdom, a period before the final judgment in which the saints would enjoy the pleasures of communion." Janice Knight, *Orthodoxies in Massachusetts: Rereading American Puritanism* (Cambridge, Mass.: Harvard University Press, 1994), pp. 154, 159.

98. Works, 9, p. 481. I am paraphrasing Gerald R. McDermott, *One Holy and Happy Society: The Public Theology of Jonathan Edwards* (University Park, Pa.: Pennsylvania State University Press, 1992), p. 63: "In religion, the millennium would be everything Northamp-

Spirit, who "in his indwelling, his influences and fruits, is the sum of all grace, holiness, comfort and joy," had up to this time been "but very sparingly" given.[99] In the millennium, as "the *chief* time" for the gift of the Spirit on earth, love would be preeminent:

> And then shall all the world be united in peace and love in one amiable society; all nations, in all parts, on every side of the globe, shall then be knit together in sweet harmony, all parts of God's church assisting and promoting the knowledge and spiritual good one of another. . . . all the world [shall then be] as one church, one orderly, regular, beautiful society, one body, all the members in beautiful proportion.[100]

In that time, not only will the Father and Son "be most eminently glorified on earth"; the saints will appear in "glorious beauty" by being "united as one holy city, one heavenly family, men of all nations shall as it were dwell together, and sweetly correspond one with another as brethren and children of the same father."[101]

Edwards's millennial hopes were nurtured by his *Humble Attempt* to bring Christians across the colonies and abroad into "visible union" through a concert of prayer. "Union is one of the most amiable things that pertains to human society; yea, it is one of the most beautiful and happy things on earth, which indeed makes earth most like heaven."[102] Christians united in prayer for the flourishing of religion would, by the grace of the Holy Spirit, constitute "one family, one holy and happy society," and so hasten the day when "the church on earth will become more like the blessed society in heaven, and vast assembly of saints and angels there."[103]

---

ton was not. It would embody every virtue and every mark of piety that Edwards longed to see among his parishioners."

99. Works, 5, pp. 341-42.

100. Works, 9, pp. 483-84.

101. Works, 5, pp. 337, 339. McDermott, *One Holy and Happy Society*, pp. 42-43, "[I]t was in the 'one amiable society' of the millennium, not his own, that Edwards was absorbed. It was the 'one holy city, one heavenly family' that looms in the background of nearly every treatise and many of his sermons, and that fills many pages of his private notebooks."

102. Works, 5, pp. 364-65.

103. Works, 5, p. 446. Cf. Richard Sibbes, "If he pray in faith, [the Christian] desires that God would pull down all opposite kingdoms to the kingdom of his Son Christ;

The millennium, however glorious, was only God's penultimate gift to the church: the enduring blessedness of saints would occur in heaven. Between the two was the final apostasy, in which the Spirit's influence would drastically wane, followed by the second coming of Christ and the second resurrection. After this came the final judgment, the consignment of the damned to hell, and the glorious return of Christ, accompanied by his elect, to heaven. Only in heaven, with the work of redemption completed, would the perfect union between God, angels, and saints be free from threats of diminution.[104]

Love is the criterion in the final separation of the damned from the elect: the final judgment distinguishes those who hate God from those who love God. In hell, the Spirit's utter absence is signaled by intense, enduring hatred: its inhabitants "hate God, and hate Christ, and hate angels and saints in heaven."[105] Although those in hell are united in "enmity and opposition to God, yet there is no union among themselves,"[106] and so the hatred that the damned share also turns them against each other. The inhabitants of hell hate each other as much as they hate God. The hatred and divisiveness of hell represent the complete antithesis of the Spirit's redemptive work.[107]

Though God's Spirit is absent from hell, God is not. "In hell God manifests his being and perfections only in hatred and wrath, and hatred without love."[108] Given the identification of the Holy Spirit with love, it is hard to see how these perfections of God could be trinitarian perfections. In his treatment of hell, as in his treatment of sin, Edwards's trinitarian harmony faltered. His attempts to fit hell into the

that the kingdom of Christ may come, more and more in the hearts of his people; that he may reign everywhere more freely and largely than he doth. Every one may help forward the kingdom of Christ; he may help forward Jerusalem and pull down Jericho; every one that hath a fervent devotion of prayer." *Complete Works*, 7, p. 471.

104. Even for the angels, heaven was a spiritually perilous place before the ascension of Christ. See Amy Plantinga Pauw, "Where Theologians Fear to Tread," *Modern Theology* 16, no. 1 (January 2000): 39-59.

105. Works, 8, p. 391.

106. Works, 8, p. 390.

107. Cf. Sibbes, "What is it that makes hell so horrible? Because there is an utter and eternal separation from the chiefest and choicest good, God himself. . . . But now the joining to God, the fountain of all good in heaven, makes heaven to be heaven indeed." *Complete Works*, 4, p. 293.

108. Works, 8, p. 390.

basic soteriological story line, according to which God "from eternity from his infinite goodness designed to communicate himself to creatures,"[109] only replicated this trinitarian discord among the saints in an appalling way. "Goodness is the only end why [God] has created the world, and the ultimate end of every dispensation of whatever nature, even the damnation of the wicked for the happiness of the blessed."[110] The misery of the damned is a manifestation of divine goodness because it enhances the saints' enjoyment of God: the saints' vision of God's hatred and wrath toward others "raise[s] their sense of the riches and excellency of his love to them." If it did not, there would be "a visible defect, an inharmoniousness" between God's eternal punishment of sinners and the saints' enjoyment of God's glory.[111] But the price of preserving this harmony is extremely high: God's hatred of the damned deforms the saints into creatures who find their own happiness increased by the eternal torment of others. This happiness in God's partiality seems to have little to do with the saints' glorification by the Holy Spirit, the personified Love of God.

In contrast with hell, heaven's true happiness is explicitly rooted in the happiness of the triune life, namely "pure, humble, heavenly, divine love."[112] Heaven is a "world of love," because it is the dwelling place of the persons of the Trinity: there the Father and Son "are united in infinitely dear and incomprehensible mutual love," and the Holy Spirit, who is "the spirit of divine love," flows forth to all heaven's inhabitants:[113]

> in heaven this fountain of love, this eternal three in one, is set open without any obstacle to hinder access to it. There this glorious God is manifested and shines forth in full glory, in beams of love; there the fountain overflows in streams and rivers of love and delight, enough for all to drink at, and to swim in, yea, so as to overflow the world as it were with a deluge of love.[114]

---

109. Works, 18, p. 389 (no. 744).

110. Works, 5, p. 137.

111. *Misc.*, no. 866.

112. Works, 16, p. 796. See Amy Plantinga Pauw, "'Heaven Is a World of Love': Edwards on Heaven and the Trinity," *Calvin Theological Journal* 30 (1995): 392-401.

113. Works, 8, p. 369. This excerpt is from Edwards's fifteenth sermon in the series "Charity and Its Fruits," entitled "Heaven Is a World of Love."

114. Works, 8, p. 370.

God and Christ join with the saints and angels to form a society over-flowing with mutual love and joy. In heaven, the relationship between God and humanity is no longer dominated by the dynamics of sin and judgment, either corporate or individual. The ambiguous, conflict-ridden drama of the earthly work of the redemption is over, crowned by the saints' joyful participation in the eternal, overflowing love of the divine life. In heaven the redemptive work of the Spirit achieves a dynamic and unhindered fullness.

What distinguishes the heavenly state of the church from its earthly state is not only that the Holy Spirit shall be given perfectly, but that love

> shall be, as it were, the only gift or fruit of the Spirit, as being the most perfect and glorious, and which being brought to perfection renders others, which God was wont to communicate to his church on earth, needless.[115]

Edwards drew on the larger Puritan tradition of depicting the heavenly love between God and the saints in frankly erotic imagery inspired by the Song of Songs.[116] In his youthful apostrophe to Sarah Pierpont, he noted that her earthly union with God was such that she expected after a while to be "caught up into heaven," there to dwell with God, and "to be ravished with his love, favor and delight, forever."[117] Such is the heavenly intimacy of the saints with Christ, that "there will be no restraint to his love, no restraint to their enjoyment of himself; nothing will be too full, too inward and intimate for them to be admitted to."[118]

The influence of the Holy Spirit, "or divine charity in the heart," is the basis not only for the saints' intimate fellowship with God and Christ, but for their perfect communion with each other. In heaven, as on earth, religious experience in its highest form is intrinsically communal. As Richard Baxter noted, "not so singular will the Christian be, as to

115. Works, 8, p. 368.
116. Cf. Sibbes, "the Spirit speaks to us by a secret kind of whispering and intimation, that the soul feels better than I can express. . . . There is, I say, a sweet joining, a sweet kiss given to the soul. 'I am thine and thou art mine,' Cant. vi.3." Complete Works, 3, p. 456.
117. Works, 16, pp. 789-90.
118. Works, 18, p. 372 (no. 741).

be solitary." Intimacies between family members and friends will endure in heaven. This conviction is reflected in Edwards's note to Sarah from his deathbed: "give my kindest Love to my dear Wife & tell her that the uncommon Union that has so long subsisted between us has been of such a Nature as I trust is Spiritual and therefore will continue for ever."[119] Social harmonies on a larger scale will also be enhanced. Baxter described the "Family of Heaven" as a society of perfect consent, "where there is no division, nor dissimilitude, nor differing Judgments, nor disaffection, nor strangeness, but all are one in Christ, who is one with the Father."[120] Even the theological differences dividing the earthly church, Baxter predicted, would be resolved into a perfect heavenly ecumenism. Through the unhindered outpouring of the Holy Spirit, the "holy and happy society" of the saints on earth finds its fulfillment in heaven.

Edwards depicted the heaven where Christ and the saints dwell in quite literal terms as "a particular place or part of the universe, and the highest or outermost part of it."[121] Heaven is a robustly physical world, whose bodily inhabitants engage in singing, conversation, and even travel:

> They shall employ themselves in singing God's praise, or expressing their thoughts to God and Christ, and also to one another; and in going from one part of heaven to another, to behold the glories of God shining in the various parts of it.[122]

The capacities of the saints' resurrected bodies will be gloriously transformed, so as to aid their happy communion with each other. "The eye may be so much more sensible," Edwards speculated, "that for aught we know they may distinctly see the beauty of one another's countenance and smiles, and hold a delightful and most intimate conversation, at a thousand miles' distance."[123] All the "external beauties and harmonies" of heaven, Edwards thought, "will appear chiefly on the

119. Ola Elizabeth Winslow, *Jonathan Edwards: 1703-1758* (New York: Macmillan, 1941), p. 319. Edwards was clear that what is spiritual is not what relates "to the spirit or soul of man, as the spiritual part of man, in opposition to the body." Works, 2, p. 198. Persons as a whole are spiritual, as the Spirit indwells them according to its proper nature as love.
120. Richard Baxter, *The Saints Everlasting Rest* (London, 1650), pp. 83, 81.
121. Works, 18, p. 381 (no. 743).
122. Works, 13, p. 296 (no. 137).
123. Works, 13, p. 369 (no. 263).

bodies of the man Christ Jesus and of the saints."[124] Joy in the glorified humanity of Christ and the community of saints was at the center of Edwards's vision of heavenly blessedness. The saints' heavenly joy in Christ is matched only by his joy in them.[125]

The heavenly love of the saints for each other and for God is safe from diminution, but it is not a static perfection. In a notebook entry inspired by his courtship with Sarah, Edwards exclaimed at how soon "earthly lovers" are

> united as near as 'tis possible, and have communion as intimate as possible. . . . And how happy is that love, in which there is an eternal progress in all these things; wherein new beauties are continually discovered, and more and more loveliness, and in which we shall forever increase in beauty ourselves, where we shall be made capable of finding out and giving, and shall receive, more and more endearing expressions of love forever: our union will become more close, and communion more intimate.[126]

Heaven within Edwards's theological scheme was a place where the pilgrim's progress in loving union with God and the saints could continue eternally, where hope as well as love could flourish forever. Because "heaven is a progressive state,"[127] the heavenly joy of the saints, and even of the triune God, will forever continue to increase. Saints can look forward to an unending expansion of their knowledge and love of God, as their capacities are stretched by what they receive.[128]

God's own eternal disposition towards self-knowledge and self-love is the archetype for all heavenly dynamism.[129] This immanent divine

---

124. Works, 13, p. 328 (no. 182).

125. Cf. Sibbes, "For the mystical body of Christ is his fulness. Christ is our fulness, and we are his fulness." *Complete Works,* 6, p. 547.

126. Works, 13, p. 337 (no. 198).

127. This phrase is the title of Appendix III in Edwards, Works, 8, p. 706.

128. Kathryn Tanner, *Jesus, Humanity and the Trinity: A Brief Systematic Theology* (Minneapolis: Fortress Press, 2001), p. 42, uses this language to describe Gregory of Nyssa's view of heaven. The striking similarities between Gregory of Nyssa and Edwards on this point are noted by Paul Ramsey, Works, 8, pp. 706-38.

129. I am indebted to Lee, *Philosophical Theology,* for this "dispositional" view of increase in heaven. In my estimation, his general argument is most convincing in its account of Edwards's eschatology.

disposition is repeated by being expressed outwardly. And the primary way in which God's knowledge and love are outwardly expressed is in the increasing knowledge and love of God by saints created in the divine image. As the saints' heavenly enjoyment of God progressively increases, their capacity to enjoy God increases as well. Because the saints become capable of progressively more love and knowledge of God, there is no intrinsic limit to their joy in heaven. The psychological model for the Trinity provided a solid foundation for Edwards's hopes for eternal "increase" in heaven.

But Edwards's vision of heaven went beyond satisfying human hopes about the afterlife. It is not only the saints who enjoy increase in heaven; in the exercise of their disposition to know and love God, the inner triune being of God is repeated and the divine beauty itself is enlarged. The saints' continual increase represents an increase in God's glory as well. As the saints continue to increase in knowledge and love of God, God receives more and more glory. This heavenly reciprocity will never cease, because the glory God deserves is infinite, and the capacity of the saints to perceive this glory and praise God for it is ever increasing. As Stephen Holmes asserts, "the being and history of the world is a generous overflowing of the being and life of the Triune God, and finds its meaning in the eschatological enlargement of that life."[130] Edwards's trinitarian notion of *divine* increase in heaven is by far the most innovative aspect of his reflections on heaven. The dynamic role of the Holy Spirit in the eternal emanations and remanations of love justified the hope of eternal increase in heavenly joy and union, both for the saints and for God.

---

130. Stephen Holmes, *God of Grace and God of Glory: An Account of the Theology of Jonathan Edwards* (Grand Rapids: Eerdmans, 2001), p. 245.

Chapter 6

A COBBLED TRINITARIANISM

"The gospel brings to light the love between the Father and the Son, and declares how that love has been manifested in mercy."

EDWARDS, *Charity and Its Fruits*

This study of Edwards has been an exercise in "ambidextrous" theology. I have shown, on the one hand, how Edwards's trinitarian reflection tied together aspects of his thought and life that have often seemed unrelated and have been studied in isolation. His philosophical musings about beauty and excellency, his debts to a larger Puritan heritage, his admiration for Sarah's mystical piety, and his pastoral failures all come into new focus through the lens of his trinitarian theology. On the other hand, I have indicated various points at which Edwards's reflection on the Trinity intersects with contemporary theological concerns, such as appropriate names for God, the propriety of *persons* language for the Trinity, and the relations between the triune life and Christian life. More broadly, I have emphasized themes of union and grace in Edwards's trinitarian reflection, so as to bring him into conversation with contemporary theologians such as William Placher, Kathryn Tanner, and Rowan Williams, who have not drawn on Edwards in their constructive work. In this chapter I expand briefly on the theological resources of Edwards's thought and reflect on the challenges of constructive historical retrieval.

A major challenge in drawing on Edwards for constructive work is that his theological writings do not reflect the same concern for coherence evident in modern "systematic" or even "dogmatic" theologies. Edwards was deeply steeped in Scripture and explored diverse biblical genres and images beyond any easy harmonization. His immediate pastoral context often defined the contours of his approach to scriptural texts and his treatment of theological themes. His catholic tastes in reading and his penchant for polemical theology frequently shifted the setting and terms of his own theological reflection. Unlike contemporary narrative theologians, Edwards appeared unconcerned to render a coherent biblical portrait of God or Christ. In one notebook entry he could probe what he saw as pride's natural inclination to "despise a crucified Savior, one that suffered such disgrace, and humbled himself so low."[1] But this compelling portrait of a "vulnerable God" could be set aside in a later entry in favor of his evident delight in Christ's "infinite majesty and the terribleness of his wrath" toward the damned.[2] The "admirable conjunction" of "majesty and meekness" that Edwards set forward so beautifully in his sermon on the excellency of Christ[3] often came apart in a clash of images.

The result of this eclecticism is that I could easily have drawn a very different theological portrait of Edwards (and many others have). Interpreting Edwards's diverse writings requires an unusual self-consciousness about the selectivity and innovation that always go into the work of construing a theological tradition. In choosing the interplay between Edwards's two models for the Trinity as the focal point of my study, I have privileged what I term Edwards's basic soteriological story line, according to which the eternal, excellent being-with of God as Trinity finds its external expression in the desire to incorporate human creatures into the divine life. This is in keeping with Edwards's repeated insistence that the trinitarian work of redemption "be looked upon as the great end and drift of all God's works and dispensations from the beginning." I do not think this is a narrow, tendentious reading of Edwards. But it does mean that everything else — his apocalyptic

1. *Misc.*, no. 875.

2. *Misc.*, no. 957. William Placher has drawn an admirable portrait of a "vulnerable God" from the Markan narratives and has shown sensitivity to the irreducible plurality of scriptural narratives. See *Narratives of a Vulnerable God: Christ, Theology, and Scripture* (Louisville: Westminster/John Knox, 1994), pp. 87-133.

3. Works, 19, p. 574.

and millenarian speculations, his dispositional metaphysics, his polemics on the freedom of the will, his apologetic appeals to views of the
"ancient heathens," his revivalism, his ardent interest in hell torments
— must "be looked upon as *appendages* to this great work, or *things*
which . . . subserve that grand design."[4] Choosing the trinitarian work
of redemption as central renders other aspects of his thought periph-
eral. Indeed, Edwards's trinitarianism provides a vantage point for as-
sessment and critique of other elements in his theology.

Within this "grand design," Edwards's two models of the Trinity
have distinctive roles to play. The psychological analogy serves as the
basso continuo, anchoring the melodic flights of the salvation narrative.
This model indicates the primordial character of God as the "fullness
of every perfection, of all excellency and beauty, and of infinite happiness,"[5] whose eternal desire is to "communicate himself to creatures,"
so as to repeat in them the perfections of the triune life. Funding all of
the economic dealings with the world is God's infinite, emanating
goodness. God is perfect gift, needing nothing from creatures. God
does not engage the world in order to receive something God lacks: in
"manifesting his glory to the understanding" and "communication to
the heart," "what God has in view . . . is not that he may receive, but
that he [may] go forth."[6] Within this theological framework the divine
response to sin takes the form of an intensification of God's commitment to union with the creaturely world. The psychological analogy,
with its heightened role for the Holy Spirit, establishes the gracious,
noncompetitive character of God.

But the *basso continuo* exists only in relation to a particular melody; it
does not stand by itself. Similarly, the psychological model is not sufficient for telling the particular story of God's engagement with the
world. It tends toward impersonal, hydraulic metaphors of pouring out
and overflowing.[7] Especially in the role it accords to the Word, this
model does not adequately reflect the risk and costliness of God's engagement with humanity — it can suggest that the work of redemption
is a bloodless process of enlightenment and moral growth. Edwards's

4. Works, 18, p. 284 (no. 702).
5. Works, 8, pp. 432-33.
6. Works, 13, p. 496 (no. 448).
7. Robert Merrihew Adams, *Finite and Infinite Goods: A Framework for Ethics* (New York: Oxford University Press, 1999), p. 42.

deployment of this model at times abstracted his account of the Spirit's work from the ambiguous, unfolding historical realm of Jesus' earthly existence and the life of the church. What does God's perfect love look like in the conflictual, capricious arena of human actions and emotions? How is divine wisdom displayed in the give-and-take of God's dealings with Israel and the church? The broad picture this model renders of the intrinsic self-giving character of the triune God must not be contradicted. But more filling in is required to show how God's wisdom and love are communicated to a world marked by sin and death.

Here the social analogy of the Trinity has a crucial role to play. It takes the melody line, showing how the overflowing gifts of God are communicated to human sinners in the drama of the Son's extraordinary life for others. Sent by the Father, the incarnate Son "empties himself" to share a life of vulnerability and suffering with sinners, so as to bring them into intimate union with the triune God. What we receive in union with Christ through the power of the Spirit is not wisdom and love in general, but the grace that conforms us to the trustful wisdom and self-giving love that characterize Christ's own life. The language of the gospel narratives — the Father to whom Jesus prayed, the Son who cried from the cross, the Spirit's mysterious work in the church and the world — finds natural expression within the framework of the social analogy. There is an irreducible particularity about the economic roles of the Trinity that suggests that "The encounter with the Triune God is not only a personal encounter, but a social encounter of persons in communion."[8] Even those hostile to social vocabulary for the Trinity often find, in their articulation of God's "personal" engagement with the world, a need to speak of divine agency in "interpersonal" terms. Efforts to articulate the correspondence between the economic narrative of redemption and the immanent life of God by describing God's eternal nature as being-with, or as self-dispossession, or as identity in otherness, draw on implicitly social conceptions of the Trinity.

But the social model cannot stand by itself either. In Edwards's explicitly familial imagery and in his account of the covenant of redemp-

8. Bradford E. Hinze, "Ecclesial Repentance and the Demands of Dialogue," *Theological Studies* 61 (2000): 220.

tion, the social model could degenerate into crude anthropomorphism, "projecting onto God the limits of created identities."[9] Without the "corrective pressure"[10] of the psychological model, appropriate modesty about our grasp of God's immanent life is lost, and divine and human forms of relationality become too closely assimilated. Human power arrangements (actual or desired) are projected onto God, or a realism about the frailties of human relationships is lost. Both of these problems were noted in Edwards's trinitarian reflection. As Gary Badcock notes, "The task of developing a theology of the inner-trinitarian relations from the economy . . . has to reckon seriously with the paradox that an adequate doctrine of the immanent Trinity is only possible when an apophatic reticence about it is embraced."[11]

In the two previous chapters we noted how Edwards's trinitarianism faltered in his treatment of human sin and divine punishment, and this problem was particularly located in his deployment of the social analogy. When cut loose from its anchor in the psychological model's depiction of God's primordial graciousness, Edwards's account of the "interpersonal" agency of the Trinity drifted into treacherous waters of trinitarian discord and pitiless divine vengeance. The depiction of God's glory and beauty funded by the psychological model became warped in Edwards's social account of the divine economy, where the role of the Holy Spirit was muted. In giving glory, the saints reflect back the Father's hatred of the wicked, as well as the Son's love for sinners. What provokes delight in heaven is not only the beautiful "bodies of the man Christ Jesus and of the saints,"[12] but also the view of hell torments. These warped views of divine glory and beauty were extrapolations from Edwards's predestinarian theological inheritance. They were also fed (as were the predestinarian views of his Reformed forebears) by his reading of the apocalyptic narratives in the gospels and the book of Revelation: the weeping and gnashing of teeth of those thrown into the outer darkness (Matt. 22:13), the lake of

9. Rowan Williams, *On Christian Theology* (Oxford: Blackwell, 2000), p. 160.

10. Nicholas Lash, *Believing Three Ways in One God: A Reading of the Apostles' Creed* (London: SCM Press, 1992), p. 96. Lash uses this term in discussing the relation of the three trinitarian articles.

11. Gary Badcock, *Light of Truth and Fire of Love: A Theology of the Holy Spirit* (Grand Rapids: Eerdmans, 1997), p. 255.

12. Works, 13, p. 328 (no. 182).

fire in which "anyone whose name was not found written in the book of life" is tormented (Rev. 20:15). These aspects of the scriptural narratives that the psychological analogy could not accommodate found lodging in the social model, introducing discord between Edwards's development of the two models. Edwards's broad use of Scripture in the deployment of the social model should curb glib talk about how preserving "the" narrative identifications of Father, Son, and Holy Spirit will keep Christian theology properly trinitarian, pastorally edifying, and so on. Edwards's trinitarian theology shows how risky "narrative identifications" of God can be, when not guided by more general construals of God's gracious relationship to creation.

As feminist theologians like to say, "doctrines function." It is not enough to show the Trinity's doctrinal and metaphysical connections, to speak in the abstract about how notions of trinitarian harmony and relationality mold human community. To understand how religious doctrines function, we must produce "thick descriptions" of the cultural situations — the web of interconnected signs, relationships, and actions within which specific terms are deployed. We must inquire how, in particular contexts, trinitarian theology takes on flesh. In Edwards's ecclesiology, a vision of perfect trinitarian communion funded a fantasy of Christian community unmarred by conflict, ambiguity, or spiritual limitations. The love and society of the Trinity became an unrealizable blueprint for Edwards's church in Northampton, and the loving communion of the Trinity was transmuted into a harsh pastoral moralism. As Edwards's pastoral practice shows, the paradigm of the beautiful society of the Trinity can serve to condemn social failures and exclude those deemed unworthy. It does not necessarily foster sacramental openness and gracious human community.

Much of Edwards's explicit trinitarian reflection is found in his "Miscellanies" notebooks, rather than his published writings or sermons. The distinction between the thoughts recorded in the "Miscellanies" and Edwards's public voice should not be overstated. As Ava Chamberlain argues, the "Miscellanies" are best thought of as "quasi-public writings, having a status analogous to the letter, which in the eighteenth century was often composed for a broad audience."[13] Ed-

13. Works, 18, p. 10. The following description of the "Miscellanies" is indebted to Chamberlain's discussion, pp. 8-12.

wards wrote the notebook entries in complete sentences, using his "public hand," and lent them to colleagues and students to read and study. Both his son, Jonathan Edwards, Jr., and his foremost pupil, Samuel Hopkins, thought the notebooks should be published and made efforts to solicit financial support for the project. Yet there is a freedom and intensity to Edwards's reflections on the Trinity in the "Miscellanies" entries of the 1720s and 1730s that rarely surfaced in his sermons and later treatises. In certain polemical contexts, such as his treatise on *Freedom of the Will*, Edwards's reliance on a trinitarian conceptuality appeared in only slight, incidental ways.[14] But even where it was at the center of his public discourse, Edwards's trinitarianism retains a kind of subterranean feel — it supported and shaped what was voiced publicly, but it did not always emerge in vivid, explicit ways.

As interest in the doctrine of the Trinity continues to grow in contemporary Christian theology, so does the issue of a public theological voice. Can a theology be trinitarian if it does not identify itself as such? Can a trinitarian theology be articulated without the classical trinitarian vocabulary? Is it appropriate to theologize to different audiences in distinct but interrelated ways, so that doctrines that seem dormant in a particular context may actually be feeding what is said, because they are being nourished elsewhere? Edwards's trinitarian reflections elicit both encouragement and caution here. While Edwards slighted traditional trinitarian terminology of *processions* and *relations*, and even used the word *Trinity* less than one would expect, he exhibited a stunning ability to incorporate philosophical, ethical, and pastoral interests into his trinitarian theology. He cobbled together his doctrine of the Trinity from various language-games, so that the idioms of beauty and disposition, of religious affections and love to Being in general, of covenant and spiritual light, all funded his trinitarian reflection. From the start, there was only a rough fit among the different idioms. And, as Edwards's legacy shows, his cobbled trinitarianism easily came apart, as different readers took various pieces of his wide-ranging reflections and used them in other contexts without attention to their trinitarian inflection. The multi-lingual character of

---

14. E.g., Works, I, p. 287, where Edwards appealed to "the promise made to the Father by the Son, by the *Logos* that was with the Father from the beginning, before he took the human nature."

Edwards's trinitarian theology contributes to both its powerful appeal and its radical instability.

There is really no alternative to Edwards's multi-lingual approach. As an "essentially parasitic" way of life, Christianity has no choice but to feed off of other ways of speaking and living. "A Christian way of life . . . has to establish relations with other ways of life, it has to take from them, in order to be one itself."[15] This is how trinitarian reflection got its start in the early church, and, in order to thrive, contemporary trinitarian theology must continue the work of incorporating other modes of discourse — political, metaphysical, cultural, aesthetic. But in a time when the stories of Scripture and the language of Christian dogmatics are foreign to so many inside as well as outside the church, theologians have to be more explicit than Edwards often was about the connections they make between the traditional language of faith and the other languages they have learned to speak. Edwards's "subterranean" approach risks being misunderstood as a retreat from trinitarian conceptualities altogether. In various rhetorical contexts theologians must continue to negotiate a hearing for terms like *Word, Spirit,* and *Trinity,* not assuming that a trinitarian framework is shared, or even understood. But with Edwards, they can declare themselves "not afraid to say twenty things about the Trinity which the Scripture [and the classical tradition] never said."

Constructive engagement with a tradition is always risky, and Edwards was a theological risk-taker. "The native unity of speculation and adoration in his life"[16] upheld disciplined study as an expression of religious devotion and at the same time authorized great theological freedom. Theological reflection need not look only backwards for its authority, and authentic new expressions of it need not always coincide with previous attempts. "I utterly disclaim a dependence on Calvin," Edwards declared, "or believing the doctrines which I hold, because he believed and taught them; and cannot justly be charged with believing in everything just as he taught."[17] No doubt part of this disclaimer was a colonial declaration of theological independence. Living in a remote

15. Kathryn Tanner, *Theories of Culture: A New Agenda for Theology* (Minneapolis: Fortress Press, 1997), p. 113.

16. Robert W. Jenson, *America's Theologian: A Recommendation of Jonathan Edwards* (Oxford: Oxford University Press, 1988), p. 22.

17. Works, I, p. 131.

colonial outpost himself, Edwards was eager to defend the theological efforts of those on the margins of academic and ecclesial influence. In a preface to a book written by one of his closest students, he insisted that attempts to bring "new additions of light" to true religion

> ought not to be despised and discouraged, under a notion that it is but vanity and arrogance in such as are lately sprung up in an obscure part of the world, to pretend to add anything to this subject, to the informations we have long since received from their fathers, who have lived in former times, in New England, and more noted countries.[18]

Not all theological innovation represented an addition of light, in Edwards's view; he aimed much of his polemical theology against "the present fashionable divinity." Yet faithfulness to the dynamic presence of God in the church and in the wider world also ruled out unquestioning adherence to past tradition. If "the whole universe, heaven and earth, air and seas, and the divine constitution and history of the holy Scriptures, be full of images of divine things, as full as a language is of words,"[19] it is inevitable that ongoing theological reflection will overflow established bounds of doctrinal definition. Like learning a language, doing theology is an ongoing, assimilative process. New situations demand new vocabulary, new attempts to speak God's language beautifully, and even a willingness to change linguistic conventions when faithfulness requires it.

Writing at the end of the nineteenth century, Alexander Allen noted that though Edwards lived in an era which tended to view the Trinity as "meaningless or irrational dogma," he "appears as anticipating that feature of modern theology which finds in the doctrine of the Trinity the essence of the Christian faith."[20] Allen's own remarks anticipate the great twentieth-century flowering of trinitarian theology in figures like Karl Barth, Eberhard Jüngel, Jürgen Moltmann, Karl Rahner, Catherine La Cugna, and many others. As Robert Jenson, himself an

---

18. Joseph Bellamy, *True Religion Delineated* (Morris-town: Henry P. Russell, 1804), p. iv.

19. Works, 11, p. 152.

20. Alexander V. G. Allen, *Jonathan Edwards* (Boston: Houghton Mifflin, 1889; reprint, New York: Burt Franklin Reprints, 1975), pp. 372-73.

important contributor to contemporary trinitarian discussion has asserted, twentieth-century theology has relearned that the doctrine of Trinity "is not a separate puzzle to be solved but the framework within which all theology's puzzles are to be solved."[21] I have argued that this was true for Edwards as well. His trinitarian theology provided a framework for pondering the diverse intellectual and pastoral puzzles of his life, from the problems of substance metaphysics and deist assaults on Christian doctrine, to God's end in creating the world and the outbreak of colonial revivals. Both when it soars and when it stumbles, Edwards's theology can contribute to the contemporary reconstruction of a trinitarian framework.

21. Robert W. Jenson, "Karl Barth," in David F. Ford, ed., *The Modern Theologians: An Introduction to Christian Theology in the Twentieth Century,* 2nd ed. (Oxford: Blackwell, 1997), p. 31.

INDEX

INDEX

Keckermann, Bartholomaeus, 46
Knight, Janice, 6, 7, 95

Lash, Nicholas, 78, 187
Lee, Sang Hyun, 15, 48, 61, 80, 88-89,
  128, 134-35, 180
Locke, John, 22, 160

Mastricht, Peter van, 27-28, 30, 36-37,
  45, 58-59, 61-64, 66, 69, 74-75, 142,
  156-57
Mather, Cotton, 8, 36-37, 46-47
Maximus the Confessor, 127
Mayhew, Jonathan, 25-26
McClymond, Michael, 3, 7, 80, 87
McDermott, Gerald, 10, 174
McLachlan, H. John, 21, 24
Millennium, 120, 174-76
Miller, Perry, 98, 101
Minkema, Kenneth, 71, 170
Moltmann, Jürgen, 117, 191
Muller, Richard, 21, 27, 68

Northampton, 151, 159, 167, 188; communion controversy in, 172-75; Edwards's pastoral relations with, 3-4,
  103, 121, 168, 170-75

Olevianus, Caspar, 93-94
Owen, John, 5, 7, 43, 89, 113, 146, 147,
  156

Perkins, William, 6, 7, 27
Pettit, Norman, 7
Placher, William, 8, 50, 114, 150, 183-84
Porterfield, Amanda, 7, 33-34
Preparationism, 98, 161-62
Preston, John, 7, 63, 96, 153, 174
Proudfoot, Wayne, 160
Psychological Image, 12-13, 43-49, 52-
  53, 55, 73-75, 85-88, 121-24; as *basso
  continuo* of redemption, 185; in ten-
  sion with social image, 11, 50-51,

129-30, 187-88; rarity in Reformed
  tradition of, 30, 45-46

Ramsey, Paul, 159, 180
Reformed tradition, 3, 52, 137, 140, 143;
  and covenant theology, 31-32, 92-95;
  distrust of nonscriptural language
  in, 29-31, 96
Relational ontology, 80-89; and aes-
  thetics, 80-85; and dispositional on-
  tology, 88-89; and idealism, 85-88
Revivals, 5, 48, 192; as work of Holy
  Spirit, 160-63, 169-70; divisiveness
  of, 163-65
Richard of St. Victor, 12, 14-15, 37, 114
Ridgley, Thomas, 68, 99-101, 104-5, 108
Rutherford, Samuel, 96-98, 102

Sanctification, 8, 17, 98-99, 124, 140,
  146, 151-53, 155-57, 160, 166-69
Schafer, Thomas, 134, 142, 155
Shea, Daniel, 80
Shepard, Thomas, 7, 98, 140
Sherlock, William, 23-24
Sibbes, Richard, 5-7, 32, 34-37, 59, 82,
  95-98, 117, 120, 126-27, 143, 152-53,
  167, 169, 173-75, 178, 180
Sibbesians. *See* Spiritual Brethren
Sin, 7, 92, 94, 113, 123, 132-34, 136-39,
  149, 161, 176, 178, 185-87; against
  Holy Spirit, 137; resists union with
  God, 136-38
Social Image, 11, 14-15, 30-37, 40-41,
  44-45, 49-52, 55, 75-77, 83, 91-93, 113-
  18, 121, 123, 125, 129, 142-43, 158-59,
  186-88; as melody of redemption,
  185-86; in tension with psychological image, 11, 50-51, 129-30, 187-88;
  rarity in Reformed tradition of, 30-
  31, 34, 37
Son, as Word of God, 5, 11-13, 19, 45,
  47-48, 52-53, 74, 85-88, 114, 123-24,
  185, 190; subordination of, 93, 99-
  101, 107, 111, 115-17; union with Fa-